24-Hour
Trading

24-Hour Trading

THE GLOBAL NETWORK OF FUTURES AND OPTIONS MARKETS

Barbara B. Diamond

Mark P. Kollar

WILEY

JOHN WILEY & SONS

New York • Chichester • Brisbane
Toronto • Singapore

Library of Congress Cataloging-in-Publication Data:

Diamond, Barbara B.
24-hour trading : the global network of futures and options
markets / by Barbara B. Diamond, Mark P. Kollar.
p. cm.
Bibliography: p.
ISBN 0-471-60072-5
1. Futures market. 2. Stock options. I. Kollar, Mark P.
II. Title. III. Title: Twenty-four-hour trading.
HG6024.A3D53 1989
332.64'5—dc19   88-29980
                                                                 CIP

Printed in the United States of America

10 9 8 7 6 5 4 3 2 1

Contents

Preface   ix
Acknowledgments   xi
List of Abbreviations   xiii

Part I The Emergence of Global Futures and Options
        Markets

1 The Evolution of Futures Markets   3

   Ancient Forerunners
   Japan and the Birth of the Futures Contract
   Early Futures Trading in the United States
   The Birth of Financial Futures

2 Futures Exchanges Today   13

   Volume and Value of Contracts
   Options Trading
   Pacific Rim Markets and the Introduction of Exchange Links

3 Participants in Futures and Options Markets   27

Institutional Hedgers
Arbitragers
Institutional Market Makers
Individual Market Makers
Market Participants Around the World
Leadership

4 Information Flow in the Markets   41

The Physical Plant and Order Flow
Relay of Price Information
Options-Related Information

5 Market Regulations   47

Futures Regulation Today
Regulation of Exchanges Outside the United States

6 The Clearinghouse and Financial Safeguards   53

Worldwide Clearinghouse Links
The International Commodities Clearing House, Ltd.
Margining Systems
Fiduciary Responsibility

7 Intermarket Communications   63

Language Barriers Between Markets
British vs. American Terminology
Interest Rate and Options Terminology

8 Computers and the Decision-Making Process   73

How Market Data Are Communicated
Comparative Charting Capabilities
The Role of Computers in Market Decisions
Trading Operation Controls
Management Internal Control Systems

CONTENTS

9 *Tomorrow's Trading Environment*   *93*

   Pathways to 24-Hour Trading

 Notes   *101*

Part II The Global Trading Information Bank

1 *Futures and Options Exchanges: A Worldwide*
   Directory   *105*

2 *Major Exchanges: Contracts Listed and Other Basic*
   Data   *123*

3 *Clearinghouse Directory*   *133*

4 *Exchange-Related Agencies and Associations*   *137*

5 *Volume Distribution by Country and Exchange*   *141*

6 *Volume Listing of Contracts*   *143*

7 *Alphabetical Contracts Index*   *153*

8 *Contract Specifications by Country and Exchange*   *163*

9 *International Holidays*   *291*

 Bibliography   *293*

 Index   *297*

Preface

This book is written for those who want a greater knowledge of futures markets around the world. The text has been developed around the consulting that we have done internationally, either with executives outside the United States who suddenly find themselves in the position of having to trade in the US markets or with firms inside the US who want to internationalize their operations. The book includes basic explanations as to the history of the industry, terminology, language, practices of daily business, the functions of the exchanges and clearinghouses, and the participants who make it all happen. For the industry professional, the most useful section may be the extensive reference material in Part II, including listings of all futures exchanges, clearinghouses, and more than 275 contract specifications and their annual volumes.

As the October 1987 stock market crash showed us, the markets in New York and Chicago are closely tied to the trading floors in Tokyo, London, and Paris. Price swings in Japanese yen futures at the Chicago Mercantile Exchange (CME) often have a direct impact on the Nikkei Stock Average at the Tokyo Stock Exchange (TSE) and the yen-bond futures contract at the London International

Financial Futures Exchange (LIFFE). News of a break or rally in the US dollar in New York interbank trading does not stop at the nation's borders. Instead, it speeds through electronic information systems to influence the opening prices of the financial and commodity markets in other time zones. The cries that locals and floor brokers make as they bid and offer in the middle of the US T-bond futures pits at the Chicago Board of Trade (CBOT) are heard on the floors of the London International Financial Futures Exchange (LIFFE), the Sydney Futures Exchange (SFE), the Hong Kong Futures Exchange (HKFE) and the Marché à Terme des Instruments Financiers (MATIF) in Paris.

Although futures markets are becoming more and more "globalized," a level playing field among the exchanges and their participants has not been established. In the United States, the base of participation in the futures markets is broad, and anyone can play an active role in the marketplace. Since investment houses are setting up shop on all the major trading floors, the number of traders is now growing in other major financial centers around the world. However, information is not always easy to find. We hope this book will address many of the questions asked by the futures trader who would like to trade global markets. For the student reader, the book will serve as a valuable reference.

As a point of interest, early exchange policies did not allow female personnel to work on the trading floor and this policy remained in effect as late as 1960. Today, many women members and competent females are active in the financial industry. However, for ease of reading, "he" is used throughout the book.

BARBARA B. DIAMOND
MARK P. KOLLAR

Chicago, Illinois
January 1989

Acknowledgments

We would like to thank the clearing firms executives, exchange and clearinghouse officials, the administration at regulatory agencies, data vendors, and news services around the world. They were supportive hosts when we traveled and quick to answer our questions.

Special thanks go to Pat Arbor, Jonathan Janott, Michael Killian, John McPartland, and Barry Taylor for reading the early draft. Their excellent suggestions gave us editorial direction and focus.

B.B.D.
M.P.K.

List of Abbreviations

Acronym	Organization
AFBD	Association of Futures Brokers and Dealers (UK) [NFA in USA]
AP	Associated Person (USA)
CFTC	Commodity Futures Trading Commission (USA)
CPO	Commodity Pool Operator (USA)
CTA	Commodity Trading Advisor (USA)
CTR	Computerized Trade Reconstruction (USA)
FB	Floor Broker (USA)
FCM	Futures Commission Merchant (USA)
FIA	Futures Industry Association (USA)
IB	Introducing Broker (USA and Australia)
ICCH	International Commodities Clearing House, Ltd.
MFF	Ministry of Fisheries and Forestries (Japan)
MITI	Ministry for International Trade and Industry (Japan)
MOF	Ministry of Finance (Japan)
NASD	National Association of Securities Dealers (USA)
NCSC	National Companies and Securities Commission (Australia)

LIST OF ABBREVIATIONS

NFA	National Futures Association (USA) [AFBD in UK]
SEC	Securities and Exchange Commission (USA) [SIB in UK]
SIB	Securities and Investment Board (UK) [SEC in USA]
SRO	Self-Regulatory Organization (UK)

EXCHANGES

Acronym	Organization
AMEX	American Stock Exchange
AFFM	Australian Financial Futures Market
BBF	Bolsa Brasileira de Futuros
BFE	Baltic Futures Exchange
BMF	Bolsa Mercantil and de Futuros
BMSP	Bolsa de Mercadorias de São Paulo
CBOE	Chicago Board Options Exchange
CBOT	Chicago Board of Trade
CCA	Compagnie des Commissionaires Agrèes
CME	Chicago Mercantile Exchange
COMEX	Commodity Exchange of New York
CSCE	Coffee, Sugar & Cocoa Exchange, Inc., New York
EOE	European Options Exchange
FOX	London Futures and Options Exchange
FTA	Financiele Termijnmarket Amsterdam NV
HKFE	Hong Kong Futures Exchange
HKSE	Hong Kong Stock Exchange
IPE	International Petroleum Exchange of London Ltd.
ISE	International Stock Exchange
KCBT	Kansas City Board of Trade
KLCE	Kuala Lumpur Commodity Exchange
LIFFE	London International Financial Futures Exchange
LME	London Metal Exchange Ltd.
LPFM	Lille Potato Futures Market
LSE	London Stock Exchange
MATIF	Marché á Terme des Instruments Financiers
ME	The Montreal Exchange
MGE	Minneapolis Grain Exchange

MIDAM	Mid-America Commodity Exchange
MIFE	Manila International Futures Exchange
MSE	Midwest Stock Exchange
NYCE	New York Cotton Exchange
NYFE	New York Futures Exchange
NYMEX	New York Mercantile Exchange
NYSE	New York Stock Exchange
NZFE	New Zealand Futures Exchange
OSE	Osaka Securities Exchange
PBOT	Philadelphia Board of Trade
PHLX	Philadelphia Stock Exchange
PSE	Pacific Stock Exchange
SFE	Sydney Futures Exchange
SIMEX	Singapore International Monetary Exchange, Ltd.
SOFE	Sweden Options and Futures Exchange
SOFFEX	Swiss Options and Financial Futures Exchange
SOM	Stockholm Options Market
SSE	Sydney Stock Exchange
TCE	Tokyo Commodity Exchange
TFE	Toronto Futures Exchange
TGE	The Tokyo Grain Exchange
TSE	Tokyo Stock Exchange
TSEX	Toronto Stock Exchange
TSUE	Tokyo Sugar Exchange
VSE	Vancouver Stock Exchange
WCE	Winnipeg Commodity Exchange

DIVISIONS OF EXCHANGES

Acronym	*Organization*
AM	Associate Market (CBOT)
COM	Commodity Options Market (CBOT)
IDEM	Index Debt (CBOT)
IMM	International Monetary Market (CME)
IOM	Index and Options Market (CME)
BIFFEX	Baltic International Freight Futures Exchange (BFE)

FOFSA	Federation of Oils, Seeds and Fats Association Ltd. (BFE)
LGFM	London Grain Futures Market (BFE)
LMFM	London Meat Futures Exchange (BFE)
LPFA	London Potato Futures Association (BFE)
SOMFA	Soy Bean Meal Futures Association, Ltd. (BFE)
TOM	Traded Options Market (ISE)

I

THE EMERGENCE OF GLOBAL FUTURES AND OPTIONS MARKETS

1

The Evolution of Futures Markets

ANCIENT FORERUNNERS

Man has been trading commodities for thousands of years. Traders have bought and sold cat pelts in St. Louis; turkeys and onions in Chicago; gold and silver in Hong Kong; cotton, cocoa, and coffee in New York and London; tin in Kuala Lumpur; and sugar in Paris. The ancient forerunners of today's trading floors—the agoras of ancient Greece, the forums of the Roman Empire and the medieval fairs of western Europe—established basic principles of trading that are still important today. Three fundamental criteria for establishing a viable market were defined by Teweles, Harlow, and Stone and found in the medieval code of mercantile law: the designation of location of the marketplace, the specific rules of inspection and grading, and defined contract terms and forms of conduct.[1] Let us examine each of these criteria in turn.

First, traders have always valued the importance of specific market sites and specific times for trading. In this manner, trading was conducted in full view of the buyers and sellers, who gathered around each other to form a loosely organized pit, ensuring fair prices. Merchants needed a place not only to exchange their products but also to exchange ideas, in short, to gossip about the markets. These ancient trading arenas eventually became the leading financial centers of their governments. There were at least nineteen trading centers throughout the Roman Empire. The LIFFE building in London is built on the site of the first European commodity exchange, which was established in London in 1570 and called the Royal Exchange. This exchange was initiated to accommodate the year-round meeting places for the transaction of commodities, and lovely oversized paintings depicting life of the time still adorn the walls for private viewing. Before the Royal Exchange, the Counts of Champagne held trade fairs that rotated the type of products sold throughout the year and offered the traders protection, money changers, and storage capacities. Today, the major financial centers of Tokyo, Hong Kong, Singapore, Sydney, London, Paris, Chicago, and New York are home to successful exchanges.

Second, product representation was important and man developed specific inspection procedures and standardized grading methods for products such as sugar and wheat at the Paris Sugar Exchange, which began trading in the eighteenth century. The inspection and grades used to evaluate the product made trade among the merchants much easier since it was not necessary to transport the entire product, but only samples of the product, permitting an easier commute to the marketplace.

Third, merchants have operated under defined contract terms and forms of conduct. "Courts of the fair" assessed the violations of the merchants and settled the disputes between the merchants. A similar, present-day framework settles trading disputes and provides clearinghouses to process trade and ensure payment.

There is evidence that the first forward contracts—forerunners of today's futures contracts—were developed in Europe at the trade fairs organized by the Counts of Champagne as early as 1114. The forward contract emerged as a document known as a *lettre de faire*, which specified the delivery of goods at a later date, as defined by W. C. Labys and C. W. J. Granger. At first these documents were used only for cash transactions between two merchants; later they became transferable documents that could pass through many hands before delivery was made. The *lettre de faire* was comparable to a modern warehouse receipt or a bill of exchange. Futures trading as we know it today evolved from these natural developments.

JAPAN AND THE BIRTH OF THE FUTURES CONTRACT

The earliest developments in futures trading took place in Japan during the eighteenth century. The first recorded use of futures trading was in 1679, but the Tokugawa Shogunate government did not legally recognize trading for sixty-one years. The first known futures market in the world, the Dojima Rice Trading Board, was established in Osaka in 1730.

Osaka was the largest and most influential port city in Japan during the feudal era. Warrior classes supported themselves by selling rice to pay land taxes to their feudal lords. Because of its proximity to rice fields and its successful port, Osaka became the island's rice center. Yodoya was this city's largest rice merchant and his prices for rice actually set the going rate throughout the agricultural community. His warehouse was the meeting place for all traders, allowing the merchants a common area to discuss market prices and trade information. The warehouse actually became the first commodity exchange in Japan around 1650. The chief merchant later moved his exchange to the Dojima district in Osaka, and this became known as the Dojima Rice Market.

Only futures trading took place in this warehouse, and all transactions were required to follow the CHO-AI-MAI-A-KAI rules or rice trade book. The rules clearly illustrate that the markets were orderly and well disciplined, and similarities can be found when these rules are compared with the basic guidelines used in futures trading today. Not only were contracts standardized and grades of rice well defined, but the trading exchange of eighteenth-century Japan was controlled by a nonprofit clearing system which charged commissions for its transactions and was totally responsible for payment defaults. Most important, however, is that no physical delivery of rice was made against outstanding contracts, and differences in value were settled in cash. This important development, which took place nearly two hundred years ago, led to the growth in financial futures and was directly responsible for the introduction of options on futures in exchanges today.

It also seems that the trading board was plagued with problems of out-trades as are some of the exchanges in the United States today. Out-trades, or mismatches, are trades where the quantities or prices recorded by the traders do not match. The most difficult problem occurs when both traders are buyers or sellers on the same transaction, instead of one trader buying and the other selling. To settle these disputes, arbitration committees were formed. No contracts could be carried into the new contract period, and no new trading took place during the last three days of the contract period. Alas, the advantages and problems of futures trading markets are centuries old.

To illustrate the evolution that has taken place in these markets, the following CHO-AI-MAI-A-KAI rules are reconstructed by economics professor Henry H. Bakken in his paper, "Futures Trading —Origin, Development and Present Economic Status."[2]

CHO-AI-MAI-A-KAI RULES

1. The contract term was limited to four months.
2. The year was divided approximately into four quarters.
3. At the end of each contract period, the market was closed for a few days.
4. Trading was carried in rice only.
5. All contracts in any four-month term were standardized.
6. The basic grade for any contract period was chosen by the traders by majority vote. Four grades were available.
7. No physical delivery against outstanding contracts was permitted.
8. All differences in value had to be settled in cash.
9. All contracts had to be settled and accounts cleared on or before the last day of the trading period.
10. No contracts could be carried over into the new contract period.
11. All trades had to be cleared through a clearinghouse.
12. Every trader was required to establish a line of credit with a clearinghouse.
13. Any default in payments was borne by the clearinghouse.
14. The clearinghouses were nonprofit operations, but a commission was charged for services rendered.
15. No new contracts could be made during the last three days of any trading period. (Bakken interprets this rule to read that these days were reserved for the business of clearing any trades by matching long positions against short positions. Thus, at the end of the four-month period, all trades would be cleared of record.)
16. An arbitration committee was evidently in existence, and it was empowered to adjudicate disputes and arbitrarily settle issues concerning values and prices.

The information researched would indicate that the first exchange of record was the Royal Exchange in London in 1570; the second, almost 100 years later in Osaka in 1679; and almost 200 years after that, trading began in Chicago in 1848.

EARLY FUTURES TRADING IN THE UNITED STATES

Although Japan and England can claim the oldest contributions to the commodities futures history, Chicago exchanges can boast of making the most innovative contributions to the futures world. This city gave birth to the first American futures exchange, financial futures contracts, options trading on exchange floors, cash settlement, and the mutual-offset system, which allows trading in the same contract on two different exchanges with the long and short positions offset between the exchanges.

Over one century after the first futures contract traded in the Dojima district of Osaka, eighty-two Chicago businessmen met in the offices of the Gage and Haines flour mill on the south bank of the Chicago River to discuss the need for a central marketplace for the city's expanding grain trade. The city's leaders were dissatisfied with the inadequacies of the Chicago harbor and the Great Lakes transportation system; the existing infrastructure could not handle the influx of grain into the harbor.

By 1848 Chicago had become the crossroads for buyers and sellers of grain. Grain trade through the city was rapidly increasing due to the opening in 1848 of the Illinois–Michigan Canal, which connected the Illinois River to Lake Michigan. This new canal allowed transportation for the commodities from the farm to the market. Charles Taylor, in his history of the Chicago Board of Trade (CBOT), states that on August 16, 1848, in the port of Chicago, there were two barges, twenty-seven brigs, sixty-seven schooners, six steamboats, six propellers, and thirty-two canal boats crowding the main river.[3] This sort of disorganization caused chaos among the merchants. When supplies of grain exceeded demand, merchants dumped corn, oats, and wheat into the river and streets.

Consequently, these eighty-two businessmen—not just farmers and merchants, but civic leaders from all sectors of the business community—provided a central cash market for the buyers and sellers of grain. Early board members traded forward or "to arrive" contracts, which thereby allowed farmers to hedge or buy insurance against the risk of price swings while they were waiting to take their goods to market and to ensure that they had a buyer for their crops. These "to arrive" contracts worked similarly to the *lettre de faire* contracts that developed in Europe earlier. The first recorded time contract occurred on March 13, 1851. As described by H. S. Irwin, this time contract was for the delivery of 3000 bushels of corn in June at one cent per bushel below the March 13 price.[4] The futures contract, as it is known today, originated from the "to arrive" contract, with the first futures contract traded on the CBOT in 1865.

As the preceding scenario suggests, the need for an organized marketplace existed in Chicago, but 1848 also heralded important developments in the field of communications, the most vital aspect of successful trading. The first telegraphic message was received in Chicago in 1848, and service soon was developed between the city and New York and Buffalo. The founders of the CBOT pushed hard to begin trading at their exchange by telegraphic means. Now information could be sent and received quickly and efficiently among the nation's grain traders and processors. At its inception, electronic communications sparked the growth of the trading industry.

Whereas the CBOT listed contracts in corn, wheat, flour, oats, hay, and timothy seed, the Chicago Merchantile Exchange, or CME (which originally was called the Chicago Butter and Egg Board), developed out of the dairy merchants' need for a central marketplace. In 1874 a group of South Water Street businessmen formed the Chicago Produce Exchange, which established guidelines to settle trading disputes and provide information and education to the traders and merchants of perishable products. The board's goals were to supply daily market quotations on butter, eggs, and other products, to provide general information regarding the market for such commodities, to offer a convenient place to buy and sell commodities, and to establish the machinery to quickly adjust business disputes among its members.

A contract with a forward delivery time was further developed at the CME with the introduction of refrigeration. This new invention allowed eggs to be stored in the spring when supplies were high and sold in the fall and winter when supplies were low. In this manner, producers and processors could market eggs more efficiently, and thus risk could be protected on the futures exchange with the egg futures contract. The growth of the CME followed the success of the Chicago Butter and Egg Board by listing contracts that needed refrigeration for storage, that is, perishable commodities. In 1919, when this perishable commodities market became the Chicago Mercantile Exchange, a clearinghouse was established to handle futures transactions.

The modern development of the CME began in 1961 with the introduction of the frozen pork belly contract. Bellies became the most actively traded contract in the world, and the exchange became the leader in meat futures, adding contracts in live and feeder cattle and live hogs. Ten years later, the CME would take the next giant step in futures trading by introducing financial futures to the trading community.

THE BIRTH OF FINANCIAL FUTURES

By the 1960s, the futures contract had developed into a useful tool for the farmer and the agricultural processor, but no futures instrument existed for the financial community. A group of pork belly traders and economists, specifically the CME's Leo Melamed and the University of Chicago's Milton Friedman, realized that the end of the gold standard meant the end of stabilized currency rates. Under the Bretton Woods Agreement of 1944, which established fixed rates for foreign currencies, exchange rate fluctuation had been limited to 1 percent in either direction. In the early 1970s with the abolition of this standard, traders became exposed to great risks in foreign currency swings. The CME seized on this opportunity and approached the board of the First National Bank of Chicago with the idea of trading not corn or cattle, but cash.

At first, the financial world was not overly impressed with the vision of these pork belly traders. Bank foreign exchange traders operated as a closed club, and no one wanted to admit midwestern locals. Friedman, who later would receive the Nobel Prize for economics, added a degree of respectability to the project with his paper, "The Need for Futures Markets in Currencies,"[5] prepared for the CME and presented on December 20, 1971, at Melamed's request.

In this paper, Friedman stated that there was a great need for a futures market in currencies to permit foreign traders and investors to hedge against the occasional changes that occur in prices, especially with the expected results of a closed gold window. Friedman asserted that futures markets would enhance foreign trade. To be successful, he said, this type of contract would have to be used not only by hedgers, but also to a great extent by speculators. The futures industry received an improved air of respectability with Friedman's endorsement, and the locals could now put on coats and ties because they were considered vital to the future of foreign trade. The CME had found the best spokesperson for the industry.

The CME opened a new division, called the International Monetary Market, for the purpose of trading futures. To encourage market participation, they offered the meat traders the chance to buy IMM memberships for a mere $100, while they charged the public $10,000. Traders needed prodding to enter the new currency futures pits. Volume was light in the first few years of trading, but it picked up in the second half of the decade because of the need to hedge against rising inflation and the highly volatile foreign exchange rates.

This was the first truly innovative move in futures trading since

1848, but the new traders who filled the pit did not recognize the full potential of these markets. The new locals and order fillers had little experience with cash market fundamentals and did not fully understand the risks they were assuming. The IMM traders were instructed to trade spreads among the different currencies to increase volume and liquidity, while the influential pork belly traders also prodded the locals to make markets for all paper that entered the pits. As traders from these pits say today, the new currency pits are proof that markets are made by people who tend to them. The new traders were responsible for the market growth since bank participation increased at a slower rate than speculative participation. The cash market traders accepted the markets after the IMM reorganized and merged into the CME. The new trading pits were served by its young traders, experienced agricultural traders, and the clearing system of the CME. The entire organization would support the next stage in the evolution in futures trading.

The success and acceptance of financial futures at the CME prompted the CBOT to introduce the Ginnie Mae Government Mortgage contract (GNMA-CDR) on October 20, 1975, and then its now-famous United States Thirty-Year Treasury Bond contract on August 22, 1977. With the introduction of the bond contract, the CBOT established its Association Market (AM) membership (previously called Government Instrument Market), which focused on financial futures. During their first year, the bonds reached a daily high of 1295 contracts. Today, there are over twenty interest rate futures contracts in the world, and these contracts are usually the volume leaders at CBOT, CME, LIFFE, MATIF, TSE, and SFE.

2

Futures Exchanges Today

The majority of all futures trading in the world takes place in the Chicago pits, where roughly seventy-five different types of futures and options on those futures contracts are listed. These exchanges have a strong financial presence in the city. According to a recent study sponsored by the four Chicago exchanges—the CBOT, the CME, the Chicago Board Options Exchange (CBOE), and the Midwest Stock Exchange (MSE)—the exchanges provide 33,000 jobs in the city, spend $900 million annually on local goods and services, and deposit $4 billion in the city's banks.[6] The exchanges are well known among Chicago residents. Even Chicago cab drivers keep tabs on exchange membership prices, who went bust, and the daily settlement prices of pork belly and soybean futures.

Although trading pits are not confined to Chicago's city limits nor to the Central Standard time zone, their presence is not as strong in other financial capitals. In 1987, of more than 310 million futures contracts traded throughout the world, 66 percent were traded in Chicago. Other active futures markets exist in New York, London, Paris, Hong Kong, Tokyo, Singapore, and Sydney. We can trade nearly every commodity from greasy wool and dried cocoons to Australia's stock barometer, the All Ordinaries Index, and the London Financial Times stock index (the "Footsie"). There are about sixty-five futures and options exchanges, and plans for new futures and options exchanges in Germany, Luxembourg, Ireland, Spain, Italy, South Africa, Hong Kong, Osaka, Tokyo, and People's Republic of China are being considered. Currently, 350 different kinds of futures contracts can be traded.

Exchanges are big business. Trading floors compete fiercely for global markets, consequently developing innovative strategies to attract foreign investment. Budgets for promoting a single contract have run into the millions of dollars, and some exchanges house well-staffed international marketing departments in major financial capitals. In 1980 the CME opened its London office, becoming the first United States exchange to develop an overseas bureau. Now many major exchanges have branch offices located in other cities such as Chicago, New York, London, Hong Kong, and Tokyo.

In addition, exchanges such as the CBOT and the Philadelphia Stock Exchange (PHLX) have extended trading hours with evening sessions to attract business from the Far East. The Sydney Futures Exchange (SFE) has special evening sessions to facilitate trading when national economic statements are made by government officials. To help the London investor, the CBOT has additional plans, including early morning sessions. The CME is now planning a new transaction system called GLOBEX to trade 24 hours a day using the Reuters electronic computer network, and many exchanges have formed links to allow trading of one contract on two trading floors, or more broadly, two time zones and two capital bases.

The introduction of financial futures contracts has accelerated the stupendous growth of these global exchanges. The Chicago and New York exchanges have been trading financial futures for over a decade, but many of the overseas marketplaces have been involved with futures contracts for only the past few years. Their growth, nevertheless, has been outstanding. For example, MATIF, which opened for business in February 1986, cleared over eleven million long bonds contracts in 1987. In 1988, MATIF has merged with the

Paris Futures Exchange adding some agricultural markets to the financial offering. LIFFE began trading financial futures in September 1982 and offered seven contracts in currencies and interest rates futures. The exchange now tallies over 70,000 contracts daily, with roughly half of the volume taking place in the 20-year UK Gilt interest rate futures pit. The exchange lists twelve futures contracts, four options on futures contracts, and two options contracts. The SFE has grown from over three million contracts traded in 1986 to over five million contracts tallied in 1987. Based on volume generated in the first nine months of 1988, the SFE could easily double its volume by the end of the year. Bolsa Mercantil and de Futuros (BMF), located in São Paulo, Brazil, traded more than five million contracts in its stock exchange index in 1987. In all, twenty exchanges or affiliations of established exchanges have been formed since May 16, 1972, the day the first financial futures contract was traded at the International Monetary Market (IMM) division of the CME. The industry is surely growing, and its influence in European and Asian markets will soon be strong competition for the markets in Chicago.

Corn, wheat, soybeans, cattle, pork bellies, silk, cotton, and orange juice are among those farm products still actively traded on the various floors, but agricultural volume was low in 1986. Financial futures have been the lifeblood and growth of the large futures marketplaces. Fixed government instruments, currencies, and stock indices account for nearly 80 percent of all contracts traded. The CBOT's US T-bond futures and options on futures contract, the world's most heavily traded contract, now averages over 150,000 contracts during both the day and evening sessions. Nearly 600 traders fill the CBOT bond pits, with more than 50 percent of these players trading as locals speculating on the movement of bond prices for their own accounts.

Today the fastest growing financial futures contract is traded in one of the world's electronic futures exchanges. The Tokyo Stock Exchange (TSE) introduced the yen bond contract on October 19, 1985, after Japan's Ministry of Finance allowed futures trading to resume in its country. The Japanese yen-denominated bond futures contract at the TSE totaled over eighteen million contracts in 1987, making it one of the world's largest futures contract.

It is no surprise that this contract is so successful because Japan has the capital to invest and the need to protect this capital in the futures markets. As we have seen, this nation also has an old history in commodities trading.

VOLUME AND VALUE OF CONTRACTS

In the early days of rice trading in Japan and grain trading in Chicago, the futures market was born out of obvious economic need. Today, exchanges spend considerable time and money in research to determine the potential success of a new futures contract.

The exchanges must prove to the regulatory authorities that an economic need exists for any new product they design for the marketplace. When properly conceived, the commercial users are surveyed extensively to determine the most suitable specification details, which may include items such as contract size, minimum price movement, value, delivery points, and variation penalties of deliverable quality. Many new product committees decide to shelve an idea because they are not satisfied that the commercial or institutional users will actively participate.

Nevertheless, the growth of new contracts has been phenomenal. None of the highest volume contracts traded in the United States today was a product before 1972. The development of products in the financial futures area has broadened the base of trading and extended possibilities to major business centers in many parts of the world. Successful interest rate contracts in London, Sydney, and Paris are excellent examples of the futures market serving an economic need.

There is a constant race among the exchanges to produce the greatest volume figures. News releases immediately report a new daily volume record. Many magazines and industry publications report volume figures on a cumulative monthly and yearly basis. Open interest is reported daily to exchange members and according to Robert Wilmouth of the FIA, the open interest figures represent the true health of an exchange.[7] (For recent volume figures on major contracts, see Part II of this book. Annual open interest figures may reflect the twelve-month average using only the last day of each month or the last day of the year figure, so we did not include this information.)

Why are volume figures so important? Each exchange collects a transaction fee from members and customers for each contract traded. Thus, high volume produces more income for the exchange and its member firms. When considering the depth of a market, the dollar value of a contract must be analyzed. For example, one CME Eurodollar contract represents one million dollars' worth of Eurodollars. At the CBOT, one US Treasury bond futures contract represents $100,000 in long-term US Treasury bonds. One Eurodollar contract equals the dollar value of ten US Treasury bond futures contracts. Although bonds are the most traded futures contract, Eurodollars are the industry's most valuable contract.

Industry professionals and exchanges understand these relationships and choose to do marketing by the numbers that best establish their position in their financial community.

OPTIONS TRADING

The CBOT has always had to consider the cyclical nature of the agricultural markets that periodically causes several years of low futures trading activity. It was during such a phase in 1973 that the exchange created the Chicago Board Options Exchange (CBOE). Until then, options trading was strictly an over-the-counter stock investment tool, and its users were continually battling against critics who tried to ban this form of trading. Initially, the CBOE listed sixteen stock option *calls* in an old trading room adjacent to the CBOT bond pit.

In 1977 the Securities and Exchange Commission (SEC), the federal regulatory agency of equity-related products, finally approved the listing of the *put* side of stock transactions and then promptly declared a moratorium on additional option listings, with the halt lasting three years. Soon options not only flourished at the CBOE, but eventually they became an important instrument at US futures exchanges.

Stock option calls give the buyer the right, but not the obligation, to buy a certain number of shares (usually 100) of the underlying security at a set price before a specified time in the future. On the other hand, a put option gives the buyer the right to sell a specified number of shares of the underlying product at a fixed cost before a certain time. In general, call buyers expect the underlying stock to rally, whereas put buyers anticipate a break in the price of the underlying contract.

Today the CBOE lists options on over 1200 equities. These are generically called options on actuals. The exchange also offers options on stock indices and interest rates. The OEX, representing the Standard & Poor's 100 stock index (the CME lists the Standard & Poor's 500 stock index), was the industry's most actively traded contract in 1986 and 1987. However, volume in all stock-index–related products has suffered greatly since the October 1987 crash.

Options on actuals are also traded at the American Stock Exchange (AMEX), the Philadelphia Stock Exchange (PHLX), the Pacific Stock Exchange (PSE), and the New York Stock Exchange (NYSE). The CBOE, however, is the volume leader in this type of contract offering, accounting for nearly 60 percent of the average number of daily contracts.

Options on futures began at the New York Coffee, Sugar & Cocoa Exchange (CSCE) on October 1, 1982, as part of a pilot program by the Commodity Futures Trading Commission (CFTC). The first option on futures contract listed was the World Sugar No. 11 contract. This option contract does not show high volume when compared to the financial options now available, but the CSCE had opened the door with the CFTC for other exchanges who wanted to trade options on futures. Trading of call and put options on futures contracts works the same way as in stock options, that is, a call gives you the right to buy the futures contract at a specific price and the put gives you the right to sell the futures contract. Traders have determined that in the valuation of options on futures, volatility-based models are more effective in estimating trade price.

We will make no effort in this book to explain options valuation further as this is the lengthy theme of several good books already available.

PACIFIC RIM MARKETS AND THE INTRODUCTION OF EXCHANGE LINKS

By the end of the 1970s, active traders could speculate or protect their investments using a wide range of futures and options on futures contracts at exchanges across the world. The next steps toward global trading would be the introduction of first the mutual-offset trading system, and then exchange links.

In a link system, a trader may establish a position to be cleared on one exchange and then transferred to another exchange for offset. With a link relationship, an exchange in a different time zone is allowed to establish a position directly into the clearing system of another exchange. For example, the SFE has a link with COMEX and LIFFE.

According to Lincoln Gould, marketing manager of the New Zealand Futures Exchange (NZFE), wool futures were actually the first 24-hour contract to change hands across geographic borders.[8] In 1981, wool trading was conducted by telephone conference call between London and New Zealand after the London Wool Terminal Market Association agreed to allow New Zealand affiliate members to trade their wool contract in New Zealand during New Zealand hours. "This was quite an achievement for a country (New Zealand) which had only been trading futures for six months," Gould had said. New Zealand market participants would trade in Auckland, Wellington, Christchurch, and Napier, and at the end of the day, trades and prices would be sent to London by Telex. In London, the contract was traded on the floor of the London Commodity Exchange. At the end of trading in London, the prices and trade information would be sent to New Zealand. All trades were cleared by the International Commodities Clearing House, Ltd. (ICCH) in London.

This concept led to the mutual-offset system, developed by the CME and the Singapore International Monetary Exchange (SIMEX) in 1984. Under this system, both exchanges operate separately with their own clearing, audit, and surveillance systems. They offer interchangeable fungible futures contracts that can be initiated or liquidated on either trading floor.

According to CME literature on the subject, certain SIMEX contracts have the same terms and conditions as the CME contracts.[9] The interexchange clearing processing takes place in Chicago after the market closes in the local country; but each clearinghouse matches its own trades locally.

For the trader, the process is simple. An investor may buy Japanese yen futures at the CME during its trading hours and liquidate that position in Singapore during SIMEX trading hours, which are during the evening hours in Chicago. (Singapore is thirteen hours ahead of Chicago; for example, 10 P.M. Monday in Chicago is 11 A.M. Tuesday in Singapore.)

According to Robert K. G. Chia and Doreen Soh, in their book *SIMEX and the Globalization of Financial Futures*,[10] trading links provide cheap and efficient risk management of overnight price movements, which can be substantial in the currency markets. The mutual-offset system between CME and SIMEX is also very cost efficient because only one set of margins and commissions is required, and the link provides a liquid marketplace for both exchanges.

Eurodollar futures was the best contract to promote for this new type of trading as volume in this contract was growing in

Chicago. It had attracted the attention of dealers in Europe and Asia, and there was an active local population in the CME pits. Most important, the contract has a cash settlement.

In its report on the development of the new system, "Factors Relating to the Feasibility of a Singapore-Based Financial Futures Market," the Continental Illinois National Bank said the nation of Singapore was chosen for this experiment because it was an international business and financial center.[11] The country was politically stable, and there were good sources of speculative capital in this financial hub. The most important characteristic was the country's geographic location. As the report explains, Singapore "lies in a strategic time zone enabling it to overlap time gaps between market closing in the United States and the opening of business in Europe." Trading in Singapore is conducted from 1900 CDT to 0420 CDT. The CME admired the country's international trade reputation, extensive infrastructure, and efficient communications link—these same things were crucial to the development of the CBOT in 1848.

Volume on the Singapore exchange has been growing steadily, but the mutual-offset system has not proved to be as dynamic as the potential strengths of the two exchanges. Speculative capital and local support surely exist on both trading floors, but the marriage neither substantially increases volume in the listed contracts nor significantly expands the trading boundaries. The mutual-offset system currently lists futures contracts in Japanese yen, Deutsche marks, British pounds, and Eurodollars. SIMEX additionally offers futures contracts in gold, the Nikkei Stock Average Index, and options on futures contracts in Eurodollars and select currencies.

Exchange links currently exist between the Commodities Exchange of New York (COMEX) and SFE to trade the gold futures contract. This link operates like a licensing arrangement in that the SFE will book a trade directly into the COMEX clearing system for initial posting or offset. The SFE also has a link with LIFFE to trade the US T-bond and Eurodollar contracts. In the London situation, the trades flow through the ICCH, the clearinghouse used by both the LIFFE and the SFE exchanges.

The Major Market Index options contract between the CBOE and Amsterdam's EOE is the latest addition to the effort at exchange relationships. To date, these links have not produced large volume, and additional linked contracts are not expected.

Despite a lack of high volume at SIMEX in its mutual trading system with the CME or its own contracts, the Pacific Rim has attracted the attention of traders and exchanges around the world. The Japanese clearly have an enormous amount of capital at risk, and exchanges have been anxious to provide hedging opportunities for these investors once the Ministry of Finance (MOF) in Japan allowed financial institutions there to participate in overseas futures markets.

LIFFE reached an agreement with the Tokyo Stock Exchange (TSE) in 1987 in a memorandum of cooperation concerning the launch of a cash-settled Japanese Government Bond futures contract based on the TSE delivery settlement price. When this occurred, some in the industry expected it to provide a basis for the Japanese to make arrangements with other exchanges, and in 1988 a similar agreement was reached with the CBOT.

To attract the Japanese investors to Chicago trading floors, the CBOT began evening trading sessions on April 30, 1987. The exchange conducts evening sessions Sunday through Thursday, from 1800 CDT to 2130 CDT, listing contracts in US T-bond and T-note futures and options on those futures, as well as on gold and silver futures. The evening session corresponds to the beginning of the business day in Tokyo. The CBOT admits that it is hard to calculate how much of the evening session's volume originates from Tokyo, although dealers on the floor at night estimate that 50 percent of their orders are Japanese-based. Evening session volume averages about 15,000 contracts per session, with most of the trading taking place in the US T-bond pit. On October 22, 1987, during the stock market crash, volume reached a record high of 44,552 contracts in US T-bond futures, while over 101,000 contracts changed hands that night in all contracts listed on the CBOT floor.

In a further attempt to expand the global trading arena and

attract the Asian marketplace to the Chicago trading floors, the CBOT recently became the first US exchange to agree to develop futures products with the Tokyo Stock Exchange. First, the CBOT plans to introduce, along with the TSE, Tokyo Stock Price Index (TOPIX) futures contracts. The index is based on 1700 shares in the first tier or section of the TSE and gives the CBOT the first international stock index on its floor and the first cash-settled contract at the TSE. The TSE currently trades a 10- and 20-year yen-bond futures contract and the TOPIX contract. The two exchanges will work together to launch US government bond futures in Tokyo and Japanese government bond futures in Chicago. In addition, the CME is planning to list the Nikkei 225 Stock Average futures contract on its floor sometime during 1989.

The exchanges in Japan can be classified into three groups depending on their regulator. The Ministry of Finance (MOF) regulates the TSE for stock trading and financial futures trading. Of the 1530 stocks listed on the stock exchange, 225 stocks are traded on an open outcry trading floor and the remaining are matched using a computerized electronic system. All orders are manually matched, whether on the floor or on the computer system, by a Saitori. The Saitori companies operate as intermediaries, much like specialists on the New York Stock Exchange, and their numbers are limited to twelve in Tokyo, five in Osaka, and three in Nagoya.

The Tokyo Stock Exchange began computing the TOPIX Stock Price Index in 1969; it had previously used a Dow-formula-based average. The TSE Index now uses a weighted formula that divides the price by the number of shares outstanding. Information published by the TSE in 1988 defines the nearly 1100 companies represented in this index as First Section firms that have met specific criteria. The 420 other companies traded on the exchange are classified into the Second Section and represent smaller and newly listed firms that do not meet the specifications and are not reflected in the index.

TSE began a financial futures market in 1985, under the surveillance of the Ministry of Finance (MOF), with the trading of the

Japanese Government Bond (JGB or Yen Bond) contract and in July 1988, a 20-year bond contract. The exchange began trading the TOPIX futures contract on September 3, 1988, and expects to add a US T-bond contract in the first quarter of 1989, and then options on these contracts.

The Yen Bond does not have limits; however, it does go into suspension. This means that an order imbalance exists, and the market will not reopen until the selling or buying moves through all bids or offers to satisfy the order. For example, if a large sell order comes into the market and the market goes into suspension, all bids will be hit until the order is filled. All contracts on the completed sell order are filled at the lowest price, and all bids (no matter that the bid price was higher) are also filled at this low price. While the market is in suspension, no orders can be canceled or entered. Clearly, it is very important to understand the differences in trading practices on each exchange.

The Osaka Securities Exchange began trading the Osaka Stock Futures 50 (OSF50) in 1987. This index is a physical delivery contract that represents 50 stocks that have been chosen according to capitalization and trading volume. On September 3, 1989, this exchange began trading the Nikkei Index, similar to the one traded on SIMEX.

The Ministry for International Trade and Industry (MITI) regulates trading on the Tokyo Commodity Exchange. Gold, silver, and platinum represent the metal market on which they expect to begin trading in options on cash in 1989. In addition, they also trade rubber, cotton yarn, and wool yarn.

The Ministry of Fisheries and Forestries (MFF) regulates trading on the Tokyo Grain Exchange and other agricultural commodities such as raw sugar, imported soybeans, adzuki (or red) beans, raw silk, and dry cocoons.

The MITI and MFF markets trade on a call session system where prices are set at four specific times a day; six times a day for the metals. These markets are connected by telephone from Tokyo to smaller markets in Osaka and Nagoya.

We were able to list eighteen futures exchanges in Japan; however, many seem to have price setting auctions at specific times during the day. Any statement of exactly how each of these exchanges operates was not possible at this writing. Let us leave this detailed research for another time and move to another city in this time zone.

Futures trading began in Hong Kong in 1909 at the Hong Kong Silver and Gold Society. The exchange is operated by a closed group of men (no women are allowed on the trading floor), and the group rarely allows new participants. The members make trades by physically hitting one another. In 1979, during the frenzied height of the gold market, physical activity on the floor became rather intense leaving a few members black and blue from the experience. Nonetheless, the exchange refuses to change the style of trading.

Wishing to trade futures under less stringent and dangerous conditions, a group of Chinese businessmen, who were not allowed membership in the Hong Kong Silver and Gold Society, opened the Hong Kong Commodity Exchange in 1975 to trade gold and grains. This exchange was replaced by the Hong Kong Futures Exchange (HKFE) in May 1985 and was incorporated on December 17, 1986. The new futures exchange was established at the behest of the Hong Kong Stock Exchange (HKSE), itself a consolidation of four smaller local stock exchanges. Contracts traded at the HKFE include cotton, soybeans, sugar, and gold. In 1986, the exchange listed the Hang Seng Index, a stock index created by the HKSE to be used on the futures exchange as the Hong Kong Stock Exchange barometer.

China is also joining the race to build a strong futures industry in the Far East. Newspapers overseas have reported that China plans to open three to five pilot futures markets in Canton by the end of 1988.

As trading today is conducted around the world, the history of the futures industry also circles the globe. Futures trading began in Japan, and now the industry returns there in full force. In the next section, we will look at the participants in the exchanges today.

3

Participants in Futures and Options Markets

Individuals and institutions who have a real presence on the floor and are active in the pits account for over half of the volume of the Chicago futures markets. It is not difficult to become an individual or institutional member; no particular educational requirements are demanded. However, adequate financial standards must be met and, for many, the money required makes entry rather difficult.

There are approximately 8000 members on the trading floors throughout the world. These players, vital to the strength of all financial futures contracts, consist of institutional hedgers, abitragers, institutional market makers, and individual market makers (locals).

INSTITUTIONAL HEDGERS

An institutional hedger uses the futures market for its most basic economic purpose: to offset risk exposure from potential future cash market transactions in a physical product. A product, in this case, could mean grains, metals, currencies, interest rates, or various types of indices. For commodities such as corn and cattle the reports of sizes and expectations are readily available from government agencies internationally. The trading of interest rates and indices can be somewhat confusing because such information is diverse and influenced by policies set by governments or private and public financial institutions.

In trading, one actually becomes the owner of the product represented by a futures contract at delivery. Let's consider some examples.

An auto dealer may need five million Deutsche marks to pay for vehicles he expects to receive in twelve months. He can purchase the actual currency on the bank forward market for delivery in one year and may choose to transact the deal with his banker as part of the total financing package. This creates the need for the bank to protect itself against risk that may occur because of the commitment to the auto dealer. The bank hedges in the currency and interest rate futures markets.

A construction company may estimate a major project that will not begin for eighteen months. Upon acceptance by its client, it can purchase US Treasury bills for future delivery in order to protect the construction firm against any interest rate exposure on its financing risk. An unfavorable change in interest rates would completely change cost projections. If the company has international exposure, it may choose to find this protection in the Eurodollar futures or in the interest rates futures market of the country directly related to the building site. Long- and/or short-term interest rate futures currently trade in Australia, Canada, England, France, Japan, New Zealand, and the United States.

The grain farmer should sell his product in midsummer, at seasonally high prices. Of course, this is impossible in the cash market because the product would have to be sold before the crop is actually harvested in the fall. The farmer does have the option to sell in the futures market, before harvest, during the summer in the low-supply, high-price time. The counterpart to the farmer, the miller, may require the wheat in midsummer. However, it would disrupt his pricing schedule if he is forced to purchase wheat at that time. Via the futures market, he can anticipate his needs and buy the product during the high-supply, low-price harvest period for future delivery. The ability of the miller to keep his own costs in line and maintain a somewhat constant resale price will keep his client, the baker, happy. The baker can then market his finished product (bread) at an acceptable price to the consumer.

Clearly, the miller will not buy at the bottom of the futures market and the farmer will not sell at the top of the futures market. Their activities as an entire community will help them to achieve more attractive average prices at each extreme. Who carries the risk of these hedge operations? It is the individual market makers and institutions who speculate on the trading floors of exchanges around the world.

Firms must decide whether or not to hedge. If the Deutsche mark is currently trading at high levels against the dollar and the mark is needed to pay for German-made products that will be received in six months, the hedging manager must evaluate the direction of the market and place the appropriate positions in the market. If the exchange rate difference between the Deutsche mark and the dollar is expected to change such that the Deutsche mark is lower in six months than it is today, it would be a better decision not to purchase Deutsche marks. Not only would the wait be profitable for the company, but a move against such a futures market position would require additional capital, which undoubtedly would have to be borrowed at current interest rates, adding further to the hedging expense.

The interest rate and exchange rate fluctuations will continue to be volatile, and business must make projections daily. Unfortunately, for many international companies, the decision to hedge can make or break the annual balance sheet and ill-timed hedging can cause a firm severe cash flow problems. Even when a company is large enough to have such expertise on the staff or to pay for this valuable advice, incorrect decisions are still possible. Options on futures trading allow a firm to protect itself from such risk. If market direction is uncertain, an option contract, viewed as an insurance premium, can protect a working contract or a project. Cost is fixed, duration of time is specified, and further risk exposure to market direction is zero.

ARBITRAGERS

The arbitrager moves between markets and facilitates trade by taking advantage of irregular price movements. In theory, the arbitrager never has a one-sided position because he is always long in one market and short in another market. An opportunity presents itself to the arbitrager whenever two markets move slightly outside of their normal trading differential. The goal is to lock in a small profit as the two markets move slightly outside of the normal trading range. The arbitrager expects the two price differences to return to their usual relationship, allowing him to liquidate the trade and realize a profit.

In the gold market in the late seventies, the arbitragers were very active in the futures markets at the COMEX and the CME. Since that time, the precious metals market is no longer split between these two markets but is now centered in New York. Although gold and silver futures are listed at Chicago exchanges, the profitable and valuable arbitrage capital has moved to other markets. With the introduction of night trading at the CBOT, particularly in US Treasury bond futures, another arbitrage or basis trade market now exists between the bond contract in the Chicago pit and the cash US Treasury bond market in Tokyo.

The CME's Standard & Poor's 500 stock index (S&P 500) offers another opportunity to manage risk against the movement of the underlying 500 stocks traded on the New York Stock Exchange (NYSE). Diverse applications among other index instruments in both futures and options in several countries offer unlimited possibilities for arbitrage, spreading, and popular options strategies.

Traders follow the many spreads in the international interest rate market:

Acronym	Market
TED	US Treasury bills vs. Eurodollars
NOB	US Notes vs. US Treasury bonds
BED	US Treasury bonds vs. Eurodollars
BAB	US Treasury bonds vs. Australian bonds
TAB	US Treasury bills vs. Australian 90-day Bank bills
BAF	US Treasury bonds vs. French Notional bonds

As the international markets overlap—allowing concurrent trading opportunities—the list will be limited only by the imagination of the participants, their available capital, and the quality of their communications network.

INSTITUTIONAL MARKET MAKERS

Many banks and brokerage firms now conduct principal or house account trading. Several brokerage firms focus exclusively on principal trading, and those with a client base serve their clients' needs by operating directly into the pit. These institutions add massive liquidity to the marketplace, and many manage their own positions on the trading floor. Upstairs traders call to the floor, and their orders are executed instantly as the traders and clerks communicate with each other through hand signals. These employees, who fight for positions each morning on the outside steps of the trading pits, are referred to as "arb clerks." Communication by this method encompasses much more than just quoting price to the phone clerks and is a highly developed skill on the Chicago and New York trading floors. Arb clerks relay information such as which houses are currently buying and selling and what is the position of the locals. They have developed an intuitive feeling of the trend in the pit. Most of these clerks understand the fundamental as well as the technical language of the markets. The arb clerk is usually young, highly trained, often well schooled and market educated.

INDIVIDUAL MARKET MAKERS

The individual market maker, who is often referred to as a trader or local in Chicago and abroad, has an extremely important role in today's marketplace. Yet until recently, this position was little respected outside the Chicago futures community, and many of the individuals may not have realized how important they are to the long-term existence of the market. Traders vary on every exchange floor. Some are marginally capitalized, some are financially strong enough to continue in the markets for the long term, and a few have greater wealth than some institutional firms. It is this diversity that allows the market to distribute the risk over a broad base of individual holders. This distribution is the key to the survival of the markets through any crisis situation.

The 508-point drop in the Dow Jones Industrial Average on October 19, 1987, illustrates this point. While the NYSE remained open on October 19 and 20, many individual stocks on the floor and in the Dow ceased trading. This action is taken when the specialist (individual or firm) cannot continue to buy when he has too much inventory to sell nor to sell when he has too little inventory. A market-maker system instead of a specialist system would broaden the base of possible buyers and sellers on the floor of the NYSE, allowing the marketplace to better absorb extreme changes in price. It would also remove the substantial risk and volatility inherent in the current system.

The two important influences in this severe decline can be tied directly to the fact that the institutional participants stopped the activity of their pit traders. This affected the liquidity of the market and exacerbated the problem. First, the inability to sell the stocks that were closed forced equity users to enter sell orders in the Standard & Poor's 500 stock index (S&P 500) futures pit in an effort to find protection. Second, arbitragers were paralyzed because individual stocks had stopped trading and the capital requirements forced them out of the market. Capital requirements problems occurred because futures transactions settle every day and stock transactions settle in five days. Therefore, traders could not use credits from one transaction to cover debits on another transaction.

Why are we talking about arbitrage, here, in the individual market maker section? Because market makers, small firms and individuals, were the only ones who were left in the pit that day. The important fact is that the individual market makers continued to make a market during the entire move. This shows that a market can continue under the most extreme conditions and displays the breadth and long-term strength of the system and its participants. Large amounts of money were made and lost during this time, but the losses of individual market makers were spread out over a broad base of traders allowing the market activities to continue even though a few institutional houses lost funds that threatened their survival.

Market makers may position-trade from a minute to a few days, or they may operate much like arbitragers by spreading. The spreader, like an arbitrager, trades the price differential between two related contract markets or two different expiries of the same contract market. The function of the spreader in different expiries gives a particular contract market greater depth as professional institutions can easily put on hedge positions that expire further into the future. Clearly, this flexibility offers the physical users of the market greater protection and does not require them to "roll over" positions as often. The differential takes into consideration interest rates, current and expected, as well as price expectations for the product represented by the contract. The spreader and the arbitrager expose themselves to risk when changing market conditions cause sudden swings in the price differentials. The risk becomes greater as they choose to trade less related products.

MARKET PARTICIPANTS AROUND THE WORLD

Local memberships must be obtained for every person trading on the floor on most exchanges. At this point, locals exist at all major exchanges throughout the world except the TSE and MATIF. The SFE has multilevel memberships. A single full clearing membership allows the organization to place two persons per contract market in the pits to trade. Firm traders execute customer orders and may not trade for themselves, but brokers may trade a house account. A local membership at a lower price permits an individual to trade for himself and fill orders on an independent basis. Locals must not represent outside interests. An associate member may not execute his own business nor trade on the floor, but will receive a reduction in fees if he is also a member of the International Commodities Clearing House, Ltd. (ICCH). Institutions represent 80 percent of the trading at the SFE.

Sydney is looking at "Chicago style" pit trading and plans to build a new trading floor using many design and communication applications. Internal structure is slower to change since a revised membership would increase competition and those in power now fear loss of market share. In reality, more competition would probably increase market volume considerably, making their pits a great deal more liquid. Efficient firms would not only maintain share, but also would show overall increases in per-contract volume.

The SFE has made an extensive commitment to developing a strong local trader population with an attractive permit program. Those traders in the business for many years can attest to the fact that immense and high volumes do not necessarily mean good profits for participants. A quiet, orderly market with adequate volume can be a far more civilized environment in which to operate. As a result, the SFE has had some success in encouraging individuals from all over the world to apply for temporary trading privileges on its floor. Traders may simply want to expand their trading horizon while experiencing life in another country for a period of time, or they may want to experience trading practices of a particular floor before making a long-term commitment to an exchange.

The SIMEX has developed a strong local population of traders as a result of the mutual offset relationship with the CME. This offset arrangement, though efficient, has not produced enough volume to satisfy the participants. The number of institutional participants in this market has increased because the SIMEX is linked with the CME, and works as an extended trading session. The HKFE was developing a good local membership base until the sharp decline in the Hang Seng Index in October 1987. It was unclear at press time whether this exchange would continue unless it could begin listing the viable interest rate contracts that are awaiting approval today and could expect to begin trading before the end of the last quarter of 1989. When an exchange addresses the true economic needs of its own country's markets and communicates during that market contract design, the chance of success is greatly enhanced.

Institutional interest constitutes 85 to 95 percent of the business at the MATIF and the LIFFE. The London exchange made a weak effort to attract local traders, and the MATIF is merely entertaining the idea. MATIF officials seem to view locals as highly independent persons who are too difficult to manage. They prefer to avoid the risk of incorporating the individual speculator into the system. The mismanagement of the "old boys network" in the London Metal Exchange (LME) metals disaster may give an appropriate view of risk. The LME situation was an example of margin monies that were not called forth from firms when the market moved against their positions. The historically good families and firms that stood behind the trading had not been required to file financial reports for many years. Regardless, it is a good reminder that there is no substitute for doing business in the proper manner at all levels.

The MATIF was established by action of the government in 1985 and is regulated by the Futures Council. The council is composed of three brokers, three insurance firms, and the Central Bank of France. François Guilbert, currently Directeur du Département de l'Administration, was the exchange's first employee. In mid 1987, M. Guilbert reported that the exchange was interested in creating a local membership.[12] By October of that year, in the middle of the now-famous stock market crash and with volume at the MATIF at healthy levels, the directeur général, while in Chicago, said that the exchange was not convinced that locals were necessary or even desirable. The more than 30,000 contracts traded on the opening of the first options on futures contract at the MATIF suggests that the exchange is functioning very well without local member participation. Its sudden and surprising success may cause planning that limits growth to the narrow base of institutional business. However, institutions often act together by entering or leaving the marketplace as a group, and a broader base of public participation and local traders would give the MATIF better insurance for the future. Nevertheless, this system is working for the MATIF, and the American system, amidst a state of great technological change, is also working. It is possible to do good business in different ways.

The visual appearance and differences of the trading floors are very striking to a gallery observer. The different functions of CME floor personnel are clearly definable by jacket colors, and a tour of this exchange is especially good for market explanation. The CBOT floor uses badge definition and it is not easy to determine a person's function at a glance—even for members. All semblance of organization completely falls apart at the World Trade Center in New York, which is the home of the five New York futures exchanges. Unfortunately, when the five exchanges agreed to share space, they divided it by square footage rather than by volume, which would have been flexible and more appropriate. This has given the Coffee, Sugar & Cocoa Exchange very comfortable quarters for trading and has forced the New York Mercantile Exchange (NYMEX) into a desperately crowded space. It is difficult to imagine all five exchanges agreeing on an expensive remodeling program or a new building. Poor lighting and maintenance along with no dress code add to an already bad situation. The conditions there are stressful and can be a personal, emotional drain over several years. It is easy to see why the sophisticated equity markets in that city have little respect for the disorder on the futures side.

The rough and ruthless environment in American futures pits tends to produce a gruff individual who cannot be easily transferred into the normal business situation offered by the institutional side. His honesty and forthright opinions are to be applauded, but presentation style and finesse have often been left in university courses past. The pit etiquette in Sydney, Singapore, Paris, and London demands that business be conducted in proper dress, using appropriate language and demeanor befitting a financial institution. However, some attribute this to the lower volume in those markets.

LEADERSHIP

Exchanges vary greatly in their leadership structures. At the Chicago exchanges, the membership manages direction with committees made up of individual and institutional members who represent their own interest and the interest of their clients. The risk management and clearing operations are dictated by brokerage (clearing) firms. This ensures the financial integrity of the institution. As a result, decisions relating to the costly computerization of the clearinghouse facilities have received the priority they deserve, and those facilities run smoothly and efficiently.

The CME and the CBOT display authoritarian and democratic leadership styles, respectively. On close examination, long-term strategic planning at the highest level of management creates fierce competition between these two major exchanges. However, benefits accrue to members through programs and support services available and keep member floor trader fees low and exchange volumes high. The competition is to keep the activity and good traders at each exchange. The public benefits through a competitive fee structure. The result continues to be one that concentrates on running the business to preserve the public image of fairness and the institutional image of the economic value of risk management. Anything that damages these two primary functions is considered a major threat.

The New York futures exchanges are controlled by the floor brokers, and attention to the clearing operation has been neglected. An expensive default by a COMEX member, exacerbated by poor administrative handling, brought the extent of their problem to the attention of the CFTC. Except for the NYMEX, which instituted a continuous clearing system, progress for correction of outdated computer clearing facilities is slow. The move by the New York futures exchanges into a single building and onto a single trading floor was an excellent first step. If they would put aside their individual differences and consolidate into a single exchange, they would make powerful gains. Consolidated, the five exchanges would be one of the largest futures exchanges in the world with diverse contract selection for the investor. Their combined resources would enable them to create a strong clearing and administrative facility. Income from total per-trade transaction fees and the added credibility of the group would put the New York exchanges in a position for a broad marketing thrust. New York has not been able to bring this vision to reality.

A list follows of the key participants of the futures industry in order of clearing flow.

MARKET PARTICIPANTS

FUTURES EXCHANGE Institution established for the purpose of facilitating transactions between buyers and sellers of futures and options on futures contracts.

CLEARINGHOUSE Matches buyers to sellers. Each clearinghouse has very different procedures and levels of guarantee. The CME is the only exchange where the clearinghouse is the same legal entity as the exchange and guarantees each buyer and each seller.

CLEARING FIRM A member of an exchange(s) that has approval of the clearinghouse to enter executed trades for matching. All trades must be entered to the clearinghouse through a clearing firm. The firm may have NFA registration in the United States as a Futures Commission Merchant (FCM).

FUTURES COMMISSION MERCHANT An exchange membership is not required of an FCM. An exchange clearing member must carry the business on its books. However, an FCM may handle customer funds and issue the client account transaction statements. This registration finds a variety of operational modes.

1. Some FCMs have memberships on specific exchanges and execute trades for their clients on the floor, but prefer not to have clearing arrangements on the exchanges.
2. An FCM may operate a retail or institutional business but use a clearing firm for all executions and generation of client statements.
3. A clearing firm outside the United States must register with the NFA as an FCM in order to solicit business within the United States. SFE members are exempt from registration.

ASSOCIATE MEMBER Has different meanings in different countries. Many exchanges who use the ICCH as their clearing facility will also allow a company to become an associate member in order to clear their own trading through the ICCH. Those firms may not be active on the floor but require floor members to execute trading in their behalf. It can also refer to a specific division of an exchange to which somewhat restricted floor privileges are extended.

ADVISOR Advises clients on trading decisions and research information. Although exchange membership is not required, in the United States an advisor must be a registered Associated Person (AP).

FLOOR BROKER Executes orders in the pit (often referred to as an order filler) and must be an exchange member. Most exchanges require a broker to attend seminars and complete testing before he is allowed to do business on the floor. Although he may execute orders for many clearing firms, a broker must be approved by a single firm before doing business on the floor. In the United States, NFA registration is required for floor brokers.

MEMBER Individual, firm, or corporation who has been approved by an exchange board and purchased a membership (seat). He may or may not exercise his floor privileges. The seat may be assigned to a clearing firm or, on some exchanges, leased to another individual.

LOCAL Member who has floor privileges and makes a market (trades for his own account) on a daily basis; also referred to as a market maker.

INTRODUCING BROKER Has different meanings in different countries. Introducing brokers (IBs) may arrange institutional business that goes directly to trading floors or they may actually operate their own retail order desk. Exchange membership is not required. In the United States, IBs are registered with the NFA.

MONEY MANAGER Makes all trading decisions for customers. Exchange membership is not required. In the United States, money managers are registered with the NFA as a Commodity Trading Advisor (CTA) or Commodity Pool Operator (CPO) and are usually paid on an incentive basis.

4

Information Flow in the Markets

In this chapter, we will discuss the importance of communication and data to the trader on both the domestic and international levels; the way in which exchanges handle order flow, price information, and telecommunications; and the willingness of different trading centers to share information among themselves and with the public.

A key feature in the success of futures trading and in the success of the different exchanges around the world is the effective and efficient use of information. Not only do exchanges provide the trading floor to buy and sell pork bellies, the Footsie, bonds, and greasy wool, but they also disseminate price data to vendors who send this information around the world. Exchanges use this price information to monitor the risk exposure of their clearing firms and the clearinghouse. Information is a valuable commodity, and management of this commodity is an important aspect of the business.

Effective communication of what takes place in the pits, in other words, what is the current price of June Swiss franc futures or May corn futures requires, among other things, an efficient trading floor. The physical plant and the technological structure of the trading floor can directly influence the volume growth of an exchange. The flexibility of the Chicago floors has clearly been an advantage over the limited changes that can be made in most environments.

Moreover, since price swings can have a dramatic impact on traders and the exchanges, forecasts must be monitored carefully using highly developed price models and advanced computer software systems. Traders have always realized the need for state-of-the-art communications and forecasting techniques. As we discussed in the history of the Chicago exchanges, the founding members of the CBOT coincidentally began grain trading with the start-up of the telegraphic message. The early speculators understood the importance of quick communication. The public must know the price immediately, and they must be able to communicate with a broker to act upon that price.

Millions of dollars are budgeted for communication systems on trading floors around the world. Over $9 million was spent on the telephone system for the CME's nearly 40,000-square-foot trading floor, which reportedly uses the largest hardwired system in the world. Except for a computer malfunction that delayed an opening for two hours, the CME has never lost its floor operations due to telephone problems because the exchange operates two systems to handle the daily workload of the trading floor. A battery back-up is ready in case any complications develop. A generator back-up is not used because generators can also fail.[13]

THE PHYSICAL PLANT AND ORDER FLOW

Orders for futures and options contracts are placed over the telephone or, in some cases, sent through wire transmissions and received by phone clerks or clearing firm brokers on the trading floors. The pits at many exchanges are surrounded by trading desks or trading booths. Each booth, which is often tiered around the pits, has an array of telephones, time stamp machines, stacks of blank order forms, and various news and price information systems. The information systems used at the trading desks are chosen and installed by the clearing firms.

Clerks wear headsets or use conventional telephone receivers to take orders and relay pit information to brokers and customers around the world. In some cases, floor clerks are talking to brokers or customers through standard hand-held telephone systems. At other times, clerks give a play-by-play account of the action in the pit to a client who trades in and out of the market actively during the day.

Orders received by telephone clerks are time-stamped and relayed to clerks by hand signals or delivered by runners to brokers in the pits for execution. Once a trade is executed in the pit, the filling broker records the price, with whom the trade was made (which could be with as many traders as the total number of contracts executed per order), and the time the trade took place. Runners then return the order to the firm's phone desk.

The booths are placed around the pits so that there are clear sight lines between brokers and their assistants. Phone clerks need an unobstructed view of data boards on the floors which carry price information for contracts traded around the world. Trading floors display prices for all types of global contracts, not just those found at their exchange. To the Chicago debt futures trader, the price of the Commodity Research Bureau cash index and the long-gilt contract at the LIFFE are just as important as the price movement of the CBOT and CME interest rate contracts. Member firms demand unobstructed sight lines on trading floors in order to view the wall price boards and activity in the pits.

Glen Windstrup, president of Task Management, a Chicago-based consulting firm for exchange floor planning, explains that nearly all major trading floors throughout the world use the Feranti-Packard electronic price information boards. These boards carry real-time price changes, opening and closing ranges, and high and low prices for the current session and for the life of the contract. Some boards also feature estimated volume figures for the day. Although prices are real-time, board systems are not always quick enough to estimate volume, and systems can be slower than the market. During a fast market opening, for example, prices trade faster than they can be displayed on the boards. Space limitations on trading floors also influence how much information is displayed on the information boards.[14]

Most of the world's trading floors are high-ceiling structures, which allows for any remodeling and is psychologically more desirable for the traders and staff. The environment feels less claustrophobic as well as less tension-filled. The CME trading floor is one of the most "flexible" floors in the world. The CME uses an "interstitial" plan, which allows both floor configurations and electronic and communication set-ups to be adjusted during business hours. Although other exchanges have raised trading floors, the CME interstitial layout lets personnel actually work under the floor. A room under the trading pits enables tradesmen to work during normal business hours, which increases efficiency of repairs and adjustments.

As locals maneuver for the best "turf" position (or location) in the trading pits, clearing firms also vie for the booth space that offers the shortest route to the pit or the best view of the trading action. Exchanges determine which member firms are placed in which booth location, taking into account the firm's volume in that particular contract, the firm's overall exchange volume, whether or not the firm is conducting customer or house trading from that position, as well as the firm's political influence with the exchange. A clearing firm that is trading for the house account may be considered second to a firm conducting large customer business.

RELAY OF PRICE INFORMATION

Price is established in the pit, the heart of the information system, among the locals and brokers using the open-outcry system. In most trading arenas, pit reporters, who are exchange employees, relay the price of the futures contract as the trade takes place. Often through walkie-talkie systems, the pit reporter sends the information to floor personnel who instantly display the prices on trading boards on the floors, which in turn are picked up by vendors who send real-time prices around the world. The control and display of data have become a lucrative venture for many exchanges. At times, it has also been a controversial subject.

Maintaining the necessary computer support and tracking price information is expensive, and selling this valued commodity is very profitable. Annual reports show that selling price quotes to vendors around the world was the CBOT's number one source of revenue and the CME's second highest source of income. In fact, in 1987, the CBOT earned about $23.5 million from the sale of price quotes, a $7 million increase from the previous year, and the CME received about $19.2 million, up from $14.2 million in 1986.

Not all exchanges capture huge profits from selling price quotes. Philosophies across the Atlantic differ greatly. The LIFFE, according to officials there, feels that price quotes should be distributed for a nominal fee, if any at all, since knowledge about the marketplace generates volume and provides for the growth of the exchange.

Not only do trading exchanges market price information with highly developed communication and data systems, but exchanges and clearing firms use this data to monitor their risk. The clearinghouse is the cornerstone of financial reliability in the futures market, and they use their highly developed internal data transmission systems for control.

OPTIONS-RELATED INFORMATION

An options trader on the floor requires "trade tables" to guide his trading decisions. Trade tables indicate prices at which options positions should be added to or liquidated according to the strike price and the underlying commodity price. These tables are usually developed by off-the-floor options specialists who rely on certain data that strategists believe to be the best indicators of profitable options positioning. Most options models contain basic information such as current underlying futures price, the current interest rate, historical price volatility of the underlying commodity, strike prices, and time to expiration. Different clearing firms rely on different options models such as the Black-Scholes and binomial models of options trading, or proprietary systems.

Each trade table is based on volatility and changes constantly during the day. Consequently, the options specialist off the floor must coordinate his real-time prices around the clock, whereas options clearing firms with a strong and active presence on the floor must be able to communicate with the upstairs options specialist to expand trade tables when markets move quickly.

Trade table architects report that they rely on the pit sense of floor traders in determining points for options execution and for market direction and price volatility. Options traders as well as futures traders rely on real-time price information for effective risk management.

At the clearinghouse level, specialists monitor clearing firm positions around-the-clock to maintain stability and margin requirements. The risk manager of a clearinghouse must analyze the company's net exposure at present prices and at theoretical prices. Hypothetical trading positions are developed continually, according to most risk managers, so that clearinghouses may be prepared to increase margins or liquidate positions if market conditions threaten clearinghouse financial strength.

5

Market Regulations

In the early days of United States futures trading, the Department of Agriculture regulated the commodity pits. There was, however, no regulatory body to monitor the financial futures which began with the inception of currency futures trading. Broad and sweeping reform took place when the United States Congress formed the Commodity Futures Trading Commission (CFTC) in 1974. Futures industry leaders in Chicago helped the federal government set up the organization and educate its personnel in an effort to "clean up" the negative image of the trading community and give those already in the industry the muscle to force undesirable practices out of the large established exchanges and the smaller inefficient exchanges.

In 1982, the National Futures Association (NFA) took on the job of monitoring the self-regulation of the exchanges. The NFA gathers many statistics about the industry, assists exchanges in enforcing rules, and controls registration and testing for industry professionals. The categories of registration include Futures Commission Merchant (FCM), Floor Broker (FB), Introducing Broker (IB), Commodity Trading Advisor (CTA), and Commodity Pool Op-

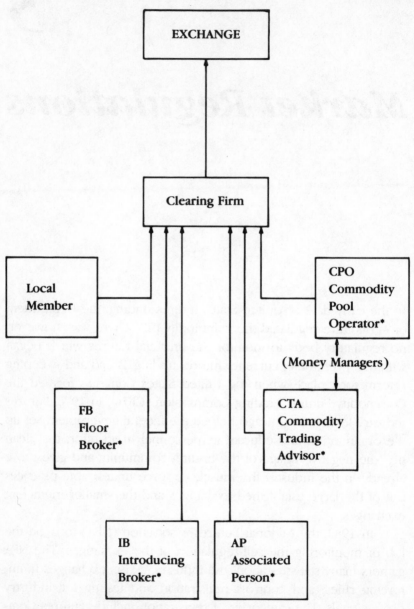

*CFTC registration required.

FIGURE 5.1 Futures transactions order flow.

erator (CPO). Individuals in each of these categories may generate futures transactions, which are always passed on to the exchanges through the appropriate clearing firm, as shown in Figure 5.1.

The high cost of meeting stringent regulatory and financial requirements as well as the need to answer legal disputes in formal court quickly squeezed out marginal operations in the brokerage community. Although some crucial image problems of trading were confronted and resolved, regulations dramatically raised the cost of doing business in the industry. Heavy volume created demands from the regulators as well as from the public for rapid price data transmission, transaction reconstruction, and good statistical research facilities. Exchanges have answered this demand by designing fast price communication systems and increasing their audit and compliance staff. Trading floors also made various non–price-related information available to the CFTC, the NFA, and the Futures Industry Association (FIA).

FUTURES REGULATION TODAY

Rules that the industry must follow in order to conduct business are extensive. They are most enforceable on the trading floor where all transactions are closely monitored and time stamped. In spite of high volume, the Chicago exchanges accurately reconstruct a trade to the minute with Computerized Trade Reconstruction (CTR).

Although international and domestic exchanges outside Chicago experience much lower volumes, many have an efficient clearing system referred to as continuous clearing. Continuous clearing is the process of matching trades during the trading day instead of waiting until the close of trading for computer processing. The International Commodities Clearing House, Ltd. (ICCH) and the LIFFE, in a joint development venture, use this procedure. The LIFFE record volume day was in excess of 180,000 contracts, matched by continuous clearing, with all mismatches corrected by 8:30 P.M. of the same day. In a Chicago interview, Barry Taylor, formerly of the LIFFE's marketing department, said, "It is no secret that these procedures (continuous clearing) are the envy of the industry and are being seriously investigated by the major exchanges in the USA."[15]

The NYMEX is the first US exchange to implement continuous clearing so that a trade processing error will appear on a screen display within fifteen minutes to an hour after the transaction has taken place. The SFE, LIFFE, and MATIF have used continuous clearing for years, even during the high-volume days of October 1987. Continuous clearing offers advantages for floor brokers because errors are corrected quickly.

High volume has not allowed the US exchanges to institute continuous clearing and remains a weak link in their clearing systems. The traders on these high-volume exchanges must arrive more than one hour before the opening in order to negotiate with other traders over the famous "out-trade sheets." There have been many problems among traders when one member acts in a less than scrupulous manner and does not turn in (or falsifies) trading cards. There have even been incidents of nonmembers entering the trading floor wearing elaborate disguises and actually trading in the commodity pits. When a member uses unacceptable business practice, there is little that can be done short of expulsion. Unfortunately, some of these undesirable persons have caused financial damage to otherwise exemplary members.

The term "bucket shop," coined in the early days of grain trading in Chicago, is still heard in various parts of the world. An Associated Person who receives an order from a client and does not pass the order through to an exchange pit to be filled is said to "bucket" the trade. The AP's clearing firm either takes the other side of the order itself or matches two clients' orders (often not even near the actual price being traded in the pit at the time). This highly illegal practice was the most blatant abuse of client confidence in the United States before strict regulation. As traders are becoming more sophisticated, the practice is finally addressed in Europe and the Far East.

REGULATION OF EXCHANGES OUTSIDE THE UNITED STATES

Exchanges in other major centers around the world are establishing guidelines similar to those in the United States. Robert Wilmouth, president of the NFA, estimates that most of his schedule is consumed with the discussion on formation of international regulatory agencies. The United States exchanges are in the unique position of having a separate futures regulatory agency to promote and safeguard their best interests. Many foreign exchanges, such as the MATIF and TSE, must confront their regulatory agencies for developments in their markets, because their agencies are biased toward the cash and equity markets. Although the American model might be flawed, traders need to function in a global community where trading practices are fairly similar from trading floor to trading floor. If a trader receives poor order placement or poor floor execution or even if reporting requirements are drastically different at a certain exchange, the trader will simply not use that particular futures market again.

The CME custom is that floor brokers operate in a "held" mode; it was this practice that built volume, and it is considered good business. This means that if the market activity trades through a price order, that order has to be filled. This policy enables off-the-floor market participants to deal with a trade decision based on market activity even before confirmations are telephoned to their office. The CBOT has never made the decision to operate on this level even though many members feel it is a good policy, especially as overseas business increases. Extreme market volatility has caused a very limited number of CME floor brokers to work on a "not held" basis. Clearing firms have been forced to divert business from these brokers in order to satisfy customer demands for this service. If the exchanges are unable to conduct orderly markets under extremely volatile conditions, the uncertainty experienced by traders will cause them to direct their business to other futures contracts or entirely different investment vehicles.

Industry and clearinghouse regulations seek to ensure financially sound exchanges, and a lack of compliance can result in the financial collapse of an exchange. For example, in October 1987, an Asian businessman defaulted on his long futures position in the Hang Seng Index at the HKFE. His true positions had not been monitored carefully by the exchange clearing system. Trading statements were carried with several brokers through various undercapitalized companies. He reportedly was responsible for nearly three quarters of the 1.2 billion (HK dollar) default suffered by the HKFE. The trader argued that because the exchange closed for four days after the initial market crash, he could not liquidate his position and thus suffered the loss. For many people in the industry, his multiple company structures and actions speak for his intentions, and the courts decided that he would have to pay back the funds over several years. In the meantime, several of the brokerage firms with whom he was dealing have been forced into liquidation or merger.

How could a default like this happen? Brokerage firms in the United States check the capital strength of individuals or corporations very thoroughly. A close watch on positions is maintained since the clearing firms assume the financial burden of the trader. In the case of the HKFE, improper regulatory control allowed one man to severely damage the entire local marketplace.

6

The Clearinghouse and Financial Safeguards

In most cases, the clearing corporation or clearinghouse is a separate body from the futures exchange. It acts as the guarantor of each contract. The clearinghouse becomes the middleman for each trade, acting as buyer to every seller and seller to every buyer. In this way, the financial integrity of the exchange is ensured.

To monitor the risk inherent in futures trading, exchanges work in conjunction with the clearinghouse to track the trading volume and positions of its member firms. Furthermore, exchanges review the back-office procedures and the daily operations of each clearing firm. Each exchange is subject to the integrity and accuracy of its accounting systems. The audit departments of the exchanges regularly inspect the books of each clearing firm to ensure that segregation requirements and other industry rules are met. Violations in customer funds segregation rules are considered serious and can result in penalties imposed by appropriate exchange committees.

This topic has received special attention lately in light of the stock market crash of October 1987. The strength of the clearinghouses in the futures industry was tested during the dramatic price swings that occurred that autumn. Although these systems were successful through this crisis, weaknesses were revealed. Immediate actions were taken to increase capital requirements and to modify programs and procedures.

A clearinghouse can only be as strong as the clearing firms and members of an exchange. To become a clearing firm at an exchange (in other words, to clear trades through the clearinghouse for customers, brokers, and locals), firms must meet certain capital requirements, own a specified number of member seats, and submit a security deposit to the clearinghouse.

To become a clearing member at the CME, for example, six memberships (two seats in each division) must be assigned to the firm. The company must have liquid assets of $1.5 million and a security deposit of $100,000 or 1 percent of the total gross margin requirement of the firm, whichever is greater, with a cap of $2 million. Financial statements are reviewed quarterly. The aggregate security deposits at the CME, as of April 1988, stood at approximately $40 million.

Other major exchanges said they also closely examine firms that are involved in businesses unrelated to the futures market. If a firm does not specialize in the futures business, only a small percentage of its total liquid assets are acceptable. The liquid assets requirement by the CBOT depends on the firm's daily volume and overnight positions. This figure is constantly monitored, and quarterly reviews set minimum requirements.

Parent company guarantee rules have recently gone into effect at some exchanges. They require a large company with a smaller and separate futures operation to guarantee, without limit, all trades for the house account of the parent company. Clearing corporations are also responsible for collecting margins and daily losses, paying out daily gains, and handling all deliveries.

Exchanges monitor risk among clearing firms by tracking the trading volume and positions of clearing firms or individual traders; maintaining margin levels to insure themselves against adverse price swings; establishing price limits as well as position limits on firms for each contract; and perhaps most recently, educating the clearing firms and traders on how to use the markets efficiently and effectively.

Many clearing firms themselves have developed sophisticated computer systems that constantly update the company's net exposure to risk in the marketplace. For instance, one particular firm maintains an order entry system at its trading booths on the exchange floors. The system allows brokers or staff to enter trades into the system on the trading floor once they are executed. In this manner, after the execution of every trade, the company's net exposure in the marketplace is automatically and instantly determined. In some cases, order entry systems not only update a specific clearing firm's position, but also send trade positions directly to the clearinghouse.

WORLDWIDE CLEARINGHOUSE LINKS

The events of the October 1987 stock market crash have highlighted the need for reliable and effective risk management. As traders become more global in their risk exposure and institutional investors begin to trade in United States, Asian, and European markets, links in clearinghouse communication will become essential. This is evident by the recent agreement among nine exchanges to share financial information about common clearing firms.

The new computerized service will gather and share data with other clearinghouses on daily profits and losses of joint member firms. In day-to-day operations, clearing firms register executed trades and settle trades with their respective exchanges. With the exception of the Chicago Board of Trade Clearing Corporation and the Chicago Mercantile Exchange, who already use the service, exchanges currently must telephone one another to keep track of a firm's position. The following exchanges will be included under the new agreement:

> Chicago Board of Trade
> Chicago Mercantile Exchange
> Coffee, Sugar & Cocoa Exchange
> Commodity Exchange of New York
> New York Futures Exchange
> New York Mercantile Exchange
> Kansas City Board of Trade
> Minneapolis Grain Exchange

The next step will be for the exchanges around the world to share clearing information to ensure financial safeguards across different time zones.

Additionally, all exchanges in the United States have elected representatives to the Joint Audit Committee. This committee keeps the exchanges in constant communication with each other to warn about possible problems arising from large, risky positions assumed by clearing firms or individuals. They also work to coordinate exchange regulation and reporting requirements required by the CFTC. A separate and new committee has been formed to discuss common regulatory concerns that include the Joint Audit Committee, the CFTC, and the SEC.

THE INTERNATIONAL COMMODITIES CLEARING HOUSE, LTD.

The most global clearing corporation and certainly one of the oldest is the International Commodities Clearing House, Ltd. (ICCH). It was founded as the London Produce Clearing House for Sugar and Coffee in 1888; its name was changed in 1973.

In a communications environment that was not conducive to

daily international electronic data transfer, the ICCH cleared for exchanges around the world. The list of exchanges is impressive:

London Futures and Options Exchange
International Petroleum Exchange of London Ltd.
London International Financial Futures Exchange
Baltic Futures Exchange
Sydney Futures Exchange
Australian Financial Futures Market
New Zealand Futures Exchange
Hong Kong Futures Exchange

The war years in Europe closed the markets from 1939 to 1945. There was a great loss of expertise and currency controls at that time, so no business took place again until the early 1950s. At that time, the United Dominion Trust put up 50,000 pounds sterling in order to reestablish the flow of business.

When the LIFFE opened for business in 1982, Trustee Savings Bank purchased the United Dominion Trust with no intention to enter the futures market. After learning that it owned the ICCH, the bank asked, "What is a future?" The decision was thus made to spread the risk among financial institutions. The following six banks: Barclays, Lloyds, Midland, National Westminster, Royal Bank of Scotland, and Standard Chartered now carry a 100-million-pound-sterling guarantee for the ICCH.

The well-designed continuous clearing software used by the ICCH, according to a spokesman there, "is so user-friendly that anyone can learn to use it in less than two hours."[16] In 1985, the ICCH developed the Automated Trading System for the NZFE, the only fully automated futures exchange in the world, as well as the computerized clearing system for INTEX, the Bermuda-based computerized trading exchange now owned by Telerate. In other related business, the ICCH reported that it owns 10 percent equity of the French clearinghouse, Banque Commerce Commercial, which clears trades for the Bourse de Commerce du Paris.

The MATIF in Paris does its own clearing, but the system was developed and is maintained for them by the ICCH. Although the MATIF system is being pushed to the limits by unexpected high volume, Bernard Pech, head of operations at the French exchange, says the system has performed quite well.

The past actions of the futures exchanges around the world point to the fact that they meet their obligations, and this has been accomplished because their systems operate on a sound footing and display sound business practices.

MARGINING SYSTEMS

Futures margins act as a good faith deposit or performance bond. Margin is the amount of money that must be deposited by the firm with the clearinghouse for each contract bought or sold at the exchange. If the market moves adversely, more margin money must be deposited. Each exchange sets minimum initial and maintenance margin levels on its futures contracts. The amount of margin also depends on whether the customer is a speculator or a hedger.

Margins are based on historical risk factors; they are not changed on a regular basis by the Board of Governors in an arbitrary manner. Margin analysts plot price movements of the underlying commodity and determine a statistical measure for a daily range in that contract. This measure is a standard deviation of price movement. One standard deviation comprises nearly two-thirds of the daily range movement of a particular commodity. Two standard deviations comprise nearly 90 percent of a daily range movement in a certain contract. Three standard deviations cover the entire price range of a commodity.

In the United States, the CFTC monitors the margin requirements for the futures industry, whereas the Securities and Exchange Commission (SEC) regulates and establishes margins for the equities industry. All margins, whether they are established for futures or equities markets, are designed to cover 90 percent of the price movements of the underlying contracts, or two standard deviations of price movement.

Clearinghouses around the world employ either gross or net margining, although many exchanges say they may convert to the gross margining system in the near future. In the gross margining system, an exchange reviews the entire market position of a clearing firm. Margins must be maintained by each clearing firm for all long and short open positions.

For example, if clearing firm A is long 150 February pork bellies and short 375 February pork bellies, according to gross margining users, clearing member A has a position worth 525 February pork bellies and the margin imposed upon that clearing member is based on 525 outstanding pork belly contracts. On the other hand, in net margining systems, clearing member A is net short 225 February pork bellies and the margin imposed upon his account is only for those positions. Margins are collected only for the firm's net long or net short position.

Gross margining ensures that the clearinghouse would have the funds on hand if a single day's loss is dramatic. The CME and the NYMEX are currently the only two exchanges in the United States that employ the gross margining system. Other exchanges in this country and the ICCH overseas base their margin requirements on the net-margining system. In January 1988 the CFTC installed new rules requiring gross margining on all foreign omnibus accounts at every exchange—unless the foreign firm can efficiently report all net positions and spreads.

In theory, today's futures positions are settled before the opening bell tomorrow morning. Trading positions are settled and risk is determined immediately. However, in the equities market, stock positions are settled in five business days. The futures participants currently need 10 to 15 percent margin money to execute trades. All positions are marked to market daily and settled with variation margin (cash) the next day before the market reopens.

Margin regulators set up minimum standards that brokerage and clearing member firms must maintain for their financial strength and integrity. Many firms require additional margin on retail accounts for their own protection. This not only reinforces the financial responsibility of the trader and the clearing firm, but also provides some "insurance time" for extreme market movement. As the volatile markets of October 1987 illustrated, margin requirements are changed by the exchange when market activity creates extreme daily ranges. For example, the CBOT adjusted margin levels more than 200 times that year.

In the options world, margins were first determined by the price movement of the underlying securities. Later, this practice changed as exchanges realized that the options contracts were subject to more dramatic price differentials than the underlying security and reacted as a separate marketplace from its underlying commodity. Options margins thus became a premium-based margining system. (Specifically, the long side of an option pays the premium, whereas the short side of the option is margined.) Virtually all options traded in the United States use premium-based or premium plus dollar add-on figure margining systems.

Exchanges apply several margin systems to the options market:

1. The "priority margin" system is based on strategies, the least risky (or least expensive, from a margin point of view) to the most risky (naked writing of puts or calls).
2. Futures style margining for options, or delta margining, and offset between futures and options positions were innovations of the LIFFE. The delta margining system is based on the delta neutral philosophy in options strategy theory and is the most cost-effective way to margin, from a trader's point of view.
3. Dollars At Risk (DAR) is a new system of margining currently being developed by the CME. The Dollars At Risk system is expected to better assess the actual risk exposure and eliminate some of the cash flow demands that are involved in the present margin policies.

As discussed, in futures trading, margins are calculated every day. The gains or losses are settled daily. Options traders pay or receive a premium for their contracts at the time of the transaction. At the time of this writing, gains from options positions cannot be used to cover losses in the futures contracts being used as a trading strategy. As hedged positions become too costly to maintain, the CME Dollars At Risk margining system may allow for broader application.

With increased use of both futures and options trading, as well as trading in different markets in different countries, the industry will need to develop a global margining system that covers risk but does not tie up credit lines.

FIDUCIARY RESPONSIBILITY

According to an NFA survey, "The CME has a $28 million trust fund that can be used for any purpose at the discretion of the Board of Governors. The CBOT has a fund of $10 million [which may be used] at the discretion of the Board of Trustees to infuse money to transfer customer positions and equities or cover customer positions and equities or to cover customer insolvency losses. The CBOT fund may not be used to benefit a clearing member firm of the CBOT."[17]

In a document printed by the CME in March 1988 and entitled "The Financial Safeguard System of the Chicago Mercantile Exchange,"[18] the procedures are clearly defined. As a general representation, in a proprietary account default, all segregated customer positions and monies are immediately moved to another clearing (firm) member. In a customer account default, all noninvolved customer positions and monies are moved to another clearing (firm) member. The document reads that if default occurs in the clearing (firm) member's customer account, "the clearinghouse has the right to apply all customer margin deposits for that account toward the default. Accordingly, the margins deposited by customers not causing the default are potentially at risk if there is a default in the customer account of their clearing firm members." Moreover, the CME would next apply its surplus funds "and the security deposits of the clearing membership, which totals 47 million." And if the default continues to be unsatisfied, the exchange would "invoke its mutual and several liability rule (Common Bond, 17 billion) which looks to all clearing (firm) members for remedy." Under no circumstances will customer margin deposits held by the clearinghouse for the segregated customer account of a clearing firm member "be used to cover either a proprietary or customer default of another clearing firm member. Customers doing business through a clearing firm member not involved in a default are insulated from losses incurred by the failure of another clearing firm member."[19]

In a survey conducted by the NFA in 1986, FCMs holding segregated customer funds had a combined net capital of nearly $6.5 billion. These firms must meet segregation requirements in excess of customer funds at a rate of 7 percent. Adjusted Net Capital (ANC) is computed using the following formula:

Current Assets − Adjusted Liabilities − Capital Charges = ANC

Any firm reporting less than 7 percent, but greater than the minimum of 4 percent is placed on an early warning list. The survey reveals that "the aggregate adjusted net capital in the industry exceeds four percent of customer funds required to be segregated." These figures are recognized as good by the industry; however, insolvency of a firm and customer protection are still issues that must be addressed.

The first area of concern in the event of insolvency is the orderly transfer of customer positions. This is especially important to a hedger who may face stringent penalties if his position were to be sold out in the defaulting firm and reestablished at a new firm. There are still unsettled legal issues regarding actions that were taken when COMEX, in response to the insolvency of Volume Investors, sold out customer positions. It is clearly understood that when something happens to injure a part of the industry, the entire industry suffers. New cooperation between exchanges and financial centers will improve services and ensure support.

7

Intermarket Communications

A common phrase in the futures industry these days is "passing the book." It is usually thought that extensive position sheets are being passed from city to city and that traders are buying and selling commodities and financial futures in this new 24-hour marketplace. This is passing the book. However, Phil Lynch of Shearson Lehman Hutton in Hong Kong says that passing the book does not always work.[20] Except for some dealer and commercial houses in London, New York, and Chicago where there are all-night trading desks, full-service 24-hour desks are not maintained in all financial centers. Lynch claims that the quality of persons available to run this type of facility is questionable at best. Consequently, to participate in overnight markets, institutions call their offices overseas and well-capitalized individuals who trade at night call their brokers at home.

Traders are individuals with specific strategies and techniques that they have developed over several years. Their market positions are usually executed after much effort and research. If it is not possible to educate two or three other persons with entirely different backgrounds in removed parts of the organization as to precisely how and why a decision was made, it is reasonable to understand why "the position book" does not move from desk to desk across time zones.

What does move between the financial control centers of firms and traders, however, is handling instructions. This is an art in itself, and there are many sad stories of how a trader in one center ruins ("blows out," in industry jargon) the position of a trader in the previous time zone simply because the handler did not follow instructions.

For example, in the middle of the night, a New York cash currency trader received a call from his Hong Kong desk when the market reached a particular price level. The trader had put on a long currency futures position during the day and wanted to monitor his position and market activity if prices reached a lower price level during the night. The key word is "monitor."

According to his instructions, the Hong Kong desk woke him up at the appointed price level and delivered an emotionally charged market report. The Hong Kong trader was obviously very bearish and the New York trader did not want to discourage him. (After all, he could be right; the Japanese yen had been declining for months.) Trying not to be influenced by an opposite opinion, the New York trader said "go for it" and hung up.

The New York trader sat in front of his computer the rest of the night monitoring his position through the London markets. Prices never reached his mental sell-stop. The market suddenly began a violent rally that would cause the futures to open sharply higher. At daybreak, with little sleep, he happily made his way to the office only to be informed that his position had been liquidated in Hong Kong.

The market in New York opened two hundred points higher, and he had missed the first leg of a two-year bull move in Japanese yen. He had no recourse, even though he always communicated buy and sell orders in precise price futures terminology. The bank had never put in place an official procedure for handling instructions or industry jargon.

Much business is done between traders in the cash financial

community with "go for it" or "do it" type instructions. Unfortunately, many assumptions are made about the intentions of the person on the other end of the telephone. Most of the futures trading business is verbal. When one considers the difficulties in normal everyday communication, coupled with cultural and language differences, it is amazing that so few errors are made. Practical considerations will cause more and more standardization in the global trading community.

LANGUAGE BARRIERS BETWEEN MARKETS

Thanks to the British, most international financial business is carried on in English. Nevertheless, trading vernacular is not always consistent among different floors and different facets of the industry. Traders, at times, have trouble understanding one another.

Investors who trade in the same country and the same markets but are not involved with each other on a daily basis often do not communicate clearly. For example, when the term "backwardation" is used, a trader will explain, "In the bank that term means discount to cash, but on the exchange floor we call it a discount market." Of course, the floor traders cannot understand why bankers feel they need to give a discount market a special name. (We will discuss this problem further as it relates to traders in different countries.) The reality is that all these small differences add to the club-like atmosphere encouraged by the various segments of the industry. Although these networks have created some healthy internal competition in the markets, group barriers will begin to break down as futures brokers, equity houses, money managers, bankers, and traders work directly with each other, rather than through the old network.

Interchange of executive personnel is the new *modus operandi* for many banks, exchanges, and brokerage firms as the intensity of the international network increases. This flow of people is already creating an increase in understanding and cooperation. In the near future, it will translate into increased market volume.

The first area of communication that must be made efficient is in order entry. In the United States the NFA lists (in order of common usage) order entry and checking terminology.[21] It will certainly be expanded as needed and as the internationalization of the marketplace requires.

TYPES OF ORDERS

MARKET "At the market" means *right now*, at the best possible price. The trader is not interested in waiting for a specified price.

PRICE LIMIT This kind of order instructs the broker to fill the customer's order at a specific price, or better.

PRICE MIT Market If Touched. This instruction is placed on a limit order where the trader wants the order filled at a price or at the market after that price has been traded.

NOT HELD This instruction is placed on a limit order when market conditions are not clear; the order may or may not be filled; but if filled, it must be at the price or better.

DRT Discretion. This order allows the broker some leeway in filling it. The order is treated like a market order that gives the broker a little more time for execution. Traders use this type of order when they have some experience with and confidence in their broker. It is especially useful when a client has a large order to be filled in a thin market and wants it fed into the market gradually so that his activity does not disrupt the pit and move the market away from him.

OPENING-ONLY Opening-only orders must be filled during opening of trading (usually the first 30 seconds).

MOC Market On Close orders must be filled only during the official close of trading (usually the last 30 seconds).

FOK Fill Or Kill. This order instructs the broker to bid or offer an order several times, but if it is not filled, it is canceled. If it

---

is a price order, the broker must first determine if the price is reasonable for the current market.

CXL Cancel. The order is canceled.

OCO Order Cancels Order (One Cancels Other). This order involves two orders and two separate order forms. The client wants to use two specific price orders, and when one is filled, the other is automatically canceled.

After an order is placed, progress checks can be made with the broker; however, there is a limited amount of communication a clerk can receive from a pit broker when the market is busy. The broker may issue the following messages as information on the progress of the order.

ORDER CHECKING

NOT FILLED The order is not filled at all. Many traders use MIT orders because, when the trader places an order to buy, he may not be filled if his price happens to be the low of the day. If he places an MIT, he probably still won't buy the bottom, but he will likely be filled near the low.

WORKING The broker is currently bidding or offering the order but has no takers.

PARTIAL FILL Part of the order is filled, and the broker should try to let the desk know how many are still working.

FILLED AND NOT ENDORSED The order is filled, but the broker has not completely filled in the required trading information. Unless the customer can check time and sales or estimate price (because he had been monitoring the activity), the customer can only wait. This message merely lets the customer know whether he is in or out of the market.

BRITISH VS. AMERICAN TERMINOLOGY

The Chicago School of Finance created a British/American glossary in early 1988 for its first equity futures options seminar in London. It is a good indicator of the learning curve that we must follow if we expect to communicate internationally.[22]

BRITISH/AMERICAN FUTURES TERMS	
British	*American*
Abandon	Expire Worthless, Expire
Agent	Floor Broker
At Best	At the Market, Market
Bargain	Trade
Board Official	Board Broker, exchange in paper
Broker Dealer	House Broker, clearing firm
Checking Clerks	Trade Checkers
Clearing Agent	Clearing Member
Closing Purchase	Closing; Transaction, Trade
Closing Sale	Closing Sale; Transaction, Trade
Dealing Slip	Order, Ticket, Paper
Expiry (Date, Cycle)	Expiration (Date, Cycle)
Floor Agent	Floor Broker
Good for the Day (GD)	Day Order
Holder	Long
Loch	Options Clearing Corporation
Mis-Matched Bargain	Out Trade
Opening Purchase	Opening Transaction; Trade
Opening Sale	Opening Transaction; Trade
Pitch	Pit
Public Limit Order Board	Book
Public Order Member	Non-Clearing Member Firm
Share Capitalization	"Stock" Dividend

INTEREST RATE AND OPTIONS TERMINOLOGY

Riding the yield curve does not take horsemanship, but it may have derived its name from the bumpy ride that it gave banks and traders in the wild interest rate period of the 1970s. In more sophisticated circles, this process may be referred to as maturity transformation —a profit is made on the difference between the long-term rates and the short-term rates. Short-term rates are normally lower than long-term rates; however, this relationship inverted in the United States when short-term rates went as high as 21 percent.

The LIBOR (London Interbank Offered Rate) refers to an interest rate at which a loan denominated in a currency of a particular country is issued. This rate is used to determine other interest rates. Much of this lending is done in London, and rates are quoted in the following currencies:

Australian dollar	Japanese yen
Austrian schilling	Netherlands guilder
Belgian franc	Norwegian krone
Canadian dollar	Spanish peseta
Danish krone	Swedish krona
French franc	Swiss franc
German Deutsche mark	UK pound sterling
Italian lira	US dollar

The United States Banker's Acceptance Rate is an interest rate for paper issued by United States banks. At the SFE, the deliverable contract titled 90-Day Bank Acceptance Rate is the eighth most actively traded interest rate futures contract in the world.

Many other potential new financial products are available for consideration in other common rates configurations. Although this terminology is more familiar on the banking side, it is included here. Some of these products are currently being considered by exchanges and may soon be futures contracts.

INTEREST RATE TERMS

FRN Floating Rate Notes determine payment rate times tied to some standard reference rate such as the LIBOR.

FRA Future Rate Agreements are actually forward contracts that fix a rate for a contemplated transaction with both the beginning and ending dates set in the future.

FSA Forward Spread Agreement is used to protect against future changes in differentials or spreads between London interbank interest rates for currency positions denominated against the US dollar.

NIF Note Issuance Facilities is referred to when a borrower raises funds by issuing floating rate notes. These issues are underwritten by commercial banks who stand ready for a predetermined period of time to loan the company funds if they cannot be raised in the credit markets.

STRIPS The trader takes both a long and short position (spread) between the delivery dates in the Eurodollar futures or forward market when that market is out of line, realizing a profit when the normal differential is in place again.

DURATION "Time it takes." This term is usually applied to cash/futures hedge or arbitrage positions in interest rates that help to determine the quantity of futures to cash required for the strategy based on time and price to expiration. The number of futures contracts may be adjusted on a daily basis, as an options position is adjusted to maintain delta or neutral conditions.

CURRENCY SWAP The exchange of two currencies at the current exchange rate with an agreement to reverse the trade at some future date.

DEBT SWAP A company may borrow in a foreign currency in order to receive a fixed lower interest rate. The currency risk must be managed. The company may gain from both the lower

---

interest rate and an appreciation of the currency in which the loan is denominated.

PARALLEL LOANS Two companies in two different countries make an agreement to loan money to each other's subsidiary located within their country. In this way, each company can avoid the premium that would be incurred by financing the foreign subsidiary through foreign exchange transactions. Each must protect itself against any risk in the movements of exchange rates, or the agreement may require that each protect the other.

INTEREST RATE SWAPS Company A issues fixed rate debt and exchanges its fixed rate with Company B which issues floating rate debt. Company B would assume the risk of the fixed rate debt, the default risk of the company, and the exchange rate risk (if the two interest payment streams are in different currencies). This risk would be reflected in the interest rate charged to the company.

ASSET FOR ASSET SWAPS This refers to banks exchanging loans from different countries or exchanging debt for real property. A company may buy the debt of a Third World nation at 70 percent of its face value. That nation's government would then make investment property in its country available to the company at face value and retire the debt.

ASSET FOR DEBT SWAPS A loan is retired by replacing it with another debt, not by payment.

OPTIONS TERMS

DELTA The futures equivalent of an options position. A trader adjusts his positions during the day if a delta neutral strategy is incorporated.

GAMMA Rate of change in options position, including interest rate and value decay to expiration. Rate of change increases as expiration approaches.

THETA Total net position by product category for all futures and options positions.

VEGA Change in value of a trader's options positions, based on an increase or decrease in volatility.

IMPLIED VOLATILITY Change in underlying futures contracts, related to sudden price moves and expectation. Unlike the equity options market, in futures options trading, implied volatility is extremely important. Traders constantly calculate this variable and incorporate the figure into their strategies.

VALUE Price of an option according to price of underlying contract, interest rates, premium, and expectations.

AMERICAN An option that can be exercised at any time during the life of the option.

EUROPEAN An option that can be exercised only at the time of expiration.

8

Computers and the Decision-Making Process

A picture is truly worth a thousand words or, perhaps, a thousand trades. Graphic presentation of prices, generated by the market during a trading day, allows a trader to make reasonable decisions on several markets. Consequently, an investor has more facts to help him make trading decisions and also a choice of various types of markets. To the futures industry, the growth in graphic price information translated into the trading floors' dramatic surge in volume.

For the investor, data lines were already in place, although the way this data traveled down the lines needed upgrading, and the invention of the personal computer opened the door for many other developments. The personal computer, however, is just the vehicle; the real secrets have been unlocked by the entrepreneurial talent of software programmers. The creativity unleashed by this rather unique group of people will continue to influence the direction of the marketplace and trading strategies as well as all society for some time. It is appropriate then for industry managers to understand some of the options available to their business using this combination of exchange-generated market information vis-à-vis software and hardware applications.

HOW MARKET DATA ARE COMMUNICATED

Market data may be sent over a broadcast system or two-way communication line. The computer can be used for the single purpose of reporting the news and turning the price data into graphics, or it can be used as a workstation for other applications determined by the user.

Two-way communication means that information flows to the user and subsequently from the user to the vendor. The user is connected by telephone lines to the vendor's mainframe computer. To receive a piece of information, the user must request data from the vendor using a request-only terminal (referred to as a dumb terminal) supplied by the vendor or a personal computer (known as an intelligent terminal), sometimes owned by the user. The user is confined to the information supplied by the vendor, and the storage capacity of the mainframe can greatly improve the quantity and variety of available information.

This application, however, has a serious downside for a trader when markets are moving actively and many users are trying to access the same mainframe information simultaneously. Ports into the mainframe are limited, and the user winds up in a queue waiting his turn. Unfortunately, this process is rarely discussed by the vendor's salesmen and is often not understood by an anxious trader. (And we are all anxious when the markets fluctuate wildly!) An investor tends to enter and reenter his request repeatedly, thus continually putting himself at the end of the line.

Broadcast systems simply send out data from the vendor to the user over telephone lines, FM signal, cable signal, or satellite dish. This is the fastest, most efficient way for a trader to receive price data. After the user has received the market information, he may use the data in any way, but he may not resell it.

Many software packages can "read" specific data lines and offer great flexibility in manipulating that data into raw bar charts, bell-curve profile charts, and point and figure charts. Prices can even be analyzed mathematically and viewed on the same screen, indicating overbought and oversold situations. Players can now look at the markets as they move tick by tick or minute by minute through various combinations of intraday, multitime graphing capabilities. The same product will produce daily, weekly, and monthly charts by contract month and nearest future charts. Using these products means climbing another learning curve, and the copious amount of data can lead to confusion. Too much unqualified information can paralyze a trader.

Most software packages require that a computer be in place exclusively for the purpose of reading the data line throughout the day and therefore cannot be used for any other application. A few packages do allow the user's personal computer to receive and retain the broadcast information in the background while the computer is being used to operate a spreadsheet and write a letter to a client on an independent word processing package. This application is called multitasking and is popular for the less intense day or position trader who wants to monitor the market but accomplish other work or pursue other interests at the same time.

The next advances in multitasking software should allow the user to capture two-way communication. While his computer receives and stores market-generated information, the user will be able to send orders and receive confirmations directly into the marketplace. Then we shall see another dynamic period of sustained volume growth on exchanges.

COMPARATIVE CHARTING CAPABILITIES

The charting capabilities of software available to run on a personal computer in the United States continue to be of greater flexibility and variety than those offered in the international marketplace.

Innovation has taken place in the small companies where traders have actually developed the software. Many of these traders had to learn how to program a personal computer as they went along.

From 1981 to 1986, institutional and brokerage firms were slow to accept the new technology, and in many instances, the small retail trader actually had better information than his broker. Progressive firms made decisions in conjunction with brokers to purchase the hardware and software and return the cost to the broker based on his or her increased volume.

Large brokerage firms viewed the products to incorporate in a mainframe application, hoping that a broad scope of applications would enhance both back office accounting and in-house communication. Firm officials rolled over with laughter when the small, newly established programmers quoted them a price for their software. Communications directors decided it must be easy and made their fatal decision to develop their own packages. Some well-known brokerage firms spent millions of dollars trying to copy these graphic products but eventually went out and acquired what they needed. In some cases, the newly hired communications director returned to the programmer and ordered several hundred units of his now successful product and data line.

The major firms involved in the international scene that supply both price data and charting are Reuters, Telerate, Quotron, ADP Comtrend, Knight Ridder, Bridge Data, Commodity Communications, Commodity Quotations, Commodity Quote Graphics, and Fiamass.

Computerization of price data generated by the markets for the public really began in 1974 when Jim Frazer, a software developer, designed a product for Comtrend that turned prices into pictures of the market. For eight years, Comtrend dominated the industry. A dumb terminal had to be hardwired directly to the mainframe unit, which provided a two-way communication line. The mainframe collected data from exchanges on a real-time basis and also provided a ten-year historical database.

Comtrend actually became a victim of its own success. Once

it became involved in many other more profitable areas of data processing and communication, its chart service suffered major access problems. An increased number of users dramatically slowed the reaction time on their two-way line, and personal computers and communications were gaining capabilities that they did not recognize. Like so many mainframe-based operations, the firm refused to recognize the value of personal computers in its development plans. Ten years after Comtrend surprised the market with its brilliant new concept, its personal computer equivalent product failed to compete in the market. While it reorganized, redeveloped, and redesigned, market share declined and competition trimmed its profitability.

Reuters, the largest financial news vendor in the world, should certainly be the best in this field, but the company has been painfully slow in the area of charting capabilities. The enormous expense of upgrading thousands of terminals, some of them very old, throughout the world to handle new capabilities was a deterrent. The further possibility of upgrading communications at all locations to 1988 standards (that is, both one-way and two-way communications) has probably given management some vivid nightmares. However, Reuters' joint venture with the CME to develop GLOBEX, discussed in Chapter 9, is bringing to the fore its deep strength and will speed the industry into the space age.

Telerate, more than half owned by Dow Jones News Service, has a graphics product that has been receiving wide acceptance in the Pacific Basin countries and Europe. It has always been at the forefront in providing cash market data for the United States Treasury bond market, United Kingdom gilts, and more recently cash currencies. Its data for financial futures are good, but agricultural and metals information has just become available. Telerate's recent purchase of a Canadian market price vendor enabled it to offer broadcast-based international price quotes on all markets, equity and futures. With its purchase of INTEX, it will most certainly negotiate relationships with exchanges in order to compete with the Reuters/CME venture.

The philosophy of some international exchanges has been to make data available to only a single vendor, and that has been Reuters. As exchanges realize that it is better to facilitate their data into the hands of any and all vendors in an inexpensive way, Telerate and Knight Ridder will be in a position to make advances in countries where their service does not currently receive high marks.

The other vendors, who are not owned by a news service, have quality graphic products and will continue to do what they do best, design efficient and effective decision-based software.

Broadcast service became widely available in the early 1980s, using an FM radio signal and a 24-inch satellite receiver. During the late 1970s, CompuTrac (now owned by Telerate) developed a graphic product that produced daily charts for the Apple II +. The system collected market data over telephone lines. In 1981, its Intraday Analyst became the first intraday graphics product to run real-time on a personal computer. The process of giving thousands of bright programmers an intelligent terminal and easy access to quick, efficient, one-way data reception created a (confused) market of some thirteen products by 1984. Competitive pricing and quality development has produced several outstanding products. Worldwide distribution is currently the new contest.

Inadequate telephone lines, national restrictions on FM radio signals, and strict governmental regulation of satellite communications continue to hamper further progress of data services in many countries. Only when governments realize that many parts of their economy depend on this technology will changes occur. A country's overall development can be directly estimated by its efficiency in communications services. When projecting the growth of a new exchange in any country or considering participation and/or membership on that exchange, it is appropriate to relate the future success of that exchange to criteria based directly on the free flow of information and communications.

THE ROLE OF COMPUTERS IN MARKET DECISIONS

The continuing conflict as to whether fundamental or technical analysis has greater importance is a debate among professionals that will never end. Our answer is that fundamental facts are indeed the most important. Still, what exactly comprises a complete list of fundamental information is rather illusive and becomes relevant when it finally impacts the marketplace. When to act is the answer the technician intends to provide. The best decisions are probably made using both fundamental and technical information.

The data management ability offered to the technician by personal computers has expanded this possibility into the hands of creative individuals all over the world. CompuTrac, the first comprehensive software package to collect daily issued data, now boasts worldwide sales of more than 5000 in the past ten years. Even where fund managers and trade system designers have written proprietary programs, many ideas were inspired by the original program. Few software programs allow users to make dramatic changes, but many now encourage parallel programming that can work in conjunction with the same database.

Even though proof cannot be offered here, it is believed by the authors that numeric analysis of market-generated price information is as old as early Japanese and Chinese trading houses. Numeric analysis of price and volume information has been practiced on the floor of the Chicago exchanges since the beginning of trading. The number of markets that traders were able to track in this manner was naturally limited, as manually updating these systems was difficult.

Technical analysis is currently available in a variety of time periods. Trade-by-trade analysis requires tick charts for intense day-trading operations. Banks and institutional trading rooms use tick charts to monitor buy and sell decisions. A few sophisticated floor traders have off-the-floor analysis operations that communicate to the floor about market extremes according to this very short-term picture of the market. Many scalpers and pit traders feel that they have lost the edge that floor membership once offered. They feel that trading is now more difficult because pit traders compete with the upstairs traders—compete with them in a way that was not possible before pictorial market graphics and instant computer analysis.

The following charts are examples of a few market graphics products available.

FIGURE 8.1 **Intraday Market graphics process real-time data tick by tick (vendors actually report changes in price) and allow traders to watch the market closely and trade actively during the day. This chart begins at the opening of market and continues until the close. It keeps the most current price data on the screen and would show a greater number of ticks for a very active and volatile day. Moving averages based on 10 and 20 ticks keep the trader aware of the trend for the day (or moment).**

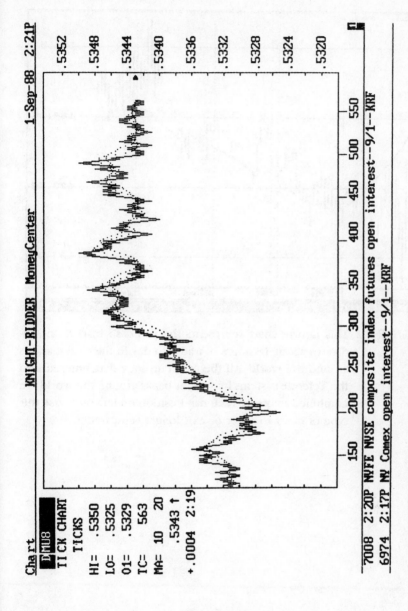

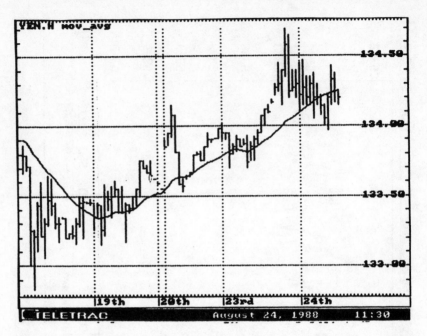

FIGURE 8.2 This hourly chart represents the yen cash market and in-
dicates about 18 hours of trading a day in the cash markets
around the world. All the cash currency data entered into
the Telerate systems by various banks around the world are
combined to create each bar. Position traders often use this
type of chart to enter or exit longer term trades.

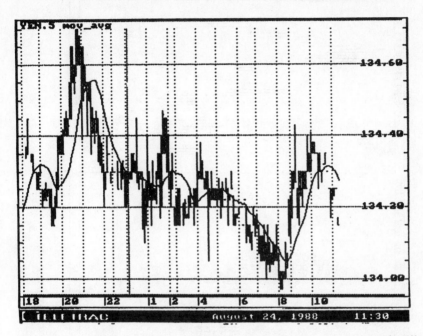

FIGURE 8.3 Often a trader needs to be more precise on entry and will
look to the hourly chart to confirm trends while using the
five-minute chart to enter the market.

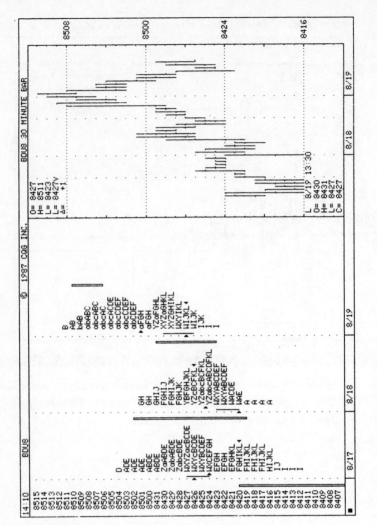

FIGURE 8.4 A popular new concept in charting, developed by a respected CBOT member, applies the laws of probability in observing the market action on a half-hour basis. The result looks something like a normal bell curve or variation on that theme. Compare this new type of chart with the half-hour bar chart.

FIGURE 8.5 Many traders are only interested in getting a feel for the market from a visual presentation. This daily gold chart gives the trader a quick view of the wave (or cycle) pattern of the market.

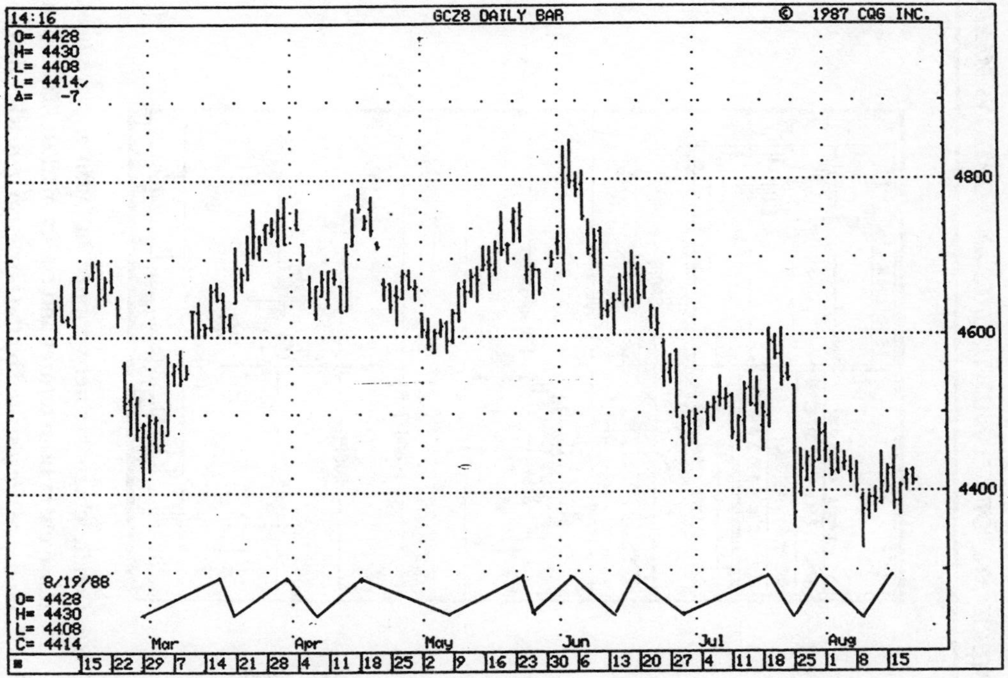

COPYRIGHT 1987 CQG INC.

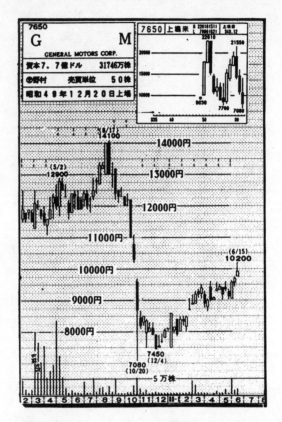

FIGURE 8.6 Candle charts are very popular in Japan and are used extensively in both futures and equity markets. The open and close are represented by the box form. A market that closed higher is white inside (the high would represent the top of the box), whereas a market that closed lower is blackened. The bars extending from the top or bottom of the box indicate the whole of the day's trading range. Compare these with the ends of the bell curve in a previous profile chart. The market probably does not trade very much at the extremes of the range, so traders would give these prices less emphasis.

Cycles, moving averages, and other numeric studies can also be optimized. This type of analysis was previously available only to very large firms with mainframe computers. The increased efficiency of research departments using applications on personal computers has allowed them to keep pace with the proliferation of new futures products without an equivalent increase in staff.

The technology necessary for futures trading, options valuation, account maintenance, and risk control makes knowledge of personal computers a necessity. Persons without this knowledge will find it more and more difficult to compete, and new talent may discover that the ability to use a computer (not program it) is a prerequisite for entry into the industry at all levels.

Although computerization has changed the way traders function and make decisions in the markets, futures traders and markets are relatively unsophisticated. The futures markets are about to make another transformation when decisions and strategies are again disrupted by technological progress as the global network shrinks and every trader has an order entry terminal on his desk.

TRADING OPERATION CONTROLS

With increased electronic access to the marketplace, internal management control systems are a continuing concern to institutions and banks running proprietary trading operations. Mitchell Fulscher, partner in charge of the Capital Markets Consulting Group at Arthur Andersen and Company in Tokyo, has definite criteria for placing controls. His observations are important and have been included here, in part, as they were presented at a seminar held in Japan in June 1987.

Fulscher commented that the need to hedge the risk of foreign exchange fluctuation and exchange rate exposure has become well established as financial managers are now becoming familiar with the use of financial futures and options as tools for hedging these risks. However, top management is concerned over the possible misuse of these financial instruments. This arises from several cases of reported losses of major banks from trade speculation and fraud. These cases usually related to "forward contracts" in foreign currencies, but top management and boards of directors often associate such failures with these new futures markets. Fulscher pointed out that before top management approves the use of futures and options markets, the fundamental question of whether this activity can be adequately monitored and controlled (by current staff and systems) must be answered. Basic internal control procedures must be established, closely monitored, and verified to win the confidence of top management.

MANAGEMENT INTERNAL CONTROL SYSTEMS

International control procedures over the use of futures and options follow the basic fundamentals. There are specific categories of controls that are summarized below:

Procedures Manual A detailed procedures manual should be prepared. This manual should outline how futures and options will be used and what specific procedures will be followed by each of the individuals involved. The manual should include examples of the forms and records and set forth in detail individual responsibilities and how each step is accomplished.

Authorized Traders Management needs to specifically designate the authorized traders. Only those individuals who are properly trained and experienced and who are being monitored should have the authority to initiate or execute trades.

Position Limits Position limits need to be established for the company. In establishing these limits, it takes careful consideration and understanding of how the markets are being used. It will be necessary to have several types of limits based upon the types of transactions and their purposes. For example, a principal amount of futures contracts related to long-term bonds has a significantly different volatility effect compared to the same principal amount of short-term instruments. Straddle positions may involve a large number of contracts, but they represent limited exposure. Limits on trading positions should be different from limits on hedging positions. Hedging is based on the concept of risk reduction. Of course, the existing exposure or risk that is being hedged needs to be first considered in establishing limits.

In addition to the overall company trading limits, there should be limitations established for each trader. This may be established based on his experience and the type of activity with which he is involved.

Authorized Brokers The outside brokers used by the institution should be formally authorized. This is important for two major reasons. First, from a credit risk point of view, it is necessary to consider the ability of the broker to perform and satisfy financial responsibilities. Second, it is extremely important to ensure that all trades and positions are properly reported to management. This requires an independent receipt of statements from all brokers being used. Therefore, a trader should not be permitted to open a new account with a broker without first receiving management approval.

Segregation of Duties As in all areas of operations, there must be adequate segregation of duties. No one individual should have total responsibility for initiating a transaction and recording the same transaction in the accounts. For example, traders should prepare a record of each trade they have executed, and this information should be sent to the accounting department for recording. The confirmations from brokers of all transactions should be sent directly to someone in the accounting department so that positions and trades can be verified. Of course, the handling and recording of related cash margin and other cash transactions should be segregated from traders' responsibility.

Verification Brokers executing transactions in futures and options are required to submit a statement each month reflecting all transactions and all open positions. This statement should be used to verify that all information has been properly recorded through the normal day-to-day process.

Internal Audit The internal auditor represents an important function in verifying that all of the controls established by management are in place and are being properly followed. In order for the internal auditor to handle this responsibility, he must understand fully all aspects of the use of futures and options along with all of the procedures required for processing the trades. As procedures are initially being designed, ideally, the internal auditor should play a key role.

Management Reporting An important aspect of the internal control system is the management reporting system. It is fundamental, of course, that management must have a complete understanding of these financial instruments and how they are being used by the institution. Once this is accomplished, there must be an adequate management reporting system designed to permit management to monitor the activity. The management information system must meet the following objectives:

Measurement of exposures
Measurement of trader performance
Measurement of hedging activity

The management reporting system must provide a summary of all of the open positions at market value and identify the amounts of unrealized gains and losses. Since there may be different accounting methods used for reporting to regulators and shareholders, management may demand a separate method of measurement.

Perhaps the most difficult challenge relates to the recognition of hedging activity. Since futures and options may be used to hedge interest rate or foreign exchange movements that are affecting the institution's cash market activities, a method must be designed to relate the futures and options gains and losses to unrealized gains and losses in the cash market. This is a most difficult challenge and will call for creativity and perhaps consultations with outside accounting experts.

Conclusion As financial institutions and other companies begin to study the use of futures markets, they must recognize that there is a substantial amount of planning and systems development that needs to be in place before the activity begins. Top management has a valid concern about fraud and speculation, particularly when a new activity such as this first begins. But this new activity can be adequately controlled. Attention to the fundamentals outlined above will help ensure the safe and profitable use of this very important financial management tool.[23]

In tomorrow's trading environment, controls will be even more important. Trading companies, investment banks, financial hedging departments of corporations, and commercial banks will need to monitor the overall risk of the firm's positions. The role of risk control managers, along with compliance positions, must soon be fulfilled by in-house staff. Computerized trading will make markets more accessible, and business will need to know who has positions and where the money is. Borders will disappear and international cooperation between exchanges and financial institutions will put political summits to shame.

9

Tomorrow's Trading Environment

Computer technology and the progressive worldwide communication network have set the course for another major advance in the futures industry. Electronic trading is about to jump from the drawing board onto the desks of traders in all parts of the world. As stated by Arthur Andersen and Company in its publication, *The Globalization of the International Financial Markets: Implications and Opportunities*, "We believe that globalization of the financial markets is not a myth—it is a reality that is here to stay. The financial market 'users' will drive the continued development of the global markets."[24] They also claim that total bonds issued in the international market in 1987 were $225 billion, compared to $38 billion less than 10 years ago, and Eurobond transactions have grown to an annual rate of $3.5 trillion.

The bankers are also moving to bring order to the marketplace as they agree on common rules. Financial market activities such as forward currency interest differential have been off balance sheet transactions and were not properly supervised in the daily risk analysis done by institutions for other areas of exposure. Central bankers will move in 1989 to correct this dilemma.

The accounting firm also believes that major developments will have taken place by 1992, corresponding to expected changes in US interstate banking and liberalization due in Europe. The efficiency of international banking, clearing, and depository functions will enable futures and equity markets to advance into the next generation of services.

Regulatory agencies, such as the CFTC in the US and the regulatory departments of the exchanges themselves, are already working together to find the common ground on which to run their business and assist one another in preventing abuses of the marketplace. Government agencies, internationally, are supporting the establishment of futures markets because they go beyond the functions of finding price, distributing goods and services, and transfer of risk. They assist in capital formation, financing, and the direction those decisions take.

PATHWAYS TO 24-HOUR TRADING

The new system was not built by politicians or economists. It was built by technology. In some respects the new world financial system is the accidental by-product of communication satellites and of engineers learning how to use the electromagnetic spectrum up to 300 gigohertz.[25]

Efficient systems are needed to establish a 24-hour electronic trading environment centered around computer technology and its marriage to high-speed, dependable communications. In addition to price information and actual transactions, market information must be passed along the same lines. In a paper entitled "Computerized Trading—A Framework for Analysis," written in 1977 while he was Chief Economist of the CFTC, Mark Powers noted that "some information, important in the bargaining process, is exchanged through the personal contact of traders in the pit.... Can that information be specified in such a way that it can be exchanged through the computer? Although some economists and others have been wont to dismiss the human element and the intuition that is purported to guide so many traders, experience and observation suggest that a good deal of subjective information is passed between bidders and offerors in the pit. This subjective information becomes the basis of an intuitive feel for the market traders rely on in their bargaining."[26] Yes, we worry about this and what to do about the beautiful new trading floors that have grown up around the world.

The answer may be as simple as it was for the Hong Kong Stock Exchange as they consolidated four exchanges on their new trading floor, where they set up computer stations on almost two-thirds of the floor space. It is the socialization of the information and the people themselves that are in danger of extinction in an isolated computer environment.

The entire industry must face the actuality that we are moving in the direction of electronic trading. As Leo Melamed of the CME stated, "To deny this direction is to forfeit the future."[27] We may always trade high volume contracts in an open-outcry trading pit, but outside of the pit and away from the outcry system, some traders will not be able to adjust to the new operational mode, and their extensive talents and experience will be lost to the industry. Most will find a new way to trade and may even be better at it.

As the labor-intensive floor operations move from pit trading to electronic systems, the numbers of persons employed will not decline, but people with well-defined skills commanding higher salaries will replace the current staff of runners.

The demise of the open-outcry trading system was put off for a time with an announcement made in September 1987 by Reuters and the Chicago Mercantile Exchange that they would form a joint venture, an electronic trading system called GLOBEX (June 20, 1988). Of greater importance than the share of the profits to be distributed to the exchange members, the real gift of the CME's innovation is the bridge it offers to members who will not change to computer trading as easily as will their sons and daughters.

GLOBEX is another try for a single offset system carried forward on a worldwide basis. The first such system was SIMEX, and it is this single offset system that Melamed believes in because it is efficient and cost effective. The CME has been pressured by the advanced tools and procedures that other financial and related markets have embraced. The exchange for physical (EFP) trading, so active in currencies, has made futures exchanges realize that their products can be successfully pirated and funneled away from the exchange floor. The banks' imaginative products that form a derivative market, although too small for pit trading, still serve an economic risk management need. The computerization of the London, Tokyo, and Hong Kong Stock Exchanges has some industry officials wondering if we might even be a step behind. However, the actual trading still takes place by telephone, and in Tokyo matching is done manually.

The CME is the first major futures institution to actually participate in and lend support toward the change to an after-hours electronic trading. An electronic system may also be an opportunity to address some current industry problems and solve the globalization difficulties foreseen in the near term.

High volume has made improvement in order routing and handling a priority matter. All the answers seem to point toward electronically moving the order between customer and clearing firm, with pass-through or routing capabilities directly to the floor.

Night trading is the chosen direction of the CBOT. Its purpose is to keep the markets for its own members; however, the initial success of nighttime trading may be short lived. The exchange does not answer the difficult question of staffing and margin transfers that must take place in the business hours of another country. More important, client trading controls cannot be put into place. The staff responsible for monitoring clients and a firm's monies (and movement of that money) generally work during the normal business day. An electronic system should be able to satisfy all these needs and risk controls, too.

The immeasurable value of an electronic system will be its

flexibility and the ability of an exchange to test a new product on the system with no additional pit traders, no expensive exchange personnel, and, if they choose, little fanfare. It will be relatively inexpensive to let a new product sit on the system for access, and if a real market need exists, the product will fly. When the volume merits, the members of the exchange can make a well-measured decision to carry on official marketing and move it into a pit trading arena. The product will have been thoroughly tested, and the process will be cost efficient. What a difference that will make to the potential number of products that might be available.

Although the open-outcry system is centuries old, it has matured in North America and been heralded as the best way to do business. Traders in other countries and among the banking community are familiar with both electronic screen trading and open outcry. Each system actually has advantages and disavantages. The point is, we may want to use both styles of trading, and we should certainly be adaptable.

As much as we would like to understand one another and have fluid conversations with all the people with whom we would like to do business, the reality of the world is that of diverse languages. In countries where English is not the native tongue, exchanges conduct business in their own language. Oddly enough, this comes as a surprise to many Americans who seem to assume that the financial markets operate in English (or American, as the French will tell you) like the airline industry. As globalization intensifies, the language barrier will become more evident to business people. The wonderful advantage of computerization is that it immediately removes the language differences. The computer will limit errors and encourage tremendous volume growth in the years ahead.

Three things could hamper the success of an electronic trading system:

1. **The markets could go flat, which would mean a general loss of activity in the economy, causing a slow start-up.**

2. Companies could be overtaxed by the cost of protecting their risk.
3. Unrealistic government regulations could slow down progress.

Although most traders expect greater volatility rather than flat markets in the future, this is really a trading decision. Internationally, governments have been decreasing taxes, some from very high levels; this should bring increased activity to the financial markets. Deregulation, on a worldwide scale, has been the order of the day.

If the GLOBEX system works, from a technical point of view, many expect it to produce good results. Every prominent exchange and financial center in the world has been in touch with the CME to inquire about participation. It is the intention of the exchange to accommodate these requests in an equitable manner that will be beneficial to the participants and protect the interest of the members of the CME.

The exchange has filled key staff positions and is in the process of amending the rule book to accept the new electronic system. Committees have been assigned for screen design, back office operations, and financial safeguards. The clearinghouse is gearing itself for 24-hour operations and money management that will allow access to margin funds several times a day.

Trading hours and a new trading date will begin after all CME markets on the floor are closed. The computer will cease trading when the first market on the floor opens in the morning. It is assumed that derivative products and products from other exchanges will be available on the system during Chicago's trading day. The opportunities for spreading from the CME markets into foreign interest rates and products will offer limitless possibilities and should dramatically increase volumes for all exchanges with related products.

Trading privileges, at this writing, will only be extended to clearing firm members and members authorized by clearing firms.

Orders will not carry from the day trading session on the floor to the GLOBEX system, and not all types of orders will be available in the electronic system. An open order, for example, will remain only in the day system unless the customer specifies that it be handled in the GLOBEX system as well.

Controls will be strictly applied, and a member who has lost his trading privileges because of a rule violation will not be allowed to trade on the GLOBEX system. The clearing firms will be responsible for how the terminals are used and will be able to terminate a trader's ability to place orders.

GLOBEX is not the only product that will be available. Others in the industry are well along in their development of electronic systems for trading, transferring orders, and providing information to the global community. Great differences will be found in the areas of software and hardware support, system controls, and integrity and dependability of service with little down time. Support products will continue to develop, enhancing users' ability to make decisions and accomplish daily work.

Traders will be able to live and travel among the major financial centers and conduct business as if from their home office. Cities will continue to house main operations, but the people will be scattered among their yachts or mountain cabins, or will be constantly on the move. Although some of us may not know what to do with the freedom, our lives will be more interesting in the new world.

The futures and options industry is young and energetic. We are standing on the threshold of a dynamic growth period that will leave the skeptics behind and carry the innovators forward.

Notes

1. Teweles, R., Harlow, C., and Stone, H. *The Commodity Futures Game: Who Wins? Who Loses? Why?* New York: McGraw-Hill, 1984, pp. 8–9.
2. Bakken, Henry H. "Futures Trading—Origin, Development and Present Economic Status." In *Futures Trading Seminar: A Commodity Marketing Forum for College Teachers of Economics*, ed. E. A. Gaumnitz, vol. 3. Madison, WI: Mimir Publishing, Inc., 1966, pp. 1–13.
3. Taylor, C. H. *History of the Board of Trade of the City of Chicago.* (3 volumes). Chicago, IL: Robert O. Law, 1917, p. 57.
4. Irwin, Harold S. *Evolution of Futures Trading.* Madison, WI: Mimir Publishing, Inc., 1954.
5. Friedman, Milton. *The Need for Futures Markets in Currencies.* Prepared for the Chicago Mercantile Exchange, December 20, 1971.
6. Financial Services Task Force of the Civic Committee of the Commercial Club of Chicago. *Economic Impact of the Chicago Exchanges.* Chicago, IL: CRESAP, 1987, Sections II and III.
7. Interview, Chicago, January 1988.
8. Interview, Auckland, April 1988.
9. CME. Mutual Offset System: SIMEX, Chicago Mercantile Exchange, 1984.
10. Chia, K. G., and Soh, Doreen. *SIMEX and the Globalization of Financial Futures.* Singapore: Times Books International (Kifford Press), 1986, pp. 50–59.

11. *Factors Relating to the Feasibility of a Singapore-Based Financial Futures Market.* Continental Illinois National Bank of Chicago. Prepared for the Chicago Mercantile Exchange, 1981.
12. Interview, Paris, June 1987.
13. Tour of CME trading floor conducted by exchange officials. Chicago, IL, November 1987.
14. Interview, Chicago, April 1988.
15. Interview, Chicago, July 1988.
16. Interview, London, June 1987.
17. Customer Account Protection Study. National Futures Association, November 20, 1986.
18. CME. The Financial Safeguard System of the Chicago Mercantile Exchange. Chicago Mercantile Exchange, April 1988.
19. Customer Account Protection Study. National Futures Association, November 20, 1986.
20. Interview, Hong Kong, March 1987.
21. *Registration Guidelines: A Compliance Guide.* National Futures Association, 1986.
22. *The Chicago School of Finance Manual*, Chicago School of Finance, 1988.
23. Fulscher, Mitchell. Seminar presentation for the Chicago Mercantile Exchange. Tokyo, Japan, June 1988.
24. Arthur Andersen. *The Globalization of the International Financial Markets: Implications and Opportunities.* Arthur Andersen, March 1988.
25. Walter Wriston, former Chairman of Citicorp. In *Innovation: The Attacher's Advantage*, Richard N. Foster. Pan Books, Sydney, Australia, 1987, p. 45.
26. Powers, Mark. *Computerized Trading—A Framework for Analysis.* Washington, D.C.: Commodity Trading Futures Commission, 1977, pp. 7–11.
27. Melamed, Leo. Announcement of GLOBEX to membership meeting of the Chicago Mercantile Exchange, September 1987. (Melamed is Special Counsel to the CME and Chairman of the Executive Committee.)

II

THE
GLOBAL TRADING
INFORMATION BANK

1

Futures and Options Exchanges: A Worldwide Directory

SYDNEY STOCK EXCHANGE LTD. (SSE)

20 Bond Street
Sydney, NS 2000
Australia
Tel: 61(02) 225 6600

SYDNEY FUTURES EXCHANGE, LTD. (SFE)

13-15 O'Connell Street
Sydney 2000
Australia
Tel: 61(02) 233 7633
Tlx: 790 126 713
Fax: 61(02) 233 6226

Offices in other cities:

Chicago
141 W. Jackson Blvd, Suite 1310A
Chicago, Il 60604
USA
Tel: 1(312) 663 5155
Tlx: 25 350 211
Fax: 1(312) 663 3657

BRAZIL

BOLSA BRASILEIRA DE FUTUROS (BBF)
(BRAZILIAN FUTURES EXCHANGE)

Avenue Rio Branco 110, 14th Fl
20040 Rio de Janeiro
Brazil
Tel: (5521) 224 6062

BOLSA DE MERCADORIAS DE SÃO PAULO (BMSP)
(SÃO PAULO COMMODITIES EXCHANGE)

Rua Libero Badaro 471, 4th Fl
São Paulo 01009
Brazil
Tel: (5511) 32 3101

BOLSA MERCANTIL AND DE FUTUROS (BMF)

Praca Antonio Prado, 48
São Paulo/SP 01010
Brazil
Tel: (5511) 239 5511
Fax: (5511) 35 2541

CANADA

THE MONTREAL EXCHANGE—BOURSE DE MONTREAL (ME)

Stock Exchange Tower
800 Square Victoria
Montreal, Quebec H4Z 1A9
Canada
Tel: 1(514) 871 2424
Tlx: 389 60586
Fax: 1(514) 871 3531

Offices in other cities:

London
Roman Wall House
1-2 Crutched Friars
London EC3N 2AN
England
Tel: 44(1) 481 8614

TORONTO FUTURES EXCHANGE (TFE)

Exchange Tower
2 First Canadian Place
Toronto, Ontario M5X 1J2
Canada
Tel: 1(416) 947 4487
Tlx: 389 17759
Fax: 1(416) 947 4585

TORONTO STOCK EXCHANGE (TSEX)

Exchange Tower
2 First Canadian Place
Toronto, Ontario M5X 1J2
Canada
Tel: 1(416) 947 4700
Tlx: 389 17759

VANCOUVER STOCK EXCHANGE (VSE)

Stock Exchange Tower
P.O. Box 10333
609 Granville Street
Vancouver, British Columbia V7Y 1H1
Canada
Tel: 1(604) 689 3334
Tlx: 389 55480
Fax: 1(604) 688 9658

WINNIPEG COMMODITY EXCHANGE (WCE)

500 Commodity Exchange Tower
360 Main Street
Winnipeg, Manitoba R3C 3Z4
Canada
Tel: 1(204) 949 0495
Tlx: 389 587778

FRANCE

LILLE POTATO FUTURES MARKET (LPTM)

Centre Mercure
445 Boulevard Gambetta
59200 Tourcoing
France
Tel:　33 2026 2213
Tlx:　842 110 155

MARCHE A TERME DES INSTRUMENTS FINANCIERS (MATIF)

Conseil du Marche a Terme
108 Rue de Richelieu
Paris 75002
France
Tel:　331 4015 2001
Tlx:　842 218 362
Fax:　331 4296 8316

COMPAGNIE DES COMMISSIONAIRES AGREES (CCA)
(PARIS FUTURES EXCHANGE)

Bourse de Commerce
2 rue de Viarmes
Paris 75001
France
Tel:　33 4508 8250
Tlx:　842 220 270 Comagre

GREAT BRITAIN

THE BALTIC FUTURES EXCHANGE (BFE)

Includes: THE BALTIC INTERNATIONAL FREIGHT FUTURES EXCHANGE LTD.
　　　(BIFFEX)
　　　FEDERATION OF OILS, SEEDS AND FATS ASSOCIATION LTD. (FOFSA
　　　INTERNATIONAL)
　　　LONDON GRAIN FUTURES MARKET (LGFM)
　　　LONDON MEAT FUTURES EXCHANGE (LMFE)
　　　LONDON POTATO FUTURES ASSOCIATION (LPFA)
　　　SOYA BEAN MEAL FUTURES ASSOCIATION LTD. (SOMFA)

24-28 St. Mary Ave
London EC3A 8EP
England

Tel: 44(1) 283 5146
Fax: 44(1) 623 2917

INTERNATIONAL PETROLEUM EXCHANGE OF LONDON LTD. (IPE)

1 Commodity Quay
St. Katherine Docks
London E1 9AX
England
Tel: 44(1) 481 2080
Tlx: 851 884 370
Fax: 44(1) 481 8485

INTERNATIONAL STOCK EXCHANGE (ISE)

Traded Options Market
Old Broad Street
London EC2N 1HP
England
Tel: 44(1) 588 2355
Tlx: 851 866 557
Fax: 44(1) 374 2355

LONDON FUTURES AND OPTIONS EXCHANGE (FOX)

Includes: TRADED OPTIONS MARKET

1 Commodity Quay
St. Katherine Docks
London E1 9AX
England
Tel: 44(1) 481 2080
Tlx: 851 844 370

THE LONDON INTERNATIONAL FINANCIAL FUTURES EXCHANGE (LIFFE)

Royal Exchange
London EC3V 3PJ
England
Tel: 44(1) 623 0444
Tlx: 851 893 893 LIFFE G
Fax: 44(1) 588 3624

THE LONDON METAL EXCHANGE LTD. (LME)

Plantation House
Fenchurch Street
London EC3M 3AP
England
Tel: 44(1) 623 0444
Tlx: 851 895 1367
Fax: 44(1) 626 1703

LONDON STOCK EXCHANGE (LSE)

Corner Old Broad and Threadneedle Street
London EC2N 1HP
England
Tel: 44(1) 588 2355

HONG KONG

HONG KONG FUTURES EXCHANGE (HKFE)

New World Trade Tower, 12th Fl/911
16-18 Queen's Road Central
Hong Kong
Tel: 852(5) 868 0338
Tlx: 780 76375 HX
Fax: 852(5) 868 0134

JAPAN

HOKKAIDO GRAIN EXCHANGE

3 Odori Nishi 5-chome
Chuo-ku Sapporo
Hokkaido 060
Japan

KANMON COMMODITY EXCHANGE
KANMON SHOHIN TORIHIKIJO

1-5, Nabecho
Shimonoseki-shi
Yamaguchi 750
Japan

KOBE GRAIN EXCHANGE
KOBE KOKUMOTSU TORIHIKIJO

2-4-16 Honmachi
Hyogo-ku, Kobe-shi
Hyogo 652
Japan

KOBE RAW SILK EXCHANGE
KOBE KIITO TORIHIKIJO

126, Higashicho
Kobe Silk Center Building, 8th Fl
Chuo-ku, Kobe-shi
Hyogo, 650
Japan

KOBE RUBBER EXCHANGE
KOBE GOMU TORIHIKIJO

49, Harimacho
Chuo-ku, Kobe-shi
Hyogo 650
Japan

MAEBASHI DRIED COCOON EXCHANGE

1-49-1 Furuichi-Machi
Maebashi City
Gunma prefecture 371
Japan

NAGOYA GRAIN AND SUGAR EXCHANGE
NAGOYA KOKUMOTSU SATO TORIHIKIJO

2-3-2 Meiekiminami
Nakamura-ku, Nagoya-shi
Aichi 450
Japan

NAGOYA TEXTILE EXCHANGE
NAGOYA SENI TORIHIKIJO

3-2-15, Nishiki
Naka-ku, Nagoya-shi
Aichi 460
Japan

OSAKA GRAIN EXCHANGE
OSAKA KOKUMOTSU TORIHIKIJO

1-10-14, Awaza
Nishi-ku, Osaka-shi
Osaka 550
Japan

OSAKA SECURITIES EXCHANGE (OSE)

Kitahama 2-chome
Higashi-ku
Osaka 541
Japan
Tel: 81(6) 203 1151

OSAKA SUGAR EXCHANGE
OSAKA SATO TORIHIKIJO

3-32-1 Kitakyutaromachi
Higashi-ku, Osaka-shi
Osaka 541
Japan

OSAKA TEXTILE EXCHANGE

3-32-1 Kitakyutaro-Machi
Higanshiku
Osaka 541
Japan
Tel: 81(6) 253 0031

TOKYO COMMODITY EXCHANGE (TCE)
TOKYO KOGYOHIN TORIHIKIJO

Tosen Building
10-8 Nihonbashi
Horidomecho 1-chome
Chuo-ku, Tokyo
Japan
Tel: 81(3) 661 9191

THE TOKYO GRAIN EXCHANGE (TGE)

12-5 Kakigara-cho
1-chome, Nihonbashi
Chuo-ku, Tokyo 103
Japan
Tel: 81(3) 668 9311

TOKYO STOCK EXCHANGE (TSE)

1-1 Nihombashi-Kayaba-Cho
2-chome, Chuo-ku
Tokyo 103
Japan
Tel: 81(3) 666 0141
Tlx: 781 02522759 TKOSE
Fax: 81(3) 661 3240

TOKYO SUGAR EXCHANGE (TSUE)
TOKYO SATO TORIHIKIJO

9-4, Koamicho
Nihonbashi, Chuo-ku
Tokyo 103
Japan

TOYOHASHI COCOON EXCHANGE

52-2 Ekimae-odori
Toyohashi City
Aichi Prefecture 440
Japan
Tel: 81(0) 532 52 6231

YOKAHAMA RAW SILK EXCHANGE

Silk Center, 4th Fl
1, Yamashitacho
Naka-ku, Yokohama-shi
Kanagawa 231
Japan

MALAYSIA

KUALA LUMPUR COMMODITY EXCHANGE (KLCE)

Podium Block, 4th Fl
Dayabumi Complex
P.O. Box 11260
50740 Kuala Lumpur
Malaysia
Tel: 60(3) 293 6822

NETHERLANDS

AMSTERDAM PORK AND POTATO EXCHANGE (APPE)

Koopmansbeurs
Damrak 62a
Amsterdam
The Netherlands
Tel: 31(20) 22 8654
Tlx: 844 16582

EUROPEAN OPTIONS EXCHANGE (EOE)
EUROPESE OPTIEBEURS

Rokin 65
1012 KK Amsterdam
The Netherlands
Tel: 31(20) 550 4550
Tlx: 844 14540
Fax: 31(20) 550 4518

> *Offices in other cities:*
>
> *London*
> P H P Naastepad
> Options and Futures Society
> 6-8 Crutched Friars
> London EC3N 2NN

FINANCIELE TERMIJNMARKT AMSTERDAM NV (FTA)

Nes 49
Amsterdam 1012 KD
PO Box 10220
1001 EE Amsterdam
The Netherlands
Tel: 31(20) 550 4550

NEW ZEALAND

NEW ZEALAND FUTURES EXCHANGE (NZFE)

PO Box 6734 Wellesley Street
Auckland
New Zealand
Tel: 64(9) 398 308

PHILIPPINES

MANILA INTERNATIONAL FUTURES EXCHANGE (MIFE)

Producers Bank Centre, 7th Fl
Paseo de Roxas
Makati, Metro Manila
Philippines
Tel: 63 818 5496

SINGAPORE

THE SINGAPORE INTERNATIONAL MONETARY EXCHANGE LTD. (SIMEX)

1 Maritime Square
09-39 World Trade Center
Singapore 0409
Tel: (65) 278 6363
Tlx: 786 RS380000 SINMEX
Fax: (65) 273 0241

SWEDEN

STOCKHOLM OPTIONS MARKET (SOM)

Birger Jarlsgatan 18
Box 5015
S-102 41, Stockholm
Sweden
Tel: 46(8) 114 070
Tlx: 854 810 6120 Options S
Fax: 46(8) 204 357

SWEDEN OPTIONS AND FUTURES EXCHANGE (SOFE)

Regeringsgatan 38
PO Box 7267

Stockholm
Sweden
Tel: 46(8) 791 4080
Fax: 46(8) 791 4075

SWITZERLAND

SWISS OPTIONS AND FINANCIAL FUTURES EXCHANGE (SOFFEX)

Talstrasse 11
Zurich 8021
Switzerland
Tel: 41(1) 21135

UNITED STATES

AMERICAN STOCK EXCHANGE (AMEX)

86 Trinity Place
New York, New York 10006
USA
Tel: 1(212) 306 1000
Tlx: 25 129 297
Fax: 1(212) 306 1802

> #### Offices in other cities:
> **Amsterdam**
> Rokin Plaza
> Papenbroeksteeg 2
> Amsterdam 1012 NW
> The Netherlands
> Tel: (20) 248 020

CHICAGO BOARD OF TRADE (CBOT)
Includes: ASSOCIATE MARKET
          COMMODITY OPTIONS MARKET
          INDEX DEBT AND EQUITY MARKET

141 West Jackson Boulevard
Chicago, Illinois 60604
USA
Tel: 1(312) 435 3500
Tlx: 25 210 286 CBOT UR
Fax: 1(312) 435 7170

Offices in other cities:

Washington DC
1455 Pennsylvania Avenue, NW, Suite 1225
Washington, DC 20004
USA
Tel: 1(202) 783 1190

London
52-54 Gracechurch Street
London EC3V OEH
England
Tel: 44(1) 929 0021
Tlx: 851 941 3558
Fax: 44(1) 929 0558

Japan
Ozma Public Relations
Aoyama Tower Building, 5th Fl
224 15 Minami-Aoyama
Minato-Ku, Tokyo 107
Japan

CHICAGO BOARD OPTIONS EXCHANGE (CBOE)

400 South LaSalle Street
Chicago, Illinois 60605
USA
Tel: 1(312) 786 5600
Tlx: 25 201 203
Fax: 1(312) 786 7413

Offices in other cities:

New York
60 Broad Street
New York, New York 10004
USA
Tel: 1(212) 943 0600

London
43 London Wall, 2nd Fl
London
Tel: 44(1) 374 8523

CHICAGO MERCANTILE EXCHANGE (CME)

Includes: INTERNATIONAL MONETARY MARKET (IMM)
INDEX AND OPTIONS MARKET (IOM)

30 South Wacker Drive
Chicago, Illinois 60696
USA
Tel: 1(312) 930 1000
Tlx: 25 212 214
Fax: 1(312) 930 8219

Offices in other cities:

New York
67 Wall Street
New York, New York 10005
USA
Tel: 1(212) 363 7000
Fax: 1(212) 425 1337

Washington DC
2000 Pennsylvania Avenue, NW
Washington, DC 20006
USA
Tel: 1(202) 223 6965
Fax: 1(202) 466 3049

London
27 Throgmorton Street
London EC2N 2AN
England
Tel: 44(1) 920 0722
Fax: 44(1) 920 0978

Japan
3-3-1 Kasumigaseki
Chiyoda-ku, Tokyo 100
Japan
Tel: 81(3) 595 2251
Tlx: 781 222 4478 CME J
Fax: 81(3) 595 2244

CHICAGO RICE AND COTTON EXCHANGE
see MIDAMERICA COMMODITY EXCHANGE

CITRUS ASSOCIATES OF NEW YORK COTTON EXCHANGE INC.
see NEW YORK COTTON EXCHANGE

COFFEE SUGAR AND COCOA EXCHANGE (CSCE)
Includes: ECONOMIC INDEX MARKET
4 World Trade Center
New York, New York 10048
USA
Tel: 1(212) 938 2800
Tlx: 25 127 066

COMMODITY EXCHANGE INC. (COMEX)
4 World Trade Center
New York, New York 10048
USA
Tel: 1(212) 938 2900
Tlx: 25 127 066
Fax: 1(212) 432 1154

Offices in other cities:
Washington DC
1331 Pennsylvania Avenue, NW, Suite 550
Washington, DC 20004
USA
Tel: 1(202) 662 8770

FINANCIAL INSTRUMENT EXCHANGE (FINEX)
see NEW YORK COTTON EXCHANGE (NYCE)

INDEX AND OPTIONS MARKET (IOM)
see CHICAGO MERCANTILE EXCHANGE (CME)

INTERNATIONAL MONETARY MARKET (IMM)

KANSAS CITY BOARD OF TRADE (KCBT)
4800 Main Street Suite 303
Kansas City, Missouri 64112
USA
Tel: 1(816) 753 7500
     1(800) 821 5228

MIDAMERICA COMMODITY EXCHANGE (MIDAM)
Includes: CHICAGO RICE AND COTTON EXCHANGE

141 West Jackson Boulevard
Chicago, Illinois 60604
USA
Tel: 1(312) 341 3078
Tlx: 210 286
Fax: 1(312) 929 0558

MINNEAPOLIS GRAIN EXCHANGE (MGE)

400 South Fourth Street
Minneapolis, Minnesota 55415
USA
Tel: 1(612) 338 6212

NEW YORK COTTON EXCHANGE (NYCE)
Includes: CITRUS ASSOCIATES OF NEW YORK COTTON EXCHANGE INC.
FINANCIAL INSTRUMENT EXCHANGE (FINEX)

4 World Trade Center
New York, New York 10048
USA
Tel: 1(212) 938 2650
      1(212) 938 2652—FINEX Division
Fax: 1(212) 839 8061

NEW YORK FUTURES EXCHANGE (NYFE)

20 Broad Street
New York, New York 10005
USA
Tel: 1(800) 221 7722
      1(212) 656 4949
Fax: 1(212) 656 8211

NEW YORK MERCANTILE EXCHANGE (NYMEX)

4 World Trade Center
New York, New York 10048
USA
Tel: 1(212) 938 2222

Offices in other cities:

London
NYMEX Information Bureau

16 John Adam Street
London WC2N 6LU
England
Tel: 44(1) 930 7642

PHILADELPHIA BOARD OF TRADE (PBOT)

1900 Market Street
Philadelphia, Pennsylvania 19103
USA
Tel: 1(215) 496 5165

PHILADELPHIA STOCK EXCHANGE (PHLX)

1900 Market Street
Philadelphia, Pennsylvania 19103
USA
Tel: 1(215) 496 5000
Fax: 1(215) 496 5514
      1(215) 496 5104

Offices in other cities:

London
Basildon House
7-11 Moorgate
London EC2R 6AD
England
Tel: 44(1) 606 2348
Tlx: 851 892 735 PHLXUK G
Fax: 44(1) 606 3548

Japan
Kyobashi Tokiwa Building 11, 4th Fl
8-5 Kyobashi 2-chome
Chuo-ku, Tokyo 104
Japan
Tel: 81(3) 561 2851
Tlx: 781 J32384 JBCTYO
Fax: 81(3) 561 2850

Hong Kong
10/F One Exchange Square
8 Connaught Place
Hong Kong
Tel: 852(5) 844 7607
Tlx: 780 81841
Fax: 852(5) 868 0149

2

Major Exchanges: Contracts Listed and Other Basic Data

CHICAGO BOARD OF TRADE (CBT)

141 West Jackson Boulevard
Chicago, Illinois 60604
1(312) 435 3500

Established in 1848
Open Outcry System
Contracts Listed: Futures and Options on Futures

Futures:	*Options on Futures:*
Corn	Corn
Oats	
Soybeans	Soybeans
Soybean Meal	Soybean Meal
Soybean Oil	Soybean Oil
Wheat (Soft Winter)	Wheat (Soft Winter)
Gold (100 troy ounces)	
Gold (One kilogram)	
Silver (5000 troy ounces)	
Silver (1000 troy ounces)	Silver (1000 troy ounces)
30-Day Fixed Rate	
US Five-Year Treasury Note	

Futures:

US 10-Year Treasury Note
US Treasury Bond

CBOE 250 Stock Index
Major Market Index
Municipal Bond Index

1986 EXCHANGE VOLUME:
1987 EXCHANGE VOLUME:

Options on Futures:

US 10-Year Treasury Note
US Treasury Bond

Municipal Bond Index

100,813,833 contracts.
127,092,990 contracts.

Memberships

All seats available for ownership or for leasing.
Fractional seats are available with no trading privileges.

Full—all contracts
Associate Market (AM)—all contracts but grain and silver
Index, Debt and Energy Market (IDEM)—all index, debt, energy contract, plus one kilo gold
Commodity Options Markets (COM)—all options contracts
Evening-session trading privileges available

CHICAGO MERCANTILE EXCHANGE (CME)

30 South Wacker Drive
Chicago, Illinois 60606
1(312) 930 1000

Established in 1903
Open Outcry System
Contracts Listed: Futures and Options on Futures

Futures:

Feeder Cattle
Live Cattle
Live Hogs
Pork Bellies (Frozen)
Lumber (Random Length)

Australian Dollar
British Pound
Canadian Dollar
Deutsche Mark
French Franc
Japanese Yen

Options on Futures:

Feeder Cattle
Live Cattle
Live Hogs
Pork Bellies (Frozen)
Lumber (Random Length)

Australian Dollar
British Pound
Canadian Dollar
Deutsche Mark

Japanese Yen

Futures:	*Options on Futures:*
Swiss Franc	Swiss Franc
European Currency Unit	
Eurodollar 90-Day Time Deposit	Eurodollar 90-Day Time Deposit
US 90-Day Treasury Bill	US 90-Day Treasury Bill
S & P 500 Stock Index	S & P 500 Stock Index

1986 EXCHANGE VOLUME:	68,775,534 contracts.
1987 EXCHANGE VOLUME:	84,367,214 contracts.

Memberships

All seats available for ownership or for leasing.
One may lease for limited period.

Full CME—all contracts
International Monetary Market (IMM)—all contracts but agricultural products.
Index and Options Market (IOM)—stock index futures, lumber, and all options on futures contracts.

COFFEE, SUGAR & COCOA EXCHANGE (CSCE)

4 World Trade Center
New York, New York 10048
1(212) 938 2800

Established in 1888
Open Outcry System
Contracts Listed: Futures and Options on Futures

Futures:	*Options on Futures:*
Cocoa	Cocoa
Coffee "C"	Coffee "C"
Sugar No. 11 (World)	Sugar No. 11
Sugar No. 14 (Domestic)	
World White Sugar	

CPI-W
(Consumer Price Index for Urban Wage Earners & Clerical Workers)

1986 EXCHANGE VOLUME:	5,535,081 contracts.
1987 EXCHANGE VOLUME:	6,256,859 contracts.

Membership

Full—all contracts
Associate—CPI-W futures and all options contracts

COMMODITY EXCHANGE INC. (COMEX)

4 World Trade Center
New York, New York 10048
1(212) 938 2900

Established in 1933
Open Outcry System
Contracts Listed: Futures and Options on Futures

Futures:

Aluminum
Copper
Gold (100 troy ounces)—SFE link
Silver (5000 troy ounces)

Moody's Corporate Bond Index

Options on Futures:

Copper
Gold (100 troy ounces)
Silver (5000 troy ounces)

1986 EXCHANGE VOLUME:	16,528,415 contracts.
1987 EXCHANGE VOLUME:	21,495,598 contracts.

Memberships

Full—all contracts
Options—all options contracts
Aluminum—aluminum only

Leasing available for Full membership only.

NEW YORK COTTON EXCHANGE (NYCE)

4 World Trade Center
New York, New York 10048
1(212) 938 2650

Established in 1870
Open Outcry System
Contracts Listed: Futures and Options on Futures

Futures:

Frozen Concentrate Orange Juice
Cotton No. 2

European Currency Unit

Five-Year US Treasury Note

US Dollar Index

Options on Futures:

Frozen Concentrate Orange Juice
Cotton No. 2

Five-Year US Treasury Note

US Dollar Index

| 1986 EXCHANGE VOLUME: | 1,477,590 contracts. |
| 1987 EXCHANGE VOLUME: | 2,498,014 contracts. |

Memberships

Full or Cotton membership—all contracts
FINEX license—financial futures and options on futures contracts

No leasing available

NEW YORK MERCANTILE EXCHANGE (NYMEX)

4 World Trade Center
New York, New York 10048
1(212) 938 2222

Established in 1884
Open Outcry System
Contracts Listed: Futures and Options on Futures

Futures:

Palladium
Platinum

Crude Oil
No. 2 Heating Oil
Propane
Leaded Gasoline

Options on Futures:

Crude Oil
No. 2 Heating Oil

| 1986 EXCHANGE VOLUME: | 25,735,271 contracts. |
| 1987 EXCHANGE VOLUME: | 14,779,679 contracts. |

Membership

Full—all contracts

No leasing available

LONDON INTERNATIONAL FINANCIAL FUTURES EXCHANGE (LIFFE)

Royal Exchange
London EC3V 3PJ
England
44(1) 623 0444

Established in 1982
Open Outcry System
Contracts Listed: Futures and Options on Futures and Options

Futures:

British Pound
Deutsche Mark
Swiss Franc
Japanese Yen
US Dollar-Deutsche Mark Currency

Eurodollar 3-Month Interest Rate
Japanese Government Bond
Long Gilt Interest Rate
Short Gilt Interest Rate
Sterling 3-Month Interest Rate
US Treasury Bond

Financial Times Stock Exchange 100
  Index

1986 EXCHANGE VOLUME:
1987 EXCHANGE VOLUME:

Options on Futures:

British Pound

US Dollar-Deutsche Mark

Eurodollar 3-Month

Long Gilt Interest Rate

Sterling 3-Month
US Treasury Bond

Financial Times Stock Exchange 100
  Index

  6,951,178 contracts.
  13,600,670 contracts.

Memberships

All memberships available for ownership or lease.

LONDON METAL EXCHANGE (LME)

Plantation House
Fenchurch Street
London EC3M 3AP
England
44(1) 626 3311

Established in 1877
Open Outcry System
Contracts Listed: Futures and Options on Futures

Futures:

Aluminum (High Grade)
Aluminum (Primary)
Copper (Grade A)
Copper (Standard)
Lead
Nickel
Silver (10,000 troy ounces)
Silver (2,000 troy ounces)
Zinc (High Grade)

Options on Futures:

Aluminum
Copper (Grade A)

Lead
Nickel
Silver

Zinc (High Grade)

Futures:

1986 EXCHANGE VOLUME:
1987 EXCHANGE VOLUME:

Options on Futures:

2,696,531 contracts.
3,284,109 contracts.

MARCHE A TERME DES INSTRUMENTS FINANCIERS (MATIF)

Chambre de Compensation des Instruments Financiers de Paris
108 Rue de Richelieu
75002 Paris
France
33 4015 2121

Established in 1986
Open Outcry System
Contracts Listed: Futures and Options on Futures

Futures:

French Government National Bond
French Treasury 90-Day Bill

Options on Futures:

French Government National Bond

1986 EXCHANGE VOLUME:
1987 EXCHANGE VOLUME:

12,018,290 contracts.

Membership

Corporate Memberships only

HONG KONG FUTURES EXCHANGE (HKFE)

Room 1211 12th Floor
New World Trade Tower
16-18 Queen's Road Central
Hong Kong
852(5) 868 0338

Established in 1976
Open Outcry System
Contracts Listed: Futures

Futures:

Sugar
Soybeans

Gold (100 troy ounces)

Hong Kong Dollar Three-Month Interest Rate

Hang Seng Index

| 1986 EXCHANGE VOLUME: | 1,435,969 contracts. |
| 1987 EXCHANGE VOLUME: | 4,535,239 contracts. |

NEW ZEALAND FUTURES EXCHANGE (NZFE)

P.O. Box 6734 Wellesley Street
Auckland
New Zealand
64(9) 398 308

Established in 1985
Electronic System
Contracts Listed: Futures

Futures:

New Zealand Crossbred Wool

United States Dollar

Five-Year Government Stock
90-Day Bank Accepted Bills

Barclays Share Price Index

| 1986 EXCHANGE VOLUME: | 112,237 contracts. |
| 1987 EXCHANGE VOLUME: | 357,174 contracts. |

SINGAPORE INTERNATIONAL MONETARY EXCHANGE (SIMEX)

1 Maritime Square
09-39 World Trade Center
Singapore 0409
65 278 6363

Established in 1983
Open Outcry System
Contracts Listed: Futures and Options on Futures

Futures:

British Pound*
Deutsche Mark*
Japanese Yen*

Eurodollar Three-Month Time
    Deposit*

Nikkei Stock Average

*denotes CME link

Options on Futures:

Eurodollar Three-Month Time Deposit
Deutsche Mark
Japanese Yen

1986 EXCHANGE VOLUME:	875,556 contracts.
1987 EXCHANGE VOLUME:	2,141,983 contracts.

Memberships

All memberships available for ownership or leasing.

SYDNEY FUTURES EXCHANGE (SFE)

13-15 O'Connell Street
Sydney N.S.W. 2000
Australia
61(2) 233 7633

Established in 1960
Open Outcry System
Contracts Listed: Futures and Options on Futures

Futures:

Live Cattle
Wool

Gold**

Australian Dollar

90-Day Bank Accepted Bills
10-Year Australian Treasury Bond
3-Year Australian Treasury Bond
Eurodollar 3-Month Time Deposit*
United States Treasury Bond*

All Ordinaries Share Price Index

*denotes LIFFE link
**denotes COMEX link

Options on Futures:

Australian Dollar

90-Day Bank Accepted Bills
10-Year Australian Treasury Bond
3-Year Australian Treasury Bond

All Ordinaries Share Price Index

1986 EXCHANGE VOLUME:	3,386,929 contracts.
1987 EXCHANGE VOLUME:	5,369,347 contracts.

Memberships

Local Membership available for ownership or leasing.
All other Memberships available for ownership only.

Local Membership—access to all markets.
Corporate Membership—access to all markets.
Associate Membership—reduced rates and direct clearing to ICCH, no floor access.
Market Membership—reduced rates and direct clearing to ICCH for specific markets, no floor access.

3

Clearinghouse
Directory

BOARD OF TRADE CLEARING CORPORATION

141 West Jackson Boulevard, Suite 1460
Chicago, Illinois 60604
USA
Tel: 1(312) 786 5700

CHAMBRE DE COMPENSATION DES INSTRUMENTS FINANCIERS DE PARIS (CCIFP)

15, Rue de la Banque
75002 Paris
France
Tel: 33(1) 4296 5365

CHICAGO MERCANTILE EXCHANGE CLEARINGHOUSE

30 South Wacker Drive
Chicago, Illinois 60606
USA
Tel: 1(312) 930 3170

COMMODITY EXCHANGE (COMEX) CLEARING ASSOCIATION INC.

4 World Trade Center, Suite 7300-D
New York, New York 10048
USA
Tel: 1(212) 775 1480

COMMODITY CLEARING CORPORATION

4 World Trade Center, Suite 7300-C
New York, New York 10048
USA
Tel: 1(212) 775 0190

COFFEE SUGAR COCOA (CSC) CLEARING CORPORATION

4 World Trade Center, Suite 7300-C
New York, New York 10048
USA
Tel: 1(212) 775 0090

EUROPEAN STOCK OPTIONS CLEARING CORPORATION (ESOCC)

Nes 49
Amsterdam 1012D
The Netherlands
Tel: 31(20) 550 4550

INTERNATIONAL COMMODITIES CLEARING HOUSE LTD. (ICCH)

Roman Wall House
1-2 Crutched Friars
London EC3N 2AN
England
Tel: 44(1) 488 3200
Tlx: 851 887 234
Fax: 44(1) 481 3462

Offices in other cities:

Sydney
Level 9, Grosvenor Place
225 George Street
Sydney, NSW 2000
Australia

Tel: 61(2) 258 8000
Tlx: 790 122 142
Fax: 61(2) 251 5152

Melbourne
Ground Floor, Bank House
11-19 Bank Place, Melbourne
Victoria 3000
Australia
Tel: 61(3) 601307

Paris
Societe Internationale de Compensation des Marches (SICM)
35 Rue des Jeuneurs
75002 Paris
France
Tel: 33(1) 4236 2769
Tlx: 842 216 366 F

c/o Banque Centrale de Compensation
22 Quai de la Megisserie
75001 Paris
France
Tel: 33(1) 4261 8195
     33(1) 4233 0904
Tlx: 842 211 526
Fax: 33(1) 4796 5095

ICCH Informatique
37 Rue du Faubourg Poissonniere
75009 Paris
France
Tel: 33(1) 4523 2557
Tlx: 842 216 366 F
Fax: 33(1) 4026 7033

Hong Kong
11221 New World Tower
6-18 Queens Road Central
Hong Kong
Tel: 852(5) 868 0338
Tlx: 842 76375 HX
Fax: 852(5) 868 0134

Auckland
105 Symonds Street, 1st Fl
Auckland
New Zealand

Tel: 64(9) 39 6281
Tlx: 791 63046 ICCH NZ
Fax: 64(9) 37 0031

INTERNATIONAL OPTIONS CLEARING CORPORATION (IOCC)

Contact: Sydney Stock Exchange, European Options Exchange, Montreal Exchange, Vancouver Exchange

KANSAS CITY BOARD OF TRADE CLEARING CORPORATION

4800 Main Street, Suite 270
Kansas City, Missouri 64112
USA
Tel: 1(816) 931 8964

MINNEAPOLIS GRAIN EXCHANGE CLEARINGHOUSE

400 South Fourth, Room 150
Minneapolis, Minnesota 55415
USA
Tel: 1(612) 333 1623

NEW YORK MERCANTILE EXCHANGE (NYMEX) CLEARINGHOUSE

4 World Trade Center, Suite 744
New York, New York 10048
USA
Tel: 1(212) 938 222

OPTIONS CLEARING CORPORATION

200 South Wacker Drive, Suite 2700
Chicago, Illinois 60606
USA
Tel: 1(312) 322 2060

TRANS-CANADA OPTIONS CORPORATION

The Exchange Tower
First Canadian Place
Toronto, Ontario M5X 1B1
Canada
Tel: 1(416) 367 2466

4

Exchange-Related Agencies and Associations

ASSOCIATION OF FUTURES BROKERS AND DEALERS (AFBD)

B Section Fifth Floor
Plantation House
4-16 Mincing Lane
London, EC3M 3DX
England
Tel: 44(1) 626 9763

ASSOCIATION FOR FUTURES INVESTMENT (AFI)

Sugar Quay
Lower Thames Street
London, EC3R 6DU
England
Tel: 44(1) 626 8788
      44(1) 481 2080

COMMODITY FUTURES TRADING COMMISSION (CFTC)

Head Office:
2033 K Street NW
Washington, DC 20581
USA
Tel: 1(202) 254 6387

Offices in other cities:

Chicago
233 South Wacker Drive, Suite 4600
Chicago, Illinois 60606
USA
Tel: 1(312) 353 6642

New York
1 World Trade Center, Suite 4747
New York, New York 10048
USA

Kansas City
4901 Main Street, Room 400
Kansas City, Missouri 63112
USA
Tel: 1(816) 374 2994

Minneapolis
510 Grain Exchange Building
Minneapolis, Minnesota 55415
USA
Tel: 1(612) 349 3257

Los Angeles
10850 Wilshire Boulevard, Suite 370
Los Angeles, California 90024
USA

FEDERATION OF COMMODITY ASSOCIATIONS

Plantation House
Mincing Lane
London EC3M 3HT
England

FUTURES INDUSTRY ASSOCIATION (FIA)

1825 Eye Street NW
Suite 1040
Washington, DC 20006
USA
Tel: 1(202) 466 5460

INTERNATIONAL FEDERATION OF STOCK EXCHANGES

22, Boulevard de Courcelles
75017 Paris
France

NATIONAL ASSOCIATION OF SECURITIES DEALERS (NASD)

Surveillance Department
1735 K Street NW
Washington, DC 20006
USA
Tel: 1(202) 728 8233

NATIONAL FUTURES ASSOCIATION

200 West Madison Street, Suite 1600
Chicago, Illinois 60606
USA
Tel: 1(312) 781 1300
       1(800) 572 8233

SECURITIES AND EXCHANGE COMMISSION

450 Fifth Street NW
Washington, DC 20549
USA
Tel: 1(202) 272 3100

SECURITIES AND INVESTMENTS BOARD

3 Royal Exchange Buildings
London, EC3V 3NL
England
Tel: 44(1) 283 2474
       44(1) 929 0433

SECURITIES DEALERS ASSOCIATION OF JAPAN
NIHON SHOKENGYO KYOKAI

1-5-8 Kayba-cho
Nihombashi, Chuo-ku
Tokyo, 103
Japan
Tel: 81(3) 667 8451

SWISS COMMODITIES, FUTURES AND OPTIONS ASSOCIATION (SCFOA)

1, Carrefour de Rive
PO Box 260
1211 Geneva 3
Switzerland
Tel: 41(2) 235 9250
Tlx: 845 27348

Volume Distribution by Country and Exchange

DISTRIBUTION BY VOLUME *(Top 10 Futures Exchanges)*

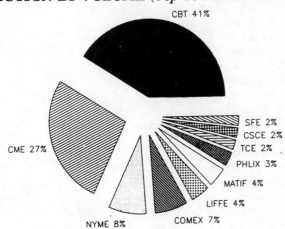

CBT 41%

SFE 2%
CSCE 2%
TCE 2%
PHLIX 3%
MATIF 4%
LIFFE 4%
COMEX 7%
NYME 8%
CME 27%

1987 Volume 313,195,991 (10 Exchanges)

VOLUME BY COUNTRY

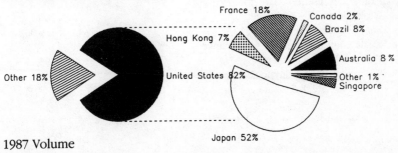

France 18%
Canada 2%
Brazil 8%
Hong Kong 7%
Australia 8%
Other 18%
United States 82%
Other 1%
Singapore
Japan 52%

1987 Volume

EXCHANGE RANK BY VOLUME 1987

	EXCHANGE	TOTAL VOLUME
1	Chicago Board of Trade	127,092,990
2	Chicago Board of Options Exchange	102,655,346
3	Chicago Mercantile Exchange	84,367,214
4	New York Mercantile Exchange	25,735,271
5	Commodity Exchange of New York	21,495,598
6	Tokyo Stock Exchange	18,284,198
7	American Stock Exchange	16,465,517
8	London International Financial Futures Exchange	13,600,670
9	March A Terme Des Instruments Financiers	12,018,290
10	Philadelphia Stock Exchange	10,570,057
11	Tokyo Commodity Exchange	6,496,804
12	Coffee Sugar & Cocoa Exchange	6,256,857
13	Sydney Futures Exchange	5,562,240
14	Bolsa Mercantil and De Futuros	5,339,126
15	Tokyo Grain Exchange	5,200,469
16	Hong Kong Futures Exchange	4,535,239
17	London Metal Exchange Ltd.	3,284,109
18	New York Futures Exchange	3,275,756
19	London Futures and Options Exchange	2,802,878
20	New York Cotton Exchange	2,498,041
21	New York Stock Exchange	2,490,303
22	MidAmerica Commodity Exchange	2,394,679
23	Singapore International Monetary Exchange, Ltd.	2,115,773
24	Kansas City Board of Trade	1,538,331
25	International Petroleum Exchange of London Ltd.	1,114,269
26	Montreal Exchange	872,496
27	Stockholm Options Market	376,771
28	New Zealand Futures Exchange	357,174
29	Minneapolis Grain Exchange	319,206
30	Toronto Stock Exchange	227,404
31	Lille Potato Futures Market	207,294
32	Osaka Securities Exchange	200,480
33	Baltic Futures Exchange	139,053
34	Kuala Lumpur Commodity Exchange	107,597
35	Toronto Futures Exchange	95,897
36	Winnipeg Commodity Exchange	74,365
37	Vancouver Stock Exchange	8,922

6

Volume Listing of Contracts

RANK	CONTRACT NAME	1987 VOLUME	OPT.	EXCH.
1	STANDARD & POOR'S 100 STOCK INDEX	101,827,077	X	CBOE
2	UNITED STATES TREASURY BONDS	66,841,474		CBOT
3	UNITED STATES TREASURY BOND	21,720,402	X	CBOT
4	EURODOLLAR NINETY DAY TIME DEPOSIT	20,416,216		CME
5	STANDARD & POOR'S 500 STOCK INDEX	19,044,673		CME
6	JAPANESE TEN YEAR GOVERNMENT BOND	18,284,198		TSE
7	CRUDE OIL	14,581,614		NYME
8	MAJOR MARKET INDEX	14,545,669	X	AMEX
9	FRENCH GOVERNMENT NOTIONAL BOND	11,911,440		MATIF
10	UK, LTOM (63 EQUITY OPTIONS)	10,782,653	X	ISE
11	GOLD	10,239,805		COMEX
12	SOYBEANS	7,378,760		CB0T
13	CORN	7,253,212		CBOT
14	UK, LONG GILT	6,995,816		LIFFE
15	OMX STOCK INDEX	6,738,654	X	SOM
16	DEUTSCHE MARK	6,037,048		CME
17	JAPANESE YEN	5,358,556		CME

RANK	CONTRACT NAME	1987 VOLUME	OPT.	EXCH.
18	SÃO PAULO STOCK EXCHANGE (BOVESPA) INDEX	5,339,122		BMF
19	SWISS FRANC	5,268,276		CME
20	UNITED STATES TEN YEAR TREASURY NOTE	5,253,791		CBOT
21	LIVE CATTLE	5,229,294		CME
22	SILVER	5,055,652		COMEX
23	NO. 2 HEATING OIL	4,293,395		NYME
24	DEUTSCHE MARK	4,263,942	X	PHLX
25	SOYBEAN OIL	3,912,417		CBOT
26	SUGAR NO. 11 (WORLD)	3,853,499		CSCE
27	SOYBEAN MEAL	3,797,970		CBOT
28	HANG SENG INDEX	3,611,329		HKFE
29	DEUTSCHE MARK	3,125,687	X	CME
30	CRUDE OIL	3,117,037	X	NYME
31	RED BEANS	3,098,437		TGE
32	NEW YORK STOCK EXCHANGE COMPOSITE STOCK INDEX	2,915,915		NYFE
33	PLATINUM	2,866,244		TCE
34	MAJOR MARKET INDEX—MAXI	2,630,887		CBOT
35	BRITISH POUND	2,592,177		CME
36	EURODOLLAR NINETY DAY TIME DEPOSIT	2,569,957	X	CME
37	COPPER	2,569,178		COMEX
38	JAPANESE YEN	2,465,026	X	PHLX
39	JAPANESE YEN	2,250,813	X	CME
40	GOLD	2,158,745		TCE
41	AUSTRALIAN TEN YEAR TREASURY BOND	2,098,246		SFE
42	AUSTRALIAN NINETY DAY BANK ACCEPTED BILLS	2,094,463		SFE
43	AMERICAN SOYBEANS	2,088,820		TGE
44	GOLD	2,080,067	X	COMEX
45	NYSE COMPOSITE INDEX	2,047,075	X	NYSE
46	LIVE HOGS	2,040,478		CME
47	WHEAT (SOFT WINTER)	1,929,306		CBOT
48	UNITED STATES NINETY DAY TREASURY BILLS	1,927,006		CME
49	BRITISH POUND	1,880,469	X	PHLX
50	STANDARD & POOR'S 500 STOCK INDEX	1,877,295	X	CME

RANK	CONTRACT NAME	1987 VOLUME	OPT.	EXCH.
51	SX 16 STOCK INDEX	1,843,272	X	SOFE
52	INSTITUTIONAL INDEX	1,780,468	X	AMEX
53	EURODOLLAR THREE MONTH TIME DEPOSIT (SFE LINK)	1,739,523		LIFFE
54	MUNICIPAL BOND INDEX	1,613,107		CBOT
55	UNITED STATES TREASURY BOND (SFE LINK)	1,557,360		LIFFE
56	EURODOLLAR NINETY DAY TIME DEPOSIT (CME LINK)	1,519,630		SIMEX
57	UK, STERLING THREE MONTH	1,507,920		LIFFE
58	SILVER	1,471,815		TCE
59	UNITED STATES TEN YEAR TREASURY NOTE	1,421,852	X	CBOT
60	COTTON NO. 2	1,395,980		NYCE
61	COPPER (GRADE A)	1,375,703		LME
62	PLATINUM	1,361,546		NYME
63	CANOLA/RAPESEED	1,358,277		WCE
64	SWISS FRANC	1,316,500	X	PHLX
65	SOYBEANS	1,242,072	X	CBOT
66	LIVE CATTLE	1,222,397	X	CME
67	GAS OIL	1,102,148		IPE
68	PORK BELLIES (FROZEN)	1,097,010		CME
69	ALUMINUM (HIGH GRADE)	1,057,024		LME
70	SWISS FRANC	1,053,323	X	CME
71	UK, STERLING THREE MONTH	1,037,306	X	LIFFE
72	UNITED STATES TREASURY BONDS	1,015,454		MIDAM
73	WHEAT (HARD RED WINTER)	971,095		KCBT
74	COFFEE "C"	964,586		CSCE
75	COCOA NO. 6	926,335		FOX
76	SILVER	918,064	X	COMEX
77	CANADIAN DOLLAR	914,563		CME
78	COFFEE (ROBUSTA)	906,930		FOX
79	COCOA	895,465		CSCE
80	FINANCIAL TIMES STOCK EXCHANGE 100 INDEX (FTSE)	883,637	X	ISE
81	SWEDISH, FIVE YEAR TREASURY NOTE	763,164	X	SOM
82	SUGAR NO. 6 (RAW)	762,053		FOX
83	CORN	661,519	X	CBOT
84	US DOLLAR	647,251	X	EOE
85	FEEDER CATTLE	645,877		CME

RANK	CONTRACT NAME	1987 VOLUME	OPT.	EXCH.
86	SOYBEANS	635,975		HKFE
87	DUTCH GOVERNMENT BONDS	634,928	X	EOE
88	ALL ORDINARIES SHARE PRICE INDEX	628,160		SFE
89	STANDARD AND POOR'S 500 STOCK INDEX	620,793	X	CBOE
90	COPPER	612,850	X	COMEX
91	DOMESTIC FEED BARLEY	599,159		WCE
92	BRITISH POUND	569,062	X	CME
93	SILVER (1,000 TROY OUNCES)	509,965		CBOT
94	VALUE LINE STOCK INDEX	505,551		KCBT
95	WHITE SUGAR	489,633		PFE
96	FINANCIAL TIMES STOCK EXCHANGE 100 INDEX (FTSE)	460,615		LIFFE
97	GOLD (10 OUNCES)—IOCC	446,585		ME
98	LUMBER (RANDOM LENGTH)	437,089		CME
99	SUGAR NO. 11 (WORLD)	432,927	X	CSCE
100	SOYBEANS	417,620		MIDAM
101	CANADIAN BONDS	415,981		ME
102	UNITED STATES DOLLAR INDEX	403,783		NYCE
103	EOE STOCK INDEX	388,576	X	EOE
104	AUSTRALIAN TEN YEAR TREASURY BOND	386,640	X	SFE
105	UNITED STATES FIVE YEAR TREASURY NOTE (FYTR®)	383,613		NYCE
106	GOLD (10 OUNCES)—IOCC	374,112	X	EOE
107	NIKKEI STOCK AVERAGE	361,982		SIMEX
108	FLAXSEED	338,050		WCE
109	DOMESTIC FEED WHEAT	320,103		WCE
110	CORN	311,722		MIDAM
111	WHEAT (HARD RED SPRING)	310,599		MGE
112	LEAD	291,680		LME
113	OATS	291,108		CBOT
114	SUGAR	282,237		HKFE
115	AUSTRALIAN DOLLAR	268,345	X	PHLX
116	FROZEN CONCENTRATE ORANGE JUICE (FCOJ)	266,641		NYCE
117	ZINC (HIGH GRADE)	238,910		LME
118	TORONTO 35 INDEX (TXO)	227,404	X	TSEX
119	CANADIAN DOLLAR	208,151	X	PHLX
120	POTATOES (CASH SETTLED)	206,850		BFE
121	NYSE COMPOSITE STOCK INDEX	206,631	X	NYFE

RANK	CONTRACT NAME	1987 VOLUME	OPT.	EXCH.
122	POTATOES (MAIN CROP)	206,196		BFE
123	OSAKA STOCK FUTURES 50	200,480		OSE
124	SUGAR NO. 5 (WHITE)	200,340		FOX
125	WHEAT (SOFT WINTER)	189,610		MIDAM
126	GOLD (ACTUALS)	177,828	X	BMF
127	UNITED STATES TREASURY BOND	174,465	X	CBOE
128	NICKEL	163,329		LME
129	PALLADIUM	160,284		NYME
130	GOLD (32.5 TROY OUNCES)	159,627		CBOT
131	OMX INDEX	159,447		SOM
132	LIVE HOGS CME	147,859	X	CME
133	NO. 2 HEATING OIL	143,605	X	NYME
134	COMMODITY RESEARCH BUREAU'S (CRB) FUTURES PRICE INDEX	136,832		NYFE
135	ALL-ORDINARIES SHARE INDEX	136,802	X	SFE
136	FEEDER CATTLE	134,830	X	CME
137	JAPANESE GOVERNMENT BOND (JGB)	133,442		LIFFE
138	CRUDE PALM OIL	131,451		KLCE
139	DEUTSCHE MARK (CME LINK)	130,807		SIMEX
140	WHEAT (SOFT WINTER)	124,598	X	CBOT
141	BARCLAYS SHARE PRICE INDEX	119,038		NZFE
142	MUNICIPAL BOND INDEX	118,632	X	CBOT
143	GOLD	118,020		BMF
144	BRAZILIAN TREASURY BOND	113,696		BMF
145	RYE	105,737		WCE
146	FRENCH TREASURY NINETY DAY BILL	104,888		MATIF
147	SWISS FRANC	97,571		MIDAM
148	JAPANESE YEN (CME LINK)	93,573		SIMEX
149	OIL INDEX	91,160	X	AMEX
150	SOYBEAN OIL	85,735	X	CBOT
151	DEUTSCHE MARK	85,009		MIDAM
152	BALTIC FREIGHT INDEX	84,862		BFE
153	VALUE LINE STOCK INDEX	84,427	X	PHLX
154	FRENCH FRANC	81,305	X	PHLX
155	SOYBEAN MEAL	81,213	X	CBOT
156	COTTON NO. 2	73,480	X	NYCE
157	SUGAR NO. 14 (DOMESTIC)	69,928		CSCE
158	DOMESTIC FEED OATS	69,573		WCE
159	EEC WHEAT	67,339		BFE

RANK	CONTRACT NAME	1987 VOLUME	OPT.	EXCH.
160	AUSTRALIAN, NINETY DAY BANK ACCEPTED BILLS	63,233	X	SFE
161	JAPANESE YEN	58,836		MIDAM
162	UNITED STATES TREASURY BONDS	54,506	X	LIFFE
163	SOYBEAN MEAL	54,063		BFE
164	AUSTRALIAN DOLLAR	53,335		CME
165	COPPER (GRADE A)	50,831	X	LME
166	ALUMINUM (PRIMARY)	49,847		LME
167	CANADIAN DOLLAR	48,690	X	CME
168	BRAZILIAN, DOMESTIC CD (60 & 90 DAY)	46,621		BMF
169	LIVE HOGS	44,364		MIDAM
170	BRITISH POUND	44,176	X	EOE
171	LIVE CATTLE	44,112		MIDAM
172	ALUMINUM (PRIMARY)	43,986	X	LME
173	EUROPEAN CURRENCY UNIT (ECU)	42,198		NYCE
174	EURODOLLAR THREE MONTH TIME DEPOSIT (SFE LINK)	39,866	X	LIFFE
175	MAJOR MARKET INDEX	39,529	X	EOE
176	NEW ZEALAND, NINETY DAY BANK ACCEPTED BILLS	37,774		NZFE
177	TORONTO 35 INDEX	35,524		TFE
178	SILVER (100 OUNCES)	35,186	X	TFE
179	WHEAT (HARD RED WINTER)	33,228	X	KCBT
180	UNITED STATES FIVE YEAR TREASURY NOTE	33,011	X	CBOE
181	SILVER (250 OUNCES)—IOCC	32,416	X	EOE
182	ROUGH RICE—CRCE	31,114		MIDAM
183	MINI VALUE LINE STOCK INDEX	28,457		KCBT
184	COFFEE "C"	25,639	X	CSCE
185	UNITED STATES NINETY DAY TREASURY BILLS	25,592		MIDAM
186	TSE 300 SPOT CONTRACT	25,187		TFE
187	GOLD (100 TROY OUNCES)	24,893		CBOT
188	UNITED STATES TREASURY NOTES	24,662	X	AMEX
189	EEC BARLEY	24,624		BFE
190	COMPUTER TECHNOLOGY INDEX	23,558	X	AMEX
191	US DOLLAR—STERLING	21,616	X	ISE
192	NEW YORK GOLD	17,957		MIDAM
193	US DOLLAR	16,191		NZFE
194	BRITISH POUND	15,565	X	LIFFE
195	PROPANE	15,312		NYME

RANK	CONTRACT NAME	1987 VOLUME	OPT.	EXCH.
196	FROZEN PORK BELLIES	15,112	X	CME
197	UK, LONG GILT	14,949	X	LIFFE
198	UNITED STATES DOLLAR INDEX	14,538	X	NYCE
199	COCOA	13,910	X	CSCE
200	CHINESE SOYBEANS	13,212		TGE
201	BRITISH POUND	12,668		LIFFE
202	DEUTSCHE MARK	12,668		LIFFE
203	SOYBEANS	12,317	X	MIDAM
204	BROILERS (FROZEN/CHILLED)	12,125		BMF
205	SILVER (5,000 TROY OUNCES)	12,092		CBOT
206	UNITED STATES NINETY DAY TREASURY BILLS	11,634	X	CME
207	MOODY'S CORPORATE BOND INDEX	11,482		COMEX
208	BRITISH POUND	10,979		MIDAM
209	ROBUSTA COFFEE	10,910		PFE
210	RUSSELL 3000 INDEX	10,734		NYFE
211	FRENCH FRANC	10,437		CME
212	SILVER (1,000 TROY OUNCES)	10,009	X	CBOT
213	NEW YORK SILVER	9,578		MIDAM
214	SX 16 STOCK INDEX—FORWARD	9,274		SOFE
215	ALUMINUM	8,500		COMEX
216	BRITISH POUND (CME LINK)	8,324		SIMEX
217	CANADIAN DOLLAR	7,749		MIDAM
218	SILVER (10,000 OUNCES)	7,694		LME
219	GAS OIL	7,518	X	IPE
220	OATS	6,958		MIDAM
221	COFFEE (ROBUSTA)	6,744	X	FOX
222	LUMBER (RANDOM LENGTH)	6,483	X	CME
223	TIN	6,441		KLCE
224	GOLD (10 OUNCES)—IOCC	6,279	X	VSE
225	HIGH FRUCTOSE CORN SYRUP	5,963		MGE
226	LIVE CATTLE	5,921		BMF
227	JAPANESE YEN	5,863		LIFFE
228	GOLD (100 OUNCES)	5,698		HKFE
229	RUSSELL 2000 INDEX	5,644		NYFE
230	CANADIAN TREASURY BILLS	5,631		ME
231	SWISS FRANC	5,169		LIFFE
232	PLATINUM	4,342		MIDAM
233	PLATINUM (10 OUNCES)—IOCC	3,793		ME
234	GOLD (COMEX LINK)	3,574		SFE
235	COPPER (STANDARD)	3,237		LME

RANK	CONTRACT NAME	1987 VOLUME	OPT.	EXCH.
236	SOYBEAN MEAL	3,191		MIDAM
237	US DOLLAR—DEUTSCHE MARK CURRENCY	2,800	X	LIFFE
238	US DOLLAR	2,786		BMF
239	SILVER (250 OUNCES)—IOCC	2,575	X	VSE
240	UNITED STATES TREASURY BONDS (LIFFE LINK)	2,094		SFE
241	EUROPEAN CURRENCY UNIT (ECU)	1,892	X	PHLX
242	PIG	1,606		BFE
243	LIVE CATTLE	1,596		SFE
244	EURODOLLAR THREE MONTH TIME DEPOSIT (LIFFE LINK)	1,568		SFE
245	WHITE WHEAT	1,415		MGE
246	COCOA BEANS	1,290		PFE
247	WHEAT (HARD RED SPRING)	1,229	X	MGE
248	POTATOES (MAIN CROP)	1,098	X	BFE
249	ZINC (HIGH GRADE)	1,035	X	LME
250	SUGAR WORLD WHITE	903		CSCE
251	LIVE HOGS	816		BMF
252	FROZEN CONCENTRATE ORANGE JUICE (FCOJ)	685	X	NYCE
253	US DOLLAR—DEUTSCHE MARK	548	X	ISE
254	WHEAT (SOFT WINTER)	530	X	MIDAM
255	CANADIAN DOLLAR—IOCC	506		ME
256	NICKEL	457	X	LME
257	COCOA NO. 6	397	X	FOX
258	WOOL	384		SFE
259	EUROPEAN CURRENCY UNIT	300		CME
260	LIVE CATTLE	275		BFE
261	LEAD	244	X	LME
262	UK, SHORT GILT	235		LIFFE
263	AUSTRALIAN DOLLAR	196	X	SFE
264	US DOLLAR—DEUTSCHE MARK CURRENCY	116		SFE
265	ALUMINUM (HIGH GRADE)	105	X	LME
266	RUBBER (SMR 20)	79		KLCE
267	SUGAR NO. 6 (RAW)	79	X	FOX
268	GOLD	74	X	MIDAM
269	PLATINUM (10 OUNCES)—IOCC	59	X	VSE
270	RUBBER (SMR 20)	42		KLCE
271	SILVER (2,000 TROY OUNCES)	27		LME
272	ALBERTA FEED BARLEY	20		WCE

RANK	CONTRACT NAME	1987 VOLUME	OPT.	EXCH.
273	CANADIAN DOLLAR—IOCC	9	X	VSE
274	CPI-W	2		CSCE
	AUSTRALIAN DOLLAR	NT	X	CME
	AUSTRALIAN DOLLAR	NT		SFE
	AUSTRALIAN THREE YEAR TREASURY BOND	NT		SFE
	AUSTRALIAN THREE YEAR TREASURY BOND	NT	X	SFE
	BOND INDEX	NT	X	EOE
	BRAZIL COFFEE	NT		BMF
	BRAZILIAN TREASURY BOND (ACTUALS)	NT	X	BMF
	BRENT BLEND CRUDE OIL	NT		IPE
	CANADIAN BANKERS' ACCEPTANCE —THREE MONTH	NT		ME
	CBOE 250 STOCK INDEX	NT		CBOT
	COCOA	NT		KLCE
	COCOA BUTTER	NT		PFE
	COTTON YARN	NT		TCE
	DEUTSCHE MARK	NT	X	SIMEX
	DUTCH, GUILDER BOND FUTURE	NT		FTA
	JAPANESE YEN	NT	X	SIMEX
	EEC BARLEY	NT	X	BFE
	EEC WHEAT	NT	X	BFE
	EURODOLLAR NINETY DAY TIME DEPOSIT	NT	X	SIMEX
	FINANCIAL NEWS COMPOSITE INDEX (FNCI)	NT	X	PSE
	FRENCH GOVERNMENT NOTIONAL BOND	NT		MATIF
	GERMAN GOVERNMENT BOND	NT		LIFFE
	JAPANESE SOYBEANS	NT		TGE
	JAPANESE TWENTY YEAR GOVERNMENT BOND	NT		TSE
	NEW ZEALAND DOLLAR	NT		NZFE
	NEW ZEALAND, FIVE YEAR GOVERNMENT STOCK NO. 2	NT		NZFE
	NIKKEI STOCK AVERAGE	NT		OSE
	POTATO STARCH	NT		TGE
	POTATOES	NT		LPFM
	RAW SUGAR	NT		TKYSG
	REFINED WHITE SOFT SUGAR	NT		TKYSG

RANK	CONTRACT NAME	1987 VOLUME	OPT.	EXCH.
	RUBBER	NT		TCE
	TOKYO STOCK PRICE INDEX (TOPIX)	NT		TSE
	UK, MEDIUM GILT	NT		LIFFE
	UNITED STATES FIVE YEAR TREASURY NOTE	NT		CBOT
	UNITED STATES, FIVE YEAR TREASURY NOTE (FYTR™)	NT	X	NYCE
	UNITED STATES THIRTY DAY FIXED-RATE	NT		CBOT
	UNITED STATES TREASURY BILLS	NT	X	AMEX
	US DOLLAR	NT	X	BMF
	WHITE BEANS	NT		TGE
	WOOLEN YARN	NT		TCE

7

Alphabetical Contracts Index

RANK	CONTRACT NAME	1987 VOLUME	OPT.	EXCH.
272	ALBERTA FEED BARLEY	20		WCE
88	ALL ORDINARIES SHARE PRICE INDEX	628,160		SFE
135	ALL-ORDINARIES SHARE INDEX	136,802	X	SFE
215	ALUMINUM	8,500		COMEX
166	ALUMINUM (PRIMARY)	49,847		LME
172	ALUMINUM (PRIMARY)	43,986	X	LME
69	ALUMINUM (HIGH GRADE)	1,057,024		LME
265	ALUMINUM (HIGH GRADE)	105	X	LME
43	AMERICAN SOYBEANS	2,088,820		TGE
164	AUSTRALIAN DOLLAR	53,335		CME
-	AUSTRALIAN DOLLAR	NT	X	CME
115	AUSTRALIAN DOLLAR	268,345	X	PHLX
-	AUSTRALIAN DOLLAR	NT		SFE
263	AUSTRALIAN DOLLAR	196	X	SFE
42	AUSTRALIAN NINETY DAY BANK ACCEPTED BILLS	2,094,463		SFE
160	AUSTRALIAN NINETY DAY BANK ACCEPTED BILLS	63,233	X	SFE
41	AUSTRALIAN TEN YEAR TREASURY BOND	2,098,246		SFE

RANK	CONTRACT NAME	1987 VOLUME	OPT.	EXCH.
104	AUSTRALIAN TEN YEAR TREASURY BOND	386,640	X	SFE
-	AUSTRALIAN THREE YEAR TREASURY BOND	NT		SFE
-	AUSTRALIAN THREE YEAR TREASURY BOND	NT	X	SFE
152	BALTIC FREIGHT INDEX	84,862		BFE
141	BARCLAYS SHARE PRICE INDEX	119,038		NZFE
-	BOND INDEX	NT	X	EOE
-	BRAZIL COFFEE	NT		BMF
168	BRAZILIAN, DOMESTIC CD (60 & 90 DAY)	46,621		BMF
144	BRAZILIAN TREASURY BOND	113,696		BMF
-	BRAZILIAN TREASURY BOND (ACTUALS)	NT	X	BMF
-	BRENT BLEND CRUDE OIL	NT		IPE
35	BRITISH POUND	2,592,177		CME
92	BRITISH POUND	569,062	X	CME
170	BRITISH POUND	44,176	X	EOE
201	BRITISH POUND	12,668		LIFFE
194	BRITISH POUND	15,565	X	LIFFE
208	BRITISH POUND	10,979		MIDAM
49	BRITISH POUND	1,880,469	X	PHLX
216	BRITISH POUND (CME LINK)	8,324		SIMEX
204	BROILERS (FROZEN/CHILLED)	12,125		BMF
-	CANADIAN BANKERS' ACCEPTANCE —THREE MONTH	NT		ME
101	CANADIAN BONDS	415,981		ME
77	CANADIAN DOLLAR	914,563		CME
167	CANADIAN DOLLAR	48,690	X	CME
217	CANADIAN DOLLAR	7,749		MIDAM
119	CANADIAN DOLLAR	208,151	X	PHLX
255	CANADIAN DOLLAR—IOCC	506		ME
273	CANADIAN DOLLAR—IOCC	9	X	VSE
230	CANADIAN TREASURY BILLS	5,631		ME
63	CANOLA/RAPESEED	1,358,277		WCE
-	CBOE 250 STOCK INDEX	NT		CBOT
200	CHINESE SOYBEANS	13,212		TGE
79	COCOA	895,465		CSCE
199	COCOA	13,910	X	CSCE
-	COCOA	NT		KLCE

RANK	CONTRACT NAME	1987 VOLUME	OPT.	EXCH.
75	COCOA NO. 6	926,335		FOX
257	COCOA NO. 6	397	X	FOX
246	COCOA BEANS	1,290		PFE
-	COCOA BUTTER	NT		PFE
74	COFFEE "C"	964,586		CSCE
184	COFFEE "C"	25,639	X	CSCE
78	COFFEE (ROBUSTA)	906,930		FOX
221	COFFEE (ROBUSTA)	6,744	X	FOX
134	COMMODITY RESEARCH BUREAU'S (CRB) FUTURES PRICE INDEX	136,832		NYFE
190	COMPUTER TECHNOLOGY INDEX	23,558	X	AMEX
37	COPPER	2,569,178		COMEX
90	COPPER	612,850	X	COMEX
61	COPPER (GRADE A)	1,375,703		LME
165	COPPER (GRADE A)	50,831	X	LME
235	COPPER (STANDARD)	3,237		LME
13	CORN	7,253,212		CBOT
83	CORN	661,519	X	CBOT
110	CORN	311,722		MIDAM
60	COTTON NO. 2	1,395,980		NYCE
156	COTTON NO. 2	73,480	X	NYCE
-	COTTON YARN	NT		TCE
274	CPI-W	2		CSCE
7	CRUDE OIL	14,581,614		NYME
30	CRUDE OIL	3,117,037	X	NYME
138	CRUDE PALM OIL	131,451		KLCE
16	DEUTSCHE MARK	6,037,048		CME
29	DEUTSCHE MARK	3,125,687	X	CME
202	DEUTSCHE MARK	12,668		LIFFE
151	DEUTSCHE MARK	85,009		MIDAM
24	DEUTSCHE MARK	4,263,942	X	PHLX
-	DEUTSCHE MARK	NT	X	SIMEX
139	DEUTSCHE MARK (CME LINK)	130,807		SIMEX
91	DOMESTIC FEED BARLEY	599,159		WCE
158	DOMESTIC FEED OATS	69,573		WCE
109	DOMESTIC FEED WHEAT	320,103		WCE
87	DUTCH GOVERNMENT BONDS	634,928	X	EOE
-	DUTCH GUILDER BOND FUTURE	NT		FTA
189	EEC BARLEY	24,624		BFE
-	EEC BARLEY	NT	X	BFE
159	EEC WHEAT	67,339		BFE
-	EEC WHEAT	NT	X	BFE

RANK	CONTRACT NAME	1987 VOLUME	OPT.	EXCH.
103	EOE STOCK INDEX	388,576	X	EOE
4	EURODOLLAR NINETY DAY TIME DEPOSIT	20,416,216		CME
36	EURODOLLAR NINETY DAY TIME DEPOSIT	2,569,957	X	CME
56	EURODOLLAR NINETY DAY TIME DEPOSIT (CME LINK)	1,519,630		SIMEX
-	EURODOLLAR NINETY DAY TIME DEPOSIT	NT	X	SIMEX
53	EURODOLLAR THREE MONTH TIME DEPOSIT (SFE LINK)	1,739,523		LIFFE
174	EURODOLLAR THREE MONTH TIME DEPOSIT (SFE LINK)	39,866	X	LIFFE
244	EURODOLLAR THREE MONTH TIME DEPOSIT (LIFFE LINK)	1,568		SFE
259	EUROPEAN CURRENCY UNIT	300		CME
173	EUROPEAN CURRENCY UNIT (ECU)	42,198		NYCE
241	EUROPEAN CURRENCY UNIT (ECU)	1,892	X	PHLX
85	FEEDER CATTLE	645,877		CME
136	FEEDER CATTLE	134,830	X	CME
-	FINANCIAL NEWS COMPOSITE INDEX (FNCI)	NT	X	PSE
96	FINANCIAL TIMES STOCK EXCHANGE 100 INDEX (FTSE)	460,615		LIFFE
80	FINANCIAL TIMES STOCK EXCHANGE 100 INDEX (FTSE)	883,637	X	ISE
108	FLAXSEED	338,050		WCE
211	FRENCH FRANC	10,437		CME
154	FRENCH FRANC	81,305	X	PHLX
9	FRENCH GOVERNMENT NOTIONAL BOND	11,911,440		MATIF
-	FRENCH GOVERNMENT NOTIONAL BOND	NT	X	MATIF
146	FRENCH TREASURY NINETY DAY BILL	104,888		MATIF
116	FROZEN CONCENTRATE ORANGE JUICE (FCOJ)	266,641		NYCE
252	FROZEN CONCENTRATE ORANGE JUICE (FCOJ)	685	X	NYCE
67	GAS OIL	1,102,148		IPE
219	GAS OIL	7,518	X	IPE

RANK	CONTRACT NAME	1987 VOLUME	OPT.	EXCH.
-	GERMAN GOVERNMENT BOND	NT		LIFFE
126	GOLD (ACTUALS)	177,828	X	BMF
143	GOLD	118,020		BMF
130	GOLD (32.5 TROY OUNCES)	159,627		CBOT
187	GOLD (100 TROY OUNCES)	24,893		CBOT
11	GOLD	10,239,805		COMEX
44	GOLD	2,080,067	X	COMEX
106	GOLD (10 OUNCES)—IOCC	374,112	X	EOE
228	GOLD (100 OUNCES)	5,698		HKFE
97	GOLD (10 OUNCES)—IOCC	446,585		ME
268	GOLD	74	X	MIDAM
234	GOLD (COMEX LINK)	3,574		SFE
40	GOLD	2,158,745		TCE
224	GOLD (10 OUNCES)—IOCC	6,279	X	VSE
28	HANG SENG INDEX	3,611,329		HKFE
225	HIGH FRUCTOSE CORN SYRUP	5,963		MGE
52	INSTITUTIONAL INDEX	1,780,468	X	AMEX
137	JAPANESE GOVERNMENT BOND (JGB)	133,442		LIFFE
6	JAPANESE TEN YEAR GOVERNMENT BOND	18,284,198		TSE
-	JAPANESE TWENTY YEAR GOVERNMENT BOND	NT		TSE
-	JAPANESE SOYBEANS	NT		TGE
17	JAPANESE YEN	5,358,556		CME
39	JAPANESE YEN	2,250,813	X	CME
227	JAPANESE YEN	5,863		LIFFE
161	JAPANESE YEN	58,836		MIDAM
148	JAPANESE YEN (CME LINK)	93,573		SIMEX
-	JAPANESE YEN	NT	X	SIMEX
38	JAPANESE YEN	2,465,026	X	PHLX
112	LEAD	291,680		LME
261	LEAD	244	X	LME
226	LIVE CATTLE	5,921		BMF
260	LIVE CATTLE	275		BFE
21	LIVE CATTLE	5,229,294		CME
66	LIVE CATTLE	1,222,397	X	CME
171	LIVE CATTLE	44,112		MIDAM
243	LIVE CATTLE	1,596		SFE
251	LIVE HOGS	816		BMF
46	LIVE HOGS	2,040,478		CME

RANK	CONTRACT NAME	1987 VOLUME	OPT.	EXCH.
132	LIVE HOGS	147,859	X	CME
169	LIVE HOGS	44,364		MIDAM
98	LUMBER (RANDOM LENGTH)	437,089		CME
222	LUMBER (RANDOM LENGTH)	6,483	X	CME
8	MAJOR MARKET INDEX	14,545,669	X	AMEX
175	MAJOR MARKET INDEX	39,529	X	EOE
34	MAJOR MARKET INDEX—MAXI	2,630,887		CBOT
183	MINI VALUE LINE STOCK INDEX	28,457		KCBT
207	MOODY'S CORPORATE BOND INDEX	11,482		COMEX
54	MUNICIPAL BOND INDEX	1,613,107		CBOT
142	MUNICIPAL BOND INDEX	118,632	X	CBOT
213	NEW YORK SILVER	9,578		MIDAM
32	NEW YORK STOCK EXCHANGE COMPOSITE STOCK INDEX	2,915,915		NYFE
-	NEW ZEALAND DOLLAR	NT		NZFE
-	NEW ZEALAND, FIVE YEAR GOVERNMENT STOCK NO. 2	NT		NZFE
176	NEW ZEALAND, NINETY DAY BANK ACCEPTED BILLS	37,774		NZFE
192	NEW YORK GOLD	17,957		MIDAM
128	NICKEL	163,329		LME
256	NICKEL	457	X	LME
-	NIKKEI STOCK AVERAGE	NT		OSE
107	NIKKEI STOCK AVERAGE	361,982		SIMEX
23	NO. 2 HEATING OIL	4,293,395		NYME
133	NO. 2 HEATING OIL	143,605	X	NYME
45	NYSE COMPOSITE STOCK INDEX	2,047,075	X	NYSE
121	NYSE COMPOSITE STOCK INDEX	206,631	X	NYFE
220	OATS	6,958		MIDAM
113	OATS	291,108		CBOT
149	OIL INDEX	91,160	X	AMEX
131	OMX INDEX	159,447		SOM
15	OMX STOCK INDEX	6,738,654	X	SOM
123	OSAKA STOCK FUTURES 50	200,480		OSE
129	PALLADIUM	160,284		NYME
242	PIG	1,606		BFE
233	PLATINUM (10 OUNCES)—IOCC	3,793		ME
232	PLATINUM	4,342		MIDAM
62	PLATINUM	1,361,546		NYME
33	PLATINUM	2,866,244		TCE

RANK	CONTRACT NAME	1987 VOLUME	OPT.	EXCH.
269	PLATINUM (10 OUNCES)—IOCC	59	X	VSE
68	PORK BELLIES (FROZEN)	1,097,010		CME
196	PORK BELLIES (FROZEN)	15,112	X	CME
-	POTATO STARCH	NT		TGE
-	POTATOES	NT		LPFM
120	POTATOES (CASH SETTLED)	206,850		BFE
122	POTATOES (MAIN CROP)	206,196		BFE
248	POTATOES (MAIN CROP)	1,098	X	BFE
195	PROPANE	15,312		NYME
-	RAW SUGAR	NT		TKYSG
31	RED BEANS	3,098,437		TGE
-	REFINED WHITE SOFT SUGAR	NT		TKYSG
209	ROBUSTA COFFEE	10,910		PFE
182	ROUGH RICE—CRCE	31,114		MIDAM
-	RUBBER	NT		TCE
270	RUBBER (SMR 20)	42		KLCE
266	RUBBER (SMR 20)	79		KLCE
229	RUSSELL 2000 INDEX	5,644		NYFE
210	RUSSELL 3000 INDEX	10,734		NYFE
145	RYE	105,737		WCE
18	SÃO PAULO STOCK EXCHANGE (BOVESPA) INDEX	5,339,122		BMF
93	SILVER (1,000 TROY OUNCES)	509,965		CBOT
212	SILVER (1,000 TROY OUNCES)	10,009	X	CBOT
205	SILVER (5,000 TROY OUNCES)	12,092		CBOT
22	SILVER	5,055,652		COMEX
76	SILVER	918,064	X	COMEX
181	SILVER (250 OUNCES)—IOCC	32,416	X	EOE
271	SILVER (2,000 TROY OUNCES)	27		LME
218	SILVER (10,000 OUNCES)	7,694		LME
58	SILVER	1,471,815		TCE
178	SILVER (100 OUNCES)	35,186	X	TFE
239	SILVER (250 OUNCES)—IOCC	2,575	X	VSE
163	SOYBEAN MEAL	54,063		BFE
27	SOYBEAN MEAL	3,797,970		CBOT
155	SOYBEAN MEAL	81,213	X	CBOT
236	SOYBEAN MEAL	3,191		MIDAM
25	SOYBEAN OIL	3,912,417		CBOT
150	SOYBEAN OIL	85,735	X	CBOT
12	SOYBEANS	7,378,760		CBOT
65	SOYBEANS	1,242,072	X	CBOT

RANK	CONTRACT NAME	1987 VOLUME	OPT.	EXCH.
86	SOYBEANS	635,975		HKFE
100	SOYBEANS	417,620		MIDAM
203	SOYBEANS	12,317	X	MIDAM
1	STANDARD & POOR'S 100 STOCK INDEX	101,827,077	X	CBOE
89	STANDARD & POOR'S 500 STOCK INDEX	620,793	X	CBOE
5	STANDARD & POOR'S 500 STOCK INDEX	19,044,673		CME
50	STANDARD & POOR'S 500 STOCK INDEX	1,877,295	X	CME
26	SUGAR NO. 11 (WORLD)	3,853,499		CSCE
99	SUGAR NO. 11 (WORLD)	432,927	X	CSCE
157	SUGAR NO. 14 (DOMESTIC)	69,928		CSCE
250	SUGAR WORLD WHITE	903		CSCE
82	SUGAR NO. 6 (RAW)	762,053		FOX
267	SUGAR NO. 6 (RAW)	79	X	FOX
124	SUGAR NO. 5 (WHITE)	200,340		FOX
114	SUGAR	282,237		HKFE
81	SWEDISH, FIVE YEAR TREASURY NOTE	763,164	X	SOM
19	SWISS FRANC	5,268,276		CME
70	SWISS FRANC	1,053,323	X	CME
231	SWISS FRANC	5,169		LIFFE
147	SWISS FRANC	97,571		MIDAM
64	SWISS FRANC	1,316,500	X	PHLX
51	SX 16 STOCK INDEX	1,843,272	X	SOFE
214	SX 16 STOCK INDEX—FORWARD	9,274		SOFE
223	TIN	6,441		KLCE
-	TOKYO STOCK PRICE INDEX (TOPIX)	NT		TSE
177	TORONTO 35 INDEX	35,524		TFE
118	TORONTO 35 INDEX (TXO)	227,404	X	TSEX
186	TSE 300 SPOT CONTRACT	25,187		TFE
14	UK, LONG GILT	6,995,816		LIFFE
197	UK, LONG GILT	14,949	X	LIFFE
10	UK, LTOM (63 EQUITY OPTIONS)	10,782,653	X	ISE
-	UK, MEDIUM GILT	NT		LIFFE
262	UK, SHORT GILT	235		LIFFE
57	UK, STERLING THREE MONTH	1,507,920		LIFFE
71	UK, STERLING THREE MONTH	1,037,306	X	LIFFE

RANK	CONTRACT NAME	1987 VOLUME	OPT.	EXCH.
102	UNITED STATES DOLLAR INDEX	403,783		NYCE
198	UNITED STATES DOLLAR INDEX	14,538	X	NYCE
-	UNITED STATES FIVE YEAR TREASURY NOTE	NT		CBOT
180	UNITED STATES FIVE YEAR TREASURY NOTE	33,011	X	CBOE
105	UNITED STATES FIVE YEAR TREASURY NOTE (FYTR™)	383,613		NYCE
-	UNITED STATES, FIVE YEAR TREASURY NOTE (FYTR™)	NT	X	NYCE
20	UNITED STATES TEN YEAR TREASURY NOTE	5,253,791		CBOT
59	UNITED STATES TEN YEAR TREASURY NOTE	1,421,852	X	CBOT
-	UNITED STATES TREASURY BILLS	NT	X	AMEX
48	UNITED STATES NINETY DAY TREASURY BILLS	1,927,006		CME
206	UNITED STATES NINETY DAY TREASURY BILLS	11,634	X	CME
185	UNITED STATES NINETY DAY TREASURY BILLS	25,592		MIDAM
-	UNITED STATES THIRTY DAY FIXED-RATE	NT		CBOT
2	UNITED STATES TREASURY BONDS	66,841,474		CBOT
3	UNITED STATES TREASURY BOND	21,720,402	X	CBOT
127	UNITED STATES TREASURY BOND	174,465	X	CBOE
55	UNITED STATES TREASURY BOND (SFE LINK)	1,557,360		LIFFE
162	UNITED STATES TREASURY BONDS (SFE LINK)	54,506	X	LIFFE
72	UNITED STATES TREASURY BONDS	1,015,454		MIDAM
240	UNITED STATES TREASURY BONDS (LIFFE LINK)	2,094		SFE
188	UNITED STATES TREASURY NOTES	24,662	X	AMEX
238	US DOLLAR	2,786		BMF
-	US DOLLAR	NT	X	BMF
84	US DOLLAR	647,251	X	EOE
253	US DOLLAR—DEUTSCHE MARK	548	X	ISE
191	US DOLLAR—STERLING	21,616	X	ISE
237	US DOLLAR—DEUTSCHE MARK CURRENCY	2,800	X	LIFFE

RANK	CONTRACT NAME	1987 VOLUME	OPT.	EXCH.
193	US DOLLAR	16,191		NZFE
264	US DOLLAR—DEUTSCHE MARK CURRENCY	116		SFE
94	VALUE LINE STOCK INDEX	505,551		KCBT
153	VALUE LINE STOCK INDEX	84,427	X	PHLX
47	WHEAT (SOFT WINTER)	1,929,306		CBOT
140	WHEAT (SOFT WINTER)	124,598	X	CBOT
111	WHEAT (HARD RED SPRING)	310,599		MGE
247	WHEAT (HARD RED SPRING)	1,229	X	MGE
125	WHEAT (SOFT WINTER)	189,610		MIDAM
254	WHEAT (SOFT WINTER)	530	X	MIDAM
73	WHEAT (HARD RED WINTER)	971,095		KCBT
179	WHEAT (HARD RED WINTER)	33,228	X	KCBT
-	WHITE BEANS	**		TGE
245	WHITE WHEAT	1,415		MGE
95	WHITE SUGAR	489,633		PFE
258	WOOL	384		SFE
-	WOOLEN YARN	NT		TCE
117	ZINC (HIGH GRADE)	238,910		LME
249	ZINC (HIGH GRADE)	1,035	X	LME

8

Contract Specifications by Country and Exchange

Contract specifications are a key to understanding fundamental information about a marketplace. Unfortunately many important facts could not be included in this book because the data are not consistent from contract to contract. Other facts that may be of importance (and available from the exchange) are listed as follows:

Delivery Points and time rules
Grading of deliverable products
Hedge or Speculative Margins requirements
Daily Price Limits

Annual volume figures could not be included here because the figure issued by the exchange is for the last day of the year only and does not represent the true depth of the market.

The futures specifications contain the unit value, type of quotation, minimum fluctuation, last trading day, trading months, settlement, trading hours, and recent volume. The options contracts define strike price intervals, expiration date, last day exercise rules, and type of exercise during the life of the contract. We have used three codes to tell you why some information is not listed, they are:

LTD, last trading day

nt, no trading (many contracts are newly listed).

na, not applicable (cash contracts do not have first notice days).

**, this information was not furnished at time of inquiry.

Care has been taken in gathering this information and each exchange has given excellent support in proof reading and revising contracts specifications through to our deadlines. However, trading hours, months traded, contract size, and expiration rules may be adjusted to better meet the needs of commercial users of the market. Please verify important details with your clearing firm.

COUNTRY: AUSTRALIA   *1987 Volume 5,562,240 contracts.*

SYDNEY FUTURES EXCHANGE (SFE)

Established:	1960
System:	Open Outcry
Relationships:	COMEX, gold contract
	LIFFE, US T Bond and Eurodollar contracts

FUTURES

GROUP: AGRICULTURE

LIVE CATTLE

Unit:	10,000 kilograms.
Quotation:	US cents per kilogram.
Minimum Fluctuation:	0.1c/kg = $10.00.
Contract Months:	Monthly.
First Notice Day:	na
Last Trading Day:	Third Wednesday of contract month.
Settlement:	Cash.
Trading Hours:	10:30 to 12:30 and 14:00 to 16:00.
Volume—1986:	2,617 contracts.
Volume—1987:	1,596 contracts.

WOOL

Unit:	1,500 kilograms.
Quotation:	Cent per kilogram.

Minimum Fluctuation:	1c/kg = $25.00.
Contract Months:	March, May, July, October, December.
First Notice Day:	na
Last Trading Day:	Day following last day of wool auction in the physical market.
Settlement:	Cash.
Trading Hours:	10:30 to 12:30 and 14:00 to 16:00.
Volume—1986:	377 contracts.
Volume—1987:	384 contracts.

GROUP: METALS

GOLD (COMEX LINK)

Unit:	100 troy ounces.
Quotation:	US dollars per troy ounce.
Minimum Fluctuation:	US.10 = US$10.00.
Contract Months:	February, April, June, August, October, December, plus current and two nearby months.
First Notice Day:	Last business day of month preceding contract month.
Last Trading Day:	Third to last business day of contract month.
Settlement:	Physical.
Trading Hours:	8:35 to 16:00.
Volume—1986:	3,983 contracts.
Volume—1987:	3,574 contracts.

GROUP: CURRENCIES

AUSTRALIAN DOLLAR

Unit:	100,000 Australian dollars.
Quotation:	US$/A$.
Minimum Fluctuation:	US$0.0001 = US$10.00.
Contract Months:	March, June, September, December.
First Notice Day:	na
Last Trading Day:	Two business days preceding third Wednesday of contract month.
Settlement:	Physical
Trading Hours:	8:30 to 16:30.
Volume—1986:	nt
Volume—1987:	nt

Began 24 February 1988

GROUP: INTEREST RATES

AUSTRALIAN 10-YEAR TREASURY BOND

Unit:	$100,000 Australian principal.

Quotation:	100 minus annual yield.
Minimum Fluctuation:	0.005pct p.a. = $25.00.
Contract Months:	March, June, September, December.
First Notice Day:	na
Last Trading Day:	Fifteenth business day of contract month at 12-noon.
Settlement:	Cash.
Trading Hours:	8:30 to 12:30 and 14:00 to 15:30.
Volume—1986:	1,430,914 contracts.
Volume—1987:	2,098,246 contracts.

AUSTRALIAN THREE-YEAR TREASURY BOND

Unit:	$100,000 Australian principal.
Quotation:	100 minus annual yield.
Minimum Fluctuation:	0.01pct = $11.50.
Contract Months:	March, June, September, December.
First Notice Day:	na
Last Trading Day:	Fifteenth business day of contract month at 12-noon.
Settlement:	Cash.
Trading Hours:	8:30 to 12:30 and 14:00 to 16:30.
Volume—1986:	nt
Volume—1987:	nt

EURODOLLAR THREE-MONTH TIME DEPOSIT (LIFFE LINK)

Unit:	US $1,000,000 principal.
Quotation:	Percent of par in basis points.
Minimum Fluctuation:	0.01pct p.a. = US$25.00.
Contract Months:	March, June, September, December.
First Notice Day:	na
Last Trading Day:	Same as LIFFE contract.
Settlement:	Cash.
Trading Hours:	8:35 to 18:15.
Volume—1986:	1,625 contracts.
Volume—1987:	1,568 contracts.

90-DAY BANK ACCEPTED BILLS

Unit:	$500,000 Australian principal.
Quotation:	100 minus annual yield.
Minimum Fluctuation:	0.01pct p.a. = $11.50.
Contract Months:	March, June, September, December, plus spot and next six months.
First Notice Day:	na
Last Trading Day:	Wednesday preceding second Friday of contract month at 12-noon.
Settlement:	Physical.

Trading Hours:	8:30 to 12:30 and 14:00 to 16:30.
Volume—1986:	1,069,754 contracts.
Volume—1987:	2,094,463 contracts.

UNITED STATES TREASURY BONDS (LIFFE LINK)

Unit:	US $100,000 principal.
Quotation:	Percent of par in basis points.
Minimum Fluctuation:	$US 1/32 = $US31.25.
Contract Months:	March, June, September, December.
First Notice Day:	Same as LIFFE.
Last Trading Day:	Seventh business preceding last business day of contract month.
Settlement:	Physical.
Trading Hours:	8:35 to 18:15.
Volume—1986:	7,280 contracts.
Volume—1987:	2,094 contracts.

GROUP: INDEX

ALL ORDINARIES SHARE PRICE INDEX

Unit:	$100 Australian times Australian Stock Exchanges All Ordinaries Share Price Index.
Quotation:	Index points.
Minimum Fluctuation:	0.1 = $10.00.
Contract Months:	March, June, September, December.
First Notice Day:	na
Last Trading Day:	Second to last business day of contract month at 12-noon.
Settlement:	Cash.
Trading Hours:	9:30 to 12:30 and 14:00 to 15:45.
Volume—1986:	466,398 contracts.
Volume—1987:	628,160 contracts.

OPTIONS

GROUP: CURRENCIES

AUSTRALIAN DOLLAR

Unit:	One SFE Australian dollar futures contract.
Quotation:	US$/A$
Minimum Fluctuation:	$US0.0001 per $A1 = $US10.00.
Strike Price:	$.01 intervals.
Contract Months:	March, June, September, December.
Last Trading Day:	Two Fridays preceding third Wednesday of contract month.

167

Expiration: Close of business, LTD.
Exercise: Automatic.
Type: American.
Settlement: Cash.
Trading Hours: 8:30 to 16:30.
Volume—1986:   2,415 contracts.
Volume—1987:   196 contracts.

GROUP: INTEREST RATES

AUSTRALIAN 10-YEAR TREASURY BOND

Unit: One SFE Australian 10-year Treasury
                                bond futures contract.
Quotation: 100 minus annual yield.
Minimum Fluctuation: 0.005pct p.a. = $25.00.
Strike Price: 0.25 pct per annual yield intervals.
Contract Months: March, June, September, December.
Last Trading Day: Same as underlying contract at 12-
                                noon.

Expiration: Close of business, LTD.
Exercise: Automatic.
Type: American.
Settlement: Cash.
Trading Hours: 8:30 to 12:30 and 14:00 to 15:30.
Volume—1986:   186,639 contracts.
Volume—1987:   386,640 contracts.

AUSTRALIAN THREE-YEAR TREASURY BOND

Unit: One SFE three-year Treasury bond
                                futures contract.
Quotation: 100 minus annual yield.
Minimum Fluctuation: 0.01pct = $25.00.
Strike Price: 0.25 pct per annual yield intervals.
Contract Months: March, June, September, December.
Last Trading Day: Same as underlying contract at 12-
                                noon.

Expiration: Close of business, LTD.
Exercise: Automatic.
Type: American.
Settlement: Cash.
Trading Hours: 8:30 to 12:30 and 14:00 to 16:30.
Volume—1986:   nt
Volume—1987:   nt

90-DAY BANK ACCEPTED BILLS OF EXCHANGE

Unit: One SFE 90-day bank accepted bills of
                                exchange futures contract.

Quotation:	100 minus annual yield.
Minimum Fluctuation:	0.01pct p.a. = $11.50.
Strike Price:	0.50 pct per annual yield.
Contract Months:	March, June, September, December.
Last Trading Day:	Noon, one week prior to underlying contract.
Expiration:	Friday one week preceding settlement of underlying futures contract at 12-noon.
Exercise:	Automatic.
Type:	American.
Settlement:	Future
Trading Hours:	8:30 to 12:30 and 14:00 to 16:30.
Volume—1986:	31,555 contracts.
Volume—1987:	63,233 contracts.

GROUP: INDEX

ALL-ORDINARIES SHARE INDEX

Unit:	One SFE All Ordinaries Index futures contract.
Quotation:	Index points.
Minimum Fluctuation:	0.1 index point.
Strike Price:	25.0 point intervals.
Contract Months:	March, June, September, December.
Last Trading Day:	Same as underlying
Expiration:	Last trading day of underlying futures contract at 12-noon.
Exercise:	Automatic.
Type:	American.
Settlement:	Cash.
Trading Hours:	9:30 to 12:30 and 14:00 to 15:45.
Volume—1986:	26,489 contracts.
Volume—1987:	136,802 contracts.

COUNTRY: BRAZIL   1987 Volume 5,339,126 contracts.

BOLSA MERCANTIL & DE FUTUROS (BMF)

Established:	1986
System:	Open Outcry
Relationships:	None

FUTURES

GROUP: AGRICULTURE

BROILERS (FROZEN/CHILLED)

Unit:	12 Metric tonnes.
Quotation:	Cz$/kg
Minimum Fluctuation:	Cz$0.01/kg
Contract Months:	Even months.
First Notice Day:	Fifth business day prior LTD.
Last Trading Day:	Last business day of delivery month.
Settlement:	Physical.
Hours:	14:15 to 14:35 and 14:40 to 15:00.
Volume—1986:	nt
Volume—1987:	12,125 contracts (began 20 March 1987).

LIVE CATTLE

Unit:	330 net arrobas (1 arrobas = 15kg).
Quotation:	Cz$/net arroba.
Minimum Fluctuation:	Cz$0.10/arroba.
Contract Months:	Even months.
First Notice Day:	First business day of delivery month.
Last Trading Day:	Last business day of the contract month.
Settlement:	Physical.
Hours:	14:15 to 14:35 and 14:40 to 15:00.
Volume—1986:	nt
Volume—1987:	5,921 contracts (began 20 May 1987).

LIVE HOGS

Unit:	8,000 net kg.
Quotation:	Cz$/net kg.
Minimum Fluctuation:	Cz$0.01/kg.
Contract Months:	Even months.
First Notice Day:	First business day of delivery month.
Last Trading Day:	Last business day of the contract month.
Settlement:	Physical.
Hours:	14:15 to 14:35 and 14:40 to 15:00.
Volume—1986:	nt
Volume—1987:	816 contracts (began 25 September 1987).

GROUP: CURRENCIES

US DOLLAR

Unit:	US$5,000.00.

Quotation:	Cz$/US$1.00.
Minimum Fluctuation:	Cz$0.01/1US$1.00.
Contract Months:	All months.
First Notice Day:	na
Last Trading Day:	First business day of delivery month.
Settlement:	Cash.
Hours:	10:00 to 10:20 and 10:30 to 15:45.
Volume—1986:	2,873 contracts (began 19 May 1986).
Volume—1987:	2,786 contracts.

GROUP: INTEREST RATES
BRAZILIAN TREASURY BOND

Unit:	1,000 Brazilian T-bonds.
Quotation:	Cz$/bond.
Minimum Fluctuation:	Cz$0.01/bond.
Contract Months:	All months.
First Notice Day:	OTN value release day.
Last Trading Day:	First business day prior to the Brazilian T-bond's expiring date.
Settlement:	Physical.
Hours:	10:30 to 16:00.
Volume—1986:	nt
Volume—1987:	113,696 contracts (began 6 March 1987).

DOMESTIC CD (60 & 90 DAY)

Unit:	Cz$1,000,000.00.
Quotation:	Points of instrument.
Minimum Fluctuation:	.1 = Cz$10.00.
Contract Months:	Current month, next three months, & subsequent even months.
First Notice Day:	Last trading day.
Last Trading Day:	Third Wednesday of the contract month or following business day.
Settlement:	Physical.
Hours:	11:15 to 12:30 and 15:15 to 16:00.
Volume—1986:	113,696 contracts (began 6 March 1987).
Volume—1987:	46,621 contracts (halted April 1987).

GROUP: METALS
GOLD

Unit:	250g
Quotation:	Cz$/g
Minimum Fluctuation:	Cz$0.10/g

Contract Months:	Odd months.
First Notice Day:	First business day after LTD.
Last Trading Day:	Last business day of the previous month.
Settlement:	Physical and cash.
Hours:	10:00 to 16:30.
Volume—1986:	64,656 contracts (began 5 March 1986).
Volume—1987:	118,020 contracts.

GROUP: INDEX

SÃO PAULO STOCK EXCHANGE (BOVESPA) INDEX

Unit:	Index times Cz$50.00.
Quotation:	Index points.
Minimum Fluctuation:	.05 = Cz$50.00.
Contract Months:	Even months.
First Notice Day:	Fifteen days preceding LTD.
Last Trading Day:	Wednesday closest to the 15th day of the contract month.
Settlement:	Cash.
Hours:	9:30 to 13:15.
Volume—1986:	1,550,277 contracts (began 14 February 1986).
Volume—1987:	5,339,122 contracts.

GROUP: SOFTS

BRAZIL COFFEE

Unit:	100 bags.
Quotation:	Cz$/bag (60kg).
Minimum Fluctuation:	Cz$10.00/bag.
Contract Months:	March, May, July, September, December.
First Notice Day:	First business day of delivery month.
Last Trading Day:	Last business day of contract month.
Settlement:	Physical.
Hours:	10:45 to 16:00.
Volume—1986:	nt
Volume—1987:	nt

Note: Contract began trading August 1988.

OPTIONS

GROUP: CURRENCIES

US DOLLAR

Unit:	US$5,000.00.
Quotation:	Cz$/US$1.00.
Minimum Fluctuation:	Cz$0.01/US$1.00.
Strike Price:	Intervals vary.
Contract Months:	All months.
Last Trading Day:	First business day contract month.
Expiration:	Close of business, LTD.
Exercise:	By instruction.
Type:	Call/American, Put/European.
Settlement:	Future.
Trading Hours:	10:00 to 10:20 and 10:30 to 15:45.
Volume—1986:	nt
Volume—1987:	nt

Note: Contract began trading March 1988.

GROUP: METALS

GOLD (ACTUALS)

Unit:	250g.
Quotation:	Cz$/g.
Minimum Fluctuation:	Cz$0.10/g.
Strike Price:	Intervals vary.
Contract Months:	Odd months.
Last Trading Day:	Third Friday of the contract month or previous business day.
Expiration:	Close of business, LTD.
Exercise:	By instruction.
Type:	Call/American, Puts/European.
Settlement:	Cash.
Trading Hours:	10:00 to 16:30.
Volume—1986:	95,208 contracts (began 31 January 1986).
Volume—1987:	177,828 contracts.

GROUP: INTEREST RATES

BRAZILIAN TREASURY BOND (ACTUALS)

Unit:	1,000 Brazilian T-bonds.
Quotation:	Cz$/bond.
Minimum Fluctuation:	Cz$0.01/bond.
Strike Price:	Intervals vary.
Contract Months:	All months.
Last Trading Day:	First business day of contract month.

173

Expiration:	Close of business, LTD.
Exercise:	By instruction.
Type:	Call/American, Puts/European.
Settlement:	Future.
Trading Hours:	10:30 to 16:00.
Volume—1986:	nt
Volume—1987:	nt

Note: Contract began trading March 1988.

COUNTRY: CANADA   *1987 Volume 1,279,084 contracts.*

BOURSE DE MONTREAL—MONTREAL EXCHANGE (ME)

Established:	1975 (Futures 1984)
System:	Open Outcry
Relationships:	Mutual Offset with Vancouver Stock Exchange, Sydney Stock Exchange, and European Options Exchange.

FUTURES

GROUP: INTEREST RATES

CANADIAN BANKERS' ACCEPTANCE—THREE MONTH

Unit:	$1,000,000 Canadian principal.
Quotation:	Index of 100 minus yield of three-month bankers' acceptance rate.
Minimum Fluctuation:	One (.01) basis point = $25.00.
Contract Months:	March, June, September, December.
First Notice Day:	**
Last Trading Day:	Second London business day preceding third Wednesday of contract month at 10:00.
Delivery Day:	Business day following last trading day.
Settlement:	**
Trading Hours:	09:00 to 15:00.
Volume—1986:	nt
Volume—1987:	**

OPTIONS

GROUP: METALS

GOLD (10 OUNCES)—IOCC

Unit:	10 troy ounces for London delivery.

Quotation: US dollars and cents per ounce.
Minimum Fluctuation: 10 cents per ounce, 1 point = $1.00.
Strike Price: $10 intervals.
Contract Months: Next three months on February, May, August, November cycle.
Last Trading Day: Third Friday in contract month.
Expiration: Monday following third Friday in contract month.
Exercise: **
Type: **
Settlement: **
Trading Hours: IOCC schedule:
MSE: 09:00 to 14:30.
VSE: 11:30 to 16:00.
EOE: 10:30 to 16:30.
ASE: 10:30 to 16:00 (Summer).
11:00 to 16:30 (Winter).
Volume—1986: 321,593 contracts.
Volume—1987: 446,585 contracts.

PLATINUM (10 OUNCES)—IOCC
Unit: 10 troy ounces.
Quotation: US dollar and cents per ounce.
Minimum Fluctuation: 10 cents per ounce, 1 point = $1.00.
Strike Price: $10 intervals.
Contract Months: Next three months on March, June, September, December cycle.
Last Trading Day: Third Friday in contract month.
Expiration: Monday following third Friday in contract month.
Exercise: **
Type: **
Settlement: **
Trading Hours: IOCC schedule:
MSE: 09:00 to 14:30.
VSE: 11:30 to 16:00.
EOE: 10:30 to 16:30.
ASE: 10:30 to 16:00 (Summer).
11:00 to 16:30 (Winter).
Volume—1986: nt
Volume—1987: 3,793 contracts.

GROUP: CURRENCIES
CANADIAN DOLLAR—IOCC
Unit: 50,000 Canadian dollars.

Quotation: US$/CD.
Minimum Fluctuation: $0.0001 per Canadian dollar =
                               US$5.00.
Strike Price: $0.01 per Canadian dollar.
Contract Months: Next three consecutive months, plus
                               next two months on March, June,
                               September, December cycle.
Last Trading Day: Third Friday in contract month.
Expiration: Monday following third Friday in
                               contract month.
Exercise: **
Type: **
Settlement: **
Trading Hours: IOCC schedule:
                               MSE: 08:00 to 14:30.
                               VSE: 11:30 to 16:00.
Volume—1986:   2,556 contracts.
Volume—1987:   506 contracts.

GROUP: INTEREST RATES

CANADIAN BONDS

Unit: $25,000 principal.
Quotation: Dollars and cents per contract.
Minimum Fluctuation: 0.01 pct of $100 principal.
Strike Price: 2.5 point intervals.
Contract Months: Next three months, plus March, June,
                               September, December cycle.
Last Trading Day: **
Expiration: Saturday following third Friday of
                               contract month.
Exercise: **
Type: **
Settlement: **
Trading Hours: 9:00 to 16:00.
Volume—1986:   275,618 contracts.
Volume—1987:   415,981 contracts.

GROUP: INTEREST RATES

CANADIAN TREASURY BILLS

Unit: $250,000 principal. Underlying
                               security is Montreal Exchange T-bill
                               index equal to 100 minus yield of
                               91-day Canadian T-bill.
Quotation: Basis points.
Minimum Fluctuation: One (.01) basis point.

Strike Price:	50 basis points intervals.
Contract Months:	Next three months, plus two following months on March, June, September, December cycle.
Last Trading Day:	Week of third Friday in contract month on day of Government Canadian T-bill auction at 12-noon.
Expiration:	Calendar day following auction.
Exercise:	**
Type:	**
Settlement:	**
Trading Hours:	08:35 to 15:00.
Volume—1986:	2,746 contracts.
Volume—1987:	5,631 contracts.

TORONTO FUTURES EXCHANGE (TFE)

Established:	1984
System:	Open Outcry
Relationships:	None

FUTURES

GROUP: INDEX

TSE 300 SPOT CONTRACT

Unit:	$10 Canadian times TSE 300 Index.
Quotation:	Points in index.
Minimum Fluctuation:	0.01 = $10.00.
Contract Months:	Daily.
First Notice Day:	na
Last Trading Day:	na
Settlement:	Cash at end of each trading day.
Trading Hours:	9:20 to 16:10.
Volume—1986:	75,081 contracts.
Volume—1987:	25,187 contracts.

TORONTO 35 INDEX

Unit:	$500 Canadian times Toronto 35 index future.
Quotation:	Index points to two decimals.
Minimum Fluctuation:	0.02 = $10.00.
Contract Months:	Three consecutive near months.
First Notice Day:	na
Last Trading Day:	Thursday preceding third Friday of contract month.

Settlement:	Cashed based on Friday's official opening.
Trading Hours:	9:15 to 16:15.
Volume—1986:	nt
Volume—1987:	35,524 contracts.

OPTIONS

GROUP: METALS

SILVER (100 OUNCES)

Unit:	100 troy ounces.
Quotation:	US cents per ounce.
Minimum Fluctuation:	One cent for all premiums.
Strike Price:	25 cent intervals below $5.
	50 cent intervals $5 to $15.
	$1 intervals above $15.
Contract Months:	Three consecutive near months, plus six and nine months.
Last Trading Day:	Third Friday of contract month.
Expiration:	Saturday following third Friday of each contract month.
Exercise:	Automatic, if in the money.
Type:	American.
Settlement:	Physical.
Trading Hours:	9:05 to 16:00.
Volume—1986:	21,132 contracts.
Volume—1987:	35,186 contracts.

TORONTO STOCK EXCHANGE (TSEX)

Established:	1852
System:	Open Outcry
Relationships:	None.

OPTIONS

GROUP: INDEX

TORONTO 35 INDEX (TXO)

Unit:	$100 times Toronto 35 index.
Quotation:	Canadian cents per index.
Minimum Fluctuation:	One cent under 10 cents.
	Five cents under five dollars.
	12½ cents at five dollars and above.
Strike Price:	Five-point intervals.
Contract Months:	Next three months.

Last Trading Day:	Thursday before third Friday of contract month.
Expiration:	Day following last trading day.
Exercise:	Automatic, if in the money.
Type:	European.
Settlement:	Cash.
Trading Hours:	9:15 to 16:15.
Volume—1986:	nt
Volume—1987:	227,404 contracts.

VANCOUVER STOCK EXCHANGE (VSE)

Established:	
System:	Open Outcry
Relationships:	Mutual Offset with Montreal Exchange, Sydney Stock Exchange, and European Options Exchange.

OPTIONS

GROUP: METALS

GOLD (10 OUNCES)—IOCC

Unit:	10 troy ounces for London delivery.
Quotation:	US dollars and cents per ounce.
Minimum Fluctuation:	$.10 = $1.00.
Strike Price:	$10 intervals.
Contract Months:	Next three months on February, May, August, November cycle.
Last Trading Day:	Third Friday in contract month.
Expiration:	Monday following third Friday in contract month.
Exercise:	By instruction.
Type:	American.
Settlement:	Cash and physical.
Trading Hours:	IOCC schedule:
	VSE: 11:30 to 16:00.
	ME: 09:00 to 14:30.
	EOE: 10:30 to 16:30.
	ASE: 11:00 to 13:00 (Summer).
	10:30 to 12:30 (Winter).
Volume—1986:	7,597 contracts.
Volume—1987:	6,279 contracts.

PLATINUM (10 OUNCES)—IOCC

Unit:	10 troy ounces.

Quotation:	US dollars and cents per ounce.
Minimum Fluctuation:	$.10 = $1.00.
Strike Price:	$10 intervals.
Contract Months:	Next three months in March, June, September, December cycle.
Last Trading Day:	Third Friday in contract month.
Expiration:	Monday following third Friday in contract month.
Exercise:	By instruction.
Type:	American.
Settlement:	Cash and physical.
Trading Hours:	IOCC schedule:
	VSE: 11:30 to 16:00.
	ME: 09:00 to 14:30.
	EOE: 10:30 to 16:30.
	ASE: 11:00 to 13:00 (Summer).
	10:30 to 12:30 (Winter).
Volume—1986:	nt
Volume—1987:	59 contracts.

SILVER (250 OUNCES)—IOCC

Unit:	250 troy ounces.
Quotation:	US dollars and cents per ounce.
Minimum Fluctuation:	$.01 = $2.50.
Strike Price:	$0.25 for five dollars or under.
	$0.50 for five dollars to $15.
	One dollar for above $15.
Contract Months:	March, June, September, December.
Last Trading Day:	Third Friday in contract month.
Expiration:	Monday following third Friday in contract month.
Exercise:	By instruction.
Type:	American.
Settlement:	Cash and physical.
Trading Hours:	IOCC schedule:
	VSE: 07:30 to 16:30.
	EOE: 10:00 to 16:30.
	ASE: 11:00 to 13:00 (Summer).
	10:30 to 12:30 (Winter).
Volume—1986:	2,075 contracts.
Volume—1987:	2,575 contracts.

GROUP: CURRENCIES

CANADIAN DOLLAR—IOCC

Unit:	50,000 Canadian dollars.

Quotation:	US$/CD.
Minimum Fluctuation:	$0.0001 per Canadian dollar = $5.00.
Strike Price:	$0.01 per Canadian dollar.
Contract Months:	Next three consecutive months, plus next two months on March, June, September, December cycle.
Last Trading Day:	Third Friday in contract month.
Expiration:	Monday following third Friday in contract month.
Exercise:	By instruction.
Type:	American.
Settlement:	Physical.
Trading Hours:	IOCC schedule: VSE: 11:30 to 16:00. ME: 08:00 to 14:30.
Volume—1986:	169 contracts.
Volume—1987:	9 contracts.

WINNIPEG COMMODITY EXCHANGE (WCE)

Established:	1887
System:	Open Outcry
Relationships:	None

FUTURES

GROUP: AGRICULTURE

Note: Volume figures correspond to crop year.

ALBERTA FEED BARLEY

Unit:	20 metric tonnes.
Quotation:	Cents per tonne.
Minimum Fluctuation:	$.10 = $2.00.
Contract Months:	February, April, June, September, November.
First Notice Day:	Eighth business day before end of contract.
Last Trading Day:	Last business day of contract month.
Settlement:	Physical.
Trading Hours:	9:30 to 13:15.
Volume—1987:	2 contracts.
Volume—1988:	20 contracts.

CANOLA/RAPESEED

Unit:	100 metric tonnes board lot.
Quotation:	Cents per tonne.

Minimum Fluctuation: $.10 = $10.00.

Contract Months: January, March, June, September, November.

First Notice Day: Eighth business day before end of contract.

Last Trading Day: Seventh business day preceding delivery date.

Settlement: Physical.

Trading Hours: 9:30 to 13:15.

Volume—1987: 1,291,290 contracts.

Volume—1988: 1,358,277 contracts.

DOMESTIC FEED BARLEY

Unit: 100 metric tonnes board lot.

Quotation: Cents per tonne.

Minimum Fluctuation: $.10 = $10.00.

Contract Months: March, May, July, October, December.

First Notice Day: Eighth business day before end of contract.

Last Trading Day: Last business day of contract month.

Settlement: Physical.

Trading Hours: 9:30 to 13:15.

Volume—1987: 305,260 contracts.

Volume—1988: 599,159 contracts.

DOMESTIC FEED OATS

Unit: 100 metric tonnes board lot.

Quotation: Cents per tonne.

Minimum Fluctuation: $.10 = $10.00.

Contract Months: March, May, July, October, December.

First Notice Day: Eighth business day before end of contract.

Last Trading Day: Last business day of contract month.

Settlement: Physical.

Trading Hours: 9:30 to 13:15.

Volume—1987: 43,555 contracts.

Volume—1988: 69,573 contracts.

DOMESTIC FEED WHEAT

Unit: 100 metric tonnes board lot.

Quotation: Cents per tonne.

Minimum Fluctuation: $.10 = $10.00.

Contract Months: March, May, July, October, December.

First Notice Day: Eighth business day before end of contract.

Last Trading Day: Last business day of contract month.

Settlement:	Physical.
Trading Hours:	9:30 to 13:15.
Volume—1987:	219,576 contracts.
Volume—1988:	320,103 contracts.

FLAXSEED

Unit:	100 metric tonnes board lot.
Quotation:	Cents per tonne.
Minimum Fluctuation:	$.10 = $10.00.
Contract Months:	March, May, July, October, December.
First Notice Day:	Eighth business day before end of contract.
Last Trading Day:	Last business day of contract month.
Settlement:	Physical.
Trading Hours:	9:30 to 13:15.
Volume—1987:	296,891 contracts.
Volume—1988:	338,050 contracts.

RYE

Unit:	100 metric tonnes.
Quotation:	Cents per tonne.
Minimum Fluctuation:	$.10 = $10.00.
Contract Months:	March, May, July, October, December.
First Notice Day:	Eighth business day before end of contract.
Last Trading Day:	Last business day of contract month.
Settlement:	Physical.
Trading Hours:	09:30 to 13:15.
Volume—1987:	115,989 contracts.
Volume—1988:	105,737 contracts.

COUNTRY: FRANCE   *1987 Volume 12,225,584 Contracts*

LILLE POTATO FUTURES MARKET (LPFM)

Established:	**
System:	Open Outcry
Relationship:	None

FUTURES

GROUP: AGRICULTURE

POTATOES

Unit:	20 tonnes potatoes.
Quotation:	French francs per kilograms.

Minimum Fluctuation:	25 francs per 100 kilograms.
Contract Months:	February, April, May, November.
First Notice Day:	**
Last Trading Day:	Second Tuesday of contract month.
Settlement:	Physical.
Trading Hours:	11:00 to 12:45 and 15:00 to 16:30.
Volume—1986:	27,989 contracts.
Volume—1987:	**

MARCHE A TERME DES INSTRUMENT FINANCIERS (MATIF)

Established:	1986
System:	Open Outcry
Relationships:	Merger, Paris Futures Exchange

FUTURES

GROUP: INTEREST RATES

FRENCH GOVERNMENT NOTIONAL BOND

Unit:	500,000 French franc principal with 10 pct coupon and 10-year maturity.
Quotation:	Percent of par in basis points.
Minimum Fluctuation:	.05 = 250 francs.
Contract Months:	March, June, September, December.
First Notice Day:	**
Last Trading Day:	Four business days preceding last business day in contract month.
Settlement:	Physical.
Trading Hours:	10:00 to 15:00.
Volume—1986:	1,663,453 contracts.
Volume—1987:	11,911,440 contracts.

FRENCH TREASURY 90-DAY BILL

Unit:	5,000,000 French franc principal.
Quotation:	100 minus interest rate.
Minimum Fluctuation:	.01 = 125 francs.
Contract Months:	March, June, September, December.
First Notice Day:	**
Last Trading Day:	Business day following Treasury bills third monthly adjudication.
Settlement:	Physical.
Trading Hours:	10:00 to 15:00.
Volume—1986:	50,109 contracts.
Volume—1987:	104,888 contracts.

OPTIONS

GROUP: INTEREST RATES

FRENCH GOVERNMENT NOTIONAL BOND

Unit:	One MATIF French government notional bond futures contract.
Quotation:	Percent of Par in basis points.
Minimum Fluctuation:	0.01 = 50 francs.
Strike Price:	Even strike prices.
Contract Months:	March, June, September, December.
Last Trading Day:	Friday preceding contract month of underlying futures contract.
Expiration:	Last day of trading by 16:00.
Exercise:	Automatic.
Type:	American.
Settlement:	**
Trading Hours:	10:00 to 15:00
Volume—1986:	nt
Volume—1987:	**

PARIS FUTURES EXCHANGE (PFE)
COMPAGNIE DES COMMISSIONAIRES AGRÈES

Established:	1961
System:	Open Outcry
Relationships:	Merger, MATIF

FUTURES

GROUP: SOFTS

COCOA BEANS

Unit:	10 metric tonnes.
Quotation:	French francs per kilograms.
Minimum Fluctuation:	50 francs per 100 kilograms.
Contract Months:	March, May, July, September, December.
First Notice Day:	**
Last Trading Day:	Last day of contract month at 13:00.
Settlement:	Physical.
Trading Hours:	10:30 to 13:00 and 15:00 to 18:30.
Volume—1986:	4,483 contracts.
Volume—1987:	1,290 contracts.

COCOA BUTTER

Unit:	10 metric tons.

Quotation: French francs per kilograms.

Minimum Fluctuation: One franc per 100 kilograms, 1 point = 50 francs.

Contract Months: March, May, July, September, December.

First Notice Day: **

Last Trading Day: Twentieth of month preceding contract month.

Settlement: Physical.

Trading Hours: 11:15 to 13:00 and 15:00 to 18:30.

Volume—1986: **

Volume—1987: **

ROBUSTA COFFEE

Unit: Five metric tons.

Quotation: French francs per kilograms.

Minimum Fluctuation: One franc per 100 kilograms, 1 point = 50 francs.

Contract Months: January, March, May, July, September, November.

First Notice Day: **

Last Trading Day: Last day of contract month at 12-noon.

Settlement: Physical.

Trading Hours: 10:15 to 13:00 and 15:00 to 18:30.

Volume—1986: 37,469 contracts.

Volume—1987: 10,910 contracts.

WHITE SUGAR

Unit: 50 metric tons.

Quotation: French francs per metric ton. US dollars for non-residents at request.

Minimum Fluctuation: One franc per ton, 1 point = 50 francs.

Contract Months: March, May, August, October, December.

First Notice Day: **

Last Trading Day: Fifteenth day of month preceding contract month.

Settlement: Physical.

Trading Hours: 10:45 to 13:00 and 15:00 to 19:00.

Volume—1986: 520,812 contracts.

Volume—1987: 489,633 contracts.

COUNTRY: GREAT BRITAIN   *1987 Volume 20,940,979 contracts.*

BALTIC FUTURES EXCHANGE (BFE)

Established: 1987
System: Open Outcry
Relationship: None

Includes: **BALTIC INTERNATIONAL FREIGHT FUTURES EXCHANGE**
LONDON GRAIN FUTURES MARKET
LONDON MEAT FUTURES MARKET
THE LONDON POTATO FUTURES MARKET
THE SOYA BEAN MEAL FUTURES ASSOCIATION LTD.

FUTURES

GROUP: INDEX

BALTIC FREIGHT INDEX

Unit:	$10 times Baltic Freight Index point.
Quotation:	US dollars per index points.
Minimum Fluctuation:	$.05 = $5.00.
Contract Months:	January, April, July, October.
First Notice Day:	na
Last Trading Day:	Last business day of contract month.
Settlement:	Cash on last trading day at 12-noon.
Trading Hours:	10:15 to 12:30 and 14:30 to 16:15.
Volume—1986:	44,911 contracts.
Volume—1987:	84,862 contracts.

LONDON GRAIN FUTURES MARKET

FUTURES

GROUP: AGRICULTURE

EEC BARLEY

Unit:	100 metric tonnes.
Quotation:	Pence per tonne.
Minimum Fluctuation:	.05 = 5 pounds.
Contract Months:	January, March, May, September, November.
First Notice Day:	Seventh day prior to first business day of contract month.
Last Trading Day:	Twenty-third day of contract month.
Settlement:	Physical.
Trading Hours:	11:00 to 12:30 and 14:45 to 16:00.

| Volume—1986: | 32,170 contracts. |
| Volume—1987: | 24,624 contracts. |

EEC WHEAT

Unit:	100 metric tonnes.
Quotation:	Pence per tonne.
Minimum Fluctuation:	.05 = 5 pounds.
Contract Months:	January, March, May, July, September, November.
First Notice Day:	Seventh day prior to first business day of contract month.
Last Trading Day:	Twenty-third day of contract month.
Settlement:	Physical.
Trading Hours:	11:00 to 12:30 and 14:45 to 16:00.
Volume—1986:	79,927 contracts.
Volume—1987:	67,339 contracts.

OPTIONS

GROUP: AGRICULTURE

EEC WHEAT

Unit:	One EEC wheat futures contract.
Quotation:	Pence per tonne.
Minimum Fluctuation:	.05 = 5 pounds.
Strike Price:	One pound per tonne intervals.
Contract Months:	January, March, May, July, September, November.
Last Trading Day:	Second Thursday of month preceding contract month.
Expiration:	Day after last trading day.
Exercise:	By instruction.
Type:	American.
Settlement:	Futures.
Trading Hours:	11:00 to 12:30 and 14:45 to 16:00.
Volume—1986:	na
Volume—1987:	na

EEC BARLEY

Unit:	One EEC barley futures contract.
Quotation:	Pence per tonne.
Minimum Fluctuation:	.05 = 5 pounds.
Strike Price:	One pound per tonne intervals.
Contract Months:	January, March, May, November.
Last Trading Day:	Second Thursday of month preceding contract month.
Expiration:	Day after last trading day.

Exercise:	By instruction.
Type:	American.
Settlement:	Futures.
Trading Hours:	11:00 to 12:30 and 14:45 to 16:00.
Volume—1986:	na
Volume—1987:	na

LONDON MEAT FUTURES MARKET

FUTURES

GROUP: AGRICULTURE

LIVE CATTLE

Unit:	5,000 kilograms.
Quotation:	Pence per kilogram.
Minimum Fluctuation:	.05 = 5 pounds.
Contract Months:	January, February, March, April, May, June, August, September, October, November.
First Notice Day:	na
Last Trading Day:	Last Friday of contract month.
Settlement:	Cash on last trading day at 12-noon.
Trading Hours:	10:00 to 12:00 and 14:15 to 15:45.
Volume—1986:	495 contracts.
Volume—1987:	275 contracts.

PIG

Unit:	3,250 kilograms.
Quotation:	Pence per kilogram.
Minimum Fluctuation:	.01 = 3.25 pounds.
Contract Months:	February, April, June, August, October, November.
First Notice Day:	na
Last Trading Day:	Last Tuesday of contract month.
Settlement:	Cash on last trading day at 12-noon.
Trading Hours:	10:00 to 12:00 and 14:15 to 15:45.
Volume—1986:	1,073 contracts.
Volume—1987:	1,606 contracts.

LONDON POTATO FUTURES MARKET

FUTURES

GROUP: AGRICULTURE

POTATOES (MAIN CROP)

Unit:	40 metric tonnes.

Quotation:	Pence per tonne.
Minimum Fluctuation:	10 pence per tonne.
Contract Months:	February, April, May, November.
First Notice Day:	First business day of contract month.
Last Trading Day:	Tenth calendar day of contract month at 12-noon.
Settlement:	Physical.
Trading Hours:	11:00 to 12:30 and 14:45 to 16:00.
Volume—1986:	259,788 contracts.
Volume—1987:	206,196 contracts.

POTATOES (CASH SETTLED)

Unit:	40 metric tonnes.
Quotation:	Pence per tonne.
Minimum Fluctuation:	10 pence per tonne.
Contract Months:	March, July, August, September.
First Notice Day:	na
Last Trading Day:	Last Tuesday of contract month.
Settlement:	Cash on last trading day at 12-noon.
Trading Hours:	11:00 to 12:30 and 14:45 to 16:00.
Volume—1986:	259,783 contracts.
Volume—1987:	206,850 contracts.

OPTIONS

GROUP: AGRICULTURE

POTATOES (MAIN CROP)

Unit:	One 40 metric tonnes potato futures contract. (Main Crop)
Quotation:	Pence per tonne.
Minimum Fluctuation:	10 pence per tonne.
Strike Price:	5 BP, less than 95 BP.
	10 BP, 100 BP to 200 BP.
	15 BP, greater than 200 BP.
Contract Months:	March, April, May, November.
Last Trading Day:	Second Wednesday of month prior to contract month.
Expiration:	Last business day at 17:00.
Exercise:	Automatic.
Type:	American.
Settlement:	Futures.
Trading Hours:	11:00 to 12:30 and 14:45 to 16:00.
Volume—1986:	2,170 contracts.
Volume—1987:	1,098 contracts.

SOYA BEAN MEAL FUTURES ASSOCIATION LTD.

FUTURES

GROUP: AGRICULTURE

SOYBEAN MEAL

Unit:	20 metric tonnes.
Quotation:	Pounds per tonne.
Minimum Fluctuation:	10 = 2 pounds.
Contract Months:	February, April, June, August, October, December.
First Notice Day:	Seventh day prior to first business day of contract month.
Last Trading Day:	22nd calendar day of contract month.
Expiration:	Last Trading Day at 16:00.
Type:	American.
Settlement:	Futures.
Trading Hours:	10:30 to 12:00 and 14:45 to 16:00.
Volume—1986:	78,304 contracts.
Volume—1987:	54,063 contracts.

INTERNATIONAL PETROLEUM EXCHANGE OF LONDON LTD. (IPE)

Established:	1981
System:	Open Outcry
Relationships:	None

FUTURES

GROUP: ENERGY

GAS OIL

Unit:	100 tonnes gas oil.
Quotation:	US dollars and cents per tonne.
Minimum Fluctuation:	25 cents per tonne.
Contract Months:	Nine consecutive months including current month.
First Notice Day:	Last trading day.
Last Trading Day:	Three business days preceding 13th calendar day of contract month at noon.
Settlement:	Physical.
Trading Hours:	9:15 to 12:15 and 14:30 to 17:15.
Volume—1986:	938,225 contracts.
Volume—1987:	1,102,148 contracts.

BRENT BLEND CRUDE OIL

Unit:	1,000 barrels (42,000 US gallons) Brent Crude Oil.
Quotation:	US dollars and cents per barrel.
Minimum Fluctuation:	One cent (.01) per barrel.
Contract Months:	Six consecutive months following current month.
First Notice Day:	na
Last Trading Day:	Tenth day of month preceding contract month.
Settlement:	Cash based on Brent Index price.
Trading Hours:	9:15 to 12:15 and 14:30 to 17:15.
Volume—1986:	nt
Volume—1987:	nt

OPTIONS

GROUP: ENERGY

GAS OIL

Unit:	One IPE gas oil futures contract.
Quotation:	US dollars and cents per tonne.
Minimum Fluctuation:	Five cents per tonne.
Strike Price:	Five dollar intervals.
Contract Months:	Nine consecutive months, including current month.
Last Trading Day:	Third Wednesday of preceding month.
Expiration:	Same as last trading day.
Exercise:	By instruction.
Type:	American.
Trading Hours:	9:15 to 12:24 and 14:30 to 17:25.
Volume—1986:	nt
Volume—1987:	7,518 contracts.

LONDON TRADED OPTIONS MARKET
INTERNATIONAL STOCK EXCHANGE (ISE)

Established:	1978
System:	Open Outcry
Relationships:	None

OPTIONS

GROUP: CURRENCIES

US DOLLAR—STERLING

Unit:	12,000 BP.

Quotation: US$/BP.
Minimum Fluctuation: Five cents.
Strike Price: Five cent intervals.
Contract Months: March, June, September, December
                               and remaining two of next three
                               months.
Last Trading Day: Friday prior to third Wednesday.
Expiration: Close of business, LTD.
Exercise: **
Type: American.
Settlement: **
Trading Hours: 9:05 to 15:40.
Volume—1986:   41,827 contracts.
Volume—1987:   21,616 contracts.

US DOLLAR—DEUTSCHE MARK

Unit: 62,500 DM.
Quotation: US$/DM.
Minimum Fluctuation: One cent.
Strike Price: One cent intervals.
Contract Months: March, June, September, December
                               and remaining two of next three
                               months.
Last Trading Day: Friday before third Wednesday.
Expiration: Close of business, LTD.
Exercise: **
Type: American.
Settlement: **
Trading Hours: 9:00 to 15:40.
Volume—1986:   2,186 contracts.
Volume—1987:   548 contracts.

GROUP: INDEX

FINANCIAL TIMES STOCK EXCHANGE 100 INDEX (FTSE)

Unit: 10 BP times index.
Quotation: Pence per 1 pence of 10 pounds.
Minimum Fluctuation: .005 pence.
Strike Price: 25 point intervals.
Contract Months: Next four months.
Last Trading Day: Last business day of month at 11:20.
Expiration: Close of business, LTD.
Exercise: **
Type: American.
Settlement: **

Trading Hours:	9:05 to 15:40.
Volume—1986:	411,784 contracts.
Volume—1987:	883,637 contracts.

LTOM (63 UK Equity Options)

Unit:	1,000 Shares (NB Vaal Reefs 100 shares).
Quotation:	Pence per underlying share.
Minimum Fluctuation:	.0025 pence.
Strike Price:	10 point intervals to 140
	20 point intervals to 300
	30 point intervals to 420
	40 point intervals to 500
	50 point intervals to 1500
	100 point intervals to 2000
	200 point intervals to 3000
	300 point intervals above that.
Contract Months:	January, April, July, October, or February, May, August, November, or March, June, September, December.
Last Trading Day:	Two days prior to last day of trading for last complete Stock Exchange account or contract month.
Expiration:	Close of business, LTD.
Exercise:	**
Type:	American.
Settlement:	**
Trading Hours:	9:05 to 16:05.
Volume—1986:	4,826,292 contracts.
Volume—1987:	10,782,653 contracts.

LONDON FUTURES AND OPTIONS EXCHANGE (FOX)

Established:	1987
System:	Open Outcry & Electronic
Relationships:	None

FUTURES

GROUP: SOFTS

COCOA NO. 6

Unit:	10 metric tonnes.
Quotation:	Pounds per tonne.
Minimum Fluctuation:	One pound per tonne.

Contract Months: March, May, July, September, December.

First Notice Day: **

Last Trading Day: Last market day of contract month at 15:30.

Settlement: Physical.

Trading Hours: 10:00 to 12:58 and 14:30 to 16:45

Volume—1986:   837,085 contracts.

Volume—1987:   926,335 contracts.

COFFEE (ROBUSTA)

Unit: 5 tonnes.

Quotation: Pound per tonne.

Minimum Fluctuation: One Pound per tonne.

Contract Months: January, March, May, July, September, November, January.

First Notice Day: **

Last Trading Day: Last market day of contract month at 12:30.

Settlement: Physical.

Trading Hours: 9:45 to 12:32 and 14:30 to 17:02

Volume—1986:   1,510,156 contracts.

Volume—1987:   906,930 contracts.

SUGAR NO. 6 (RAW)

Unit: 50 tonnes.

Quotation: US dollars and cents per tonne FOBS.

Minimum Fluctuation: $.20 per tonne.

Contract Months: March, May, August, October, December.

First Notice Day: **

Last Trading Day: Last market day of month preceding contract month.

Settlement: Physical.

Trading Hours: 10:30 to 12:30 and 14:30 to 19:00.

Volume—1986:   706,053 contracts.

Volume—1987:   762,053 contracts.

SUGAR NO. 5 (WHITE) (Traded on automatic trading system ATS)

Unit: 50 tonnes.

Quotation: US dollars and cents per tonne FOB.

Minimum Fluctuation: $.10 per tonne.

Contract Months: March, May, August, October, December.

First Notice Day: **

Last Trading Day: Market day preceding 15th calendar day preceding first calendar of delivery period at 16:00.
Settlement: Physical.
Trading Hours: 9:45 to 19:10
Volume—1986:   210 contracts.
Volume—1987:   200,340 contracts.

OPTIONS

GROUP: SOFTS

COCOA NO. 6

Unit: One FOX 10-tonne cocoa futures contract.
Quotation: Pounds per tonne.
Minimum Fluctuation: One pound per tonne.
Strike Price: 50 pounds per tonne.
Contract Months: March, May, July, September, December, March, May.
Last Trading Day: Third Wednesday of preceding month.
Expiration: Close of business day.
Exercise: By instruction.
Type: **
Settlement: **
Trading Hours: 10:00 to 13:00 and 14:30 to 17:00.
Volume—1986:   387 contracts.
Volume—1987:   397 contracts.

COFFEE (ROBUSTA)

Unit: One FOX 5-tonne coffee futures contract.
Quotation: Pounds per tonne.
Minimum Fluctuation: One pound per tonne.
Strike Price: 50 pounds per tonne intervals.
Contract Months: January, March, May, July, September, November, January.
Last Trading Day: Close of business day to third Wednesday in preceding month.
Expiration: Last trading day.
Exercise: By instruction.
Type: **
Settlement: **
Trading Hours: 09:45 to 12:30 and 14:30 to 17:00
Volume—1986:   3,556 contracts.
Volume—1987:   6,744 contracts.

SUGAR NO. 6 (RAW)

Unit:	One FOX 50-tonne raw sugar futures contract.
Quotation:	US cents per tonne.
Minimum Fluctuation:	$.05 per tonne.
Strike Price:	$5.00 intervals.
Contract Months:	March, May, August, October, December.
Last Trading Day:	Third Wednesday in preceding month.
Expiration:	Close of business day.
Exercise:	By instruction.
Type:	**
Settlement:	**
Trading Hours:	10:30 to 12:30 and 14:30 to 19:00.
Volume—1986:	1,356 contracts.
Volume—1987:	79 contracts.

LONDON INTERNATIONAL FINANCIAL FUTURES EXCHANGE (LIFFE)

Established:	1982
System:	Open Outcry
Relationships:	Sydney Futures Exchange

FUTURES

GROUP: CURRENCIES

BRITISH POUND

Unit:	25,000 British pounds.
Quotation:	US$/BP
Minimum Fluctuation:	$.01 = $2.50.
Contract Months:	March, June, September, December.
First Notice Day:	Last trading day at 12-noon.
Delivery Day:	Third Wednesday of contract month.
Last Trading Day:	Two business days preceding delivery at 10:31.
Settlement:	Physical.
Trading Hours:	8:32 to 16:02
Volume—1986:	41,495 contracts.
Volume—1987:	12,668 contracts.

DEUTSCHE MARK

Unit:	125,000 Deutsche marks.
Quotation:	US$/DM.
Minimum Fluctuation:	$.01 = $12/50.

Contract Months:	March, June, September, December.
First Notice Day:	na
Delivery Day:	Third Wednesday of contract month.
Last Trading Day:	Two business days preceding delivery at 10:32.
Settlement:	Physical.
Trading Hours:	8:34 to 16:04
Volume—1986:	16,250 contracts.
Volume—1987:	12,668 contracts.

JAPANESE YEN

Unit:	12,500,000 Japanese yen.
Quotation:	US$/100 JY.
Minimum Fluctuation:	$.01 = $12.50.
Contract Months:	March, June, September, December.
First Notice Day:	na
Delivery day:	Third Wednesday of contract month.
Last Trading Day:	Two business days preceding delivery at 10:30.
Settlement:	Physical.
Trading Hours:	8:30 to 16:00
Volume—1986:	7,776 contracts.
Volume—1987:	5,863 contracts.

SWISS FRANC

Unit:	125,000 Swiss francs.
Quotation:	US$/SF.
Minimum Fluctuation:	$.01 = $12.50.
Contract Months:	March, June, September, December.
First Notice Day:	na
Delivery Day:	Third Wednesday of contract month.
Last Trading Day:	Two business days preceding delivery at 10:33.
Settlement:	Physical.
Trading Hours:	8:36 to 16:06
Volume—1986:	5,856 contracts.
Volume—1987:	5,169 contracts.

US DOLLAR—DEUTSCHE MARK CURRENCY

Unit:	$50,000 against DM.
Quotation:	DM/US$.
Minimum Fluctuation:	0.0001 = 5 DMarks.
Contract Months:	March, June, September, December.
First Notice Day:	na
Delivery Day:	Third Wednesday of contract month.
Last Trading Day:	Two business days preceding delivery at 10:32.

Settlement:	Physical.
Trading Hours:	8:34 to 16:04
Volume—1986:	532 contracts.
Volume—1987:	116 contracts.

GROUP: INTEREST RATES

EURODOLLAR THREE-MONTH TIME DEPOSIT (SFE LINK)

Unit:	US $1,000,000 principal.
Quotation:	100.00 minus interest rate.
Minimum Fluctuation:	0.01 = $25.00.
Contract Months:	March, June, September, December.
First Notice Day:	na
Last Trading Day:	Two business days preceding third Wednesday of contract month at 11:00.
Settlement:	Cash.
Trading Hours:	8:30 to 16:00
Volume—1986:	1,104,002 contracts.
Volume—1987:	1,739,523 contracts.

GERMAN GOVERNMENT BOND

Unit:	250,000 DM nominal value national German Government Bond with 6 pct coupon.
Quotation:	Per 100 DM nominal value.
Minimum Fluctuation:	0.01 DM = 25 DM.
Contract Months:	March, June, September, December.
First Notice Day:	**
Delivery Day:	Tenth Calendar day of contract month.
Last Trading Day:	Three Frankfurt working days before delivery day at 11:00.
Settlement:	Physical.
Trading Hours:	8:10 to 16:00.
Volume—1986:	nt
Volume—1987:	nt

JAPANESE GOVERNMENT BOND (JGB)

Unit:	100,000,000 Japanese yen government bond with 6 pct coupon.
Quotation:	Per 100 yen face value.
Minimum Fluctuation:	0.01 yen = 10,000 yen.
Contract Months:	March, June, September, December.
First Notice Day:	na
Last Trading Day:	One business day preceding last trading day of Tokyo Stock Exchange at 16:05.

Settlement:

Trading Hours:
Volume—1986:
Volume—1987:

Cash on second day following last
    trading day.
8:10 to 16:05
nt
133,761 contracts.

LONG GILT

Unit:

Quotation:
Minimum Fluctuation:
Contract Months:
First Notice Day:
Last Trading Day:

50,000 Pound national gilt with 12 pct
    coupon.
Per 100 Pound nominal.
1/32 = 15.625 pounds.
March, June, September, December.
na
Two business days preceding last
    business day in contract month at
    11:00.

Settlement:
Trading Hours:
Volume—1986:
Volume—1987:

Physical.
9:00 to 16:15
2,612,721 contracts.
6,977,908 contracts.

MEDIUM GILT

Unit:

Quotation:
Minimum Fluctuation:
Contract Months:
First Notice Day:

Last Trading Day:

Settlement:
Trading Hours:
Volume—1986:
Volume—1987:

50,000 BP notional gilt with 9 pct
    coupon.
Per 100 BP nominal.
1/32 = 15.625 pounds.
March, June, September, December.
Business day preceding delivery
    month.
Two business days prior to last
    business day in delivery month.
Physical
8:55 to 16:10.
nt
nt

SHORT GILT

Unit:

Quotation:
Minimum Fluctuation:

Contract Months:
First Notice Day:
Last Trading Day:

100,000 Pound national gilt with
    10 pct coupon.
Per 100 Pound nominal.
1/64 = 15.625 pounds = 15.625
    sterling.
March, June, September, December.
na
Two business days preceding last
    business day in contract month at
    11:00.

Settlement:	Physical.
Trading Hours:	9:05 to 16:20.
Volume—1986:	957,589 contracts.
Volume—1987:	1,495,756 contracts.

STERLING THREE-MONTH

Unit:	500,000 Pound principal.
Quotation:	100.00 minus interest rate.
Minimum Fluctuation:	0.01 = 12.50 pounds.
Contract Months:	March, June, September, December.
First Notice Day:	na
Last Trading Day:	Third Wednesday of contract month at 11:00.

Settlement:	Cash.
Trading Hours:	8:20 to 16:02
Volume—1986:	61,229 contracts.
Volume—1987:	284 contracts.

UNITED STATES TREASURY BOND (SFE LINK)

Unit:	$100,000 principal with 8 pct coupon.
Quotation:	Per US$100 par value.
Minimum Fluctuation:	1/32 = $31.25.
Contract Months:	March, June, September, December.
First Notice Day:	Two business days prior to first business day in the delivery month.
Last Trading Day:	Seven CBOT business days preceding last business day of contract month at 9:00 CST.

Settlement:	Physical.
Trading Hours:	8:15 to 16:10
Volume—1986:	1,542,331 contracts.
Volume—1987:	1,549,484 contracts.

GROUP: INDEX

FINANCIAL TIMES STOCK EXCHANGE 100 INDEX (FTSE)

Unit:	25 Pounds per full index point.
Quotation:	Index divided by 10.
Minimum Fluctuation:	0.05 = 12.50 pounds.
Contract Months:	March, June, September, December.
First Notice Day:	na
Last Trading Day:	Last business day of contract month at 11:20.

Settlement:	Cash.
Trading Hours:	9:05 to 16:05
Volume—1986:	121,608 contracts.
Volume—1987:	458,045 contracts.

OPTIONS
GROUP: INTEREST RATES

EURODOLLAR THREE-MONTH TIME DEPOSIT (SFE LINK)

Unit:	One LIFFE US $1,000,000 Eurodollar futures contract.
Quotation:	0.01 multiples.
Minimum Fluctuation:	0.01 = $25.00.
Strike Price:	0.25 intervals.
Contract Months:	March, June, September, December.
Last Trading Day:	Last trading day of underlying futures contract at 11:00.
Expiration:	Last trading day at 17:00.
Exercise:	Automatic.
Type:	American.
Settlement:	Futures.
Trading Hours:	8:32 to 16:00
Volume—1986:	38,455 contracts.
Volume—1987:	39,866 contracts.

LONG GILT

Unit:	One LIFFE 50,000 BP long gilt futures contract.
Quotation:	Multiples of 1/64.
Minimum Fluctuation:	1/64.
Strike Price:	Two Pound intervals.
Contract Months:	March, June, September, December.
Last Trading Day:	Sixth business day preceding first delivery day of underlying futures contract.
Expiration:	Last trading day at 18:00.
Exercise:	By instruction.
Type:	American.
Settlement:	Futures.
Trading Hours:	9:02 to 16:15.
Volume—1986:	nt
Volume—1987:	14,949 contracts.

STERLING THREE-MONTH

Unit:	One LIFFE 500,000 BP futures contract.
Quotation:	Multiples of 0.01.
Minimum Fluctuation:	0.01 = 12.50 pounds.
Strike Price:	0.25 intervals.
Contract Months:	March, June, September, December.
Last Trading Day:	Last trading day of underlying futures contract.

Expiration:	Last trading day at 17:00.
Exercise:	By instruction.
Type:	American.
Settlement:	Futures.
Trading Hours:	8:22 to 16:02.
Volume—1986:	274,081 contracts.
Volume—1987:	1,037,306 contracts.

UNITED STATES TREASURY BONDS (SFE LINK)

Unit:	One LIFFE US $100,000 Treasury bond futures contract.
Quotation:	Multiples of 1/64.
Minimum Fluctuation:	1/64 = US$15.625.
Strike Price:	Two bond point intervals.
Contract Months:	March, June, September, December.
Last Trading Day:	First Friday at least six CBOT working days preceding first delivery.
Expiration:	Last trading day at 20:30.
Exercise:	By instruction.
Type:	American.
Settlement:	Futures.
Trading Hours:	8:17 to 16:10.
Volume—1986:	51,790 contracts.
Volume—1987:	54,506 contracts.

OPTIONS

GROUP: CURRENCIES

BRITISH POUND

Unit:	25,000 pound traded against US dollar.
Quotation:	US$/BP.
Minimum Fluctuation:	0.01 = $2.50.
Strike Price:	$.05.
Contract Months:	March, June, September, December, with three nearby months.
Last Trading Day:	Three business days before third Wednesday of contract month.
Expiration:	Last trading day at 17:00.
Exercise:	By instruction.
Type:	American.
Settlement:	Physical.
Trading Hours:	8:34 to 16:02.
Volume—1986:	104,329 contracts.
Volume—1987:	15,565 contracts.

US DOLLAR—DEUTSCHE MARK CURRENCY

Unit:	US $50,000 traded against DM.

Quotation:	DM/US$.
Minimum Fluctuation:	0.01 pfennigs per US dollar = 5 DM.
Strike Price:	Five pfennigs per US dollar.
Contract Months:	March, June, September, December with three nearby months.
Last Trading Day:	Three business days preceding third Wednesday of contract month.
Expiration:	Two business days before third Wednesday of contract month at 10:00.
Exercise:	By instruction.
Type:	American.
Settlement:	Physical.
Trading Hours:	8:36 to 16:04.
Volume—1986:	8,286 contracts.
Volume—1987:	2,800 contracts.

LONDON METAL EXCHANGE (LME)

Established:	1877
System:	Open Outcry
Relationships:	None

FUTURES

GROUP: METALS

ALUMINUM (HIGH GRADE)

Unit:	25 metric tonnes.
Quotation:	US dollars per tonne.
Minimum Fluctuation:	0.01 = $25.00.
Contract Months:	Daily between spot and next three months.
First Notice Day:	**
Last Trading Day:	**
Settlement:	Cash and physical.
Trading Hours:	11:55 to 12:00 and 12:55 to 13:00. 15:40 to 15:45 and 16:20 to 16:25.
Volume—1986:	749,000 contracts.
Volume—1987:	1,057,024 contracts.

ALUMINUM (PRIMARY)

Unit:	25 metric tonnes.
Quotation:	Pounds per tonne.
Minimum Fluctuation:	0.50 = 12.50 pounds.
Contract Months:	Daily between spot and next three months.

First Notice Day: **
Last Trading Day: **
Settlement: Cash and physical.
Trading Hours: 11:50 to 11:55 and 12:50 to 12:55
15:35 to 15:40 and 16:15 to 16:20

Volume—1986: **
Volume—1987: 49,847 contracts.

COPPER (GRADE A)

Unit: 25 metric tonnes.
Quotation: Pounds per tonne.
Minimum Fluctuation: 0.50 = 12.50 pounds.
Contract Months: Daily between spot and next three
months.

First Notice Day: **
Last Trading Day: **
Settlement: Cash and physical.
Trading Hours: 12:00 to 12:05 and 12:30 to 12:35.
15:30 to 15:35 and 16:10 to 16:15.

Volume—1986: 720,449 contracts.
Volume—1987: 1,375,703 contracts.

COPPER (STANDARD)

Unit: 25 metric tonnes.
Quotation: Pounds per tonne.
Minimum Fluctuation: 0.50 = 12.50 pounds.
Contract Months: Daily between spot and next three
months.

First Notice Day: **
Last Trading Day: **
Settlement: Cash and physical.
Trading Hours: 12:00 to 12:05 and 12:35 to 12:40.
15:30 to 15:35 and 16:10 to 16:15.

Volume—1986: **
Volume—1987: 3,237 contracts.

LEAD

Unit: 25 metric tonnes.
Quotation: Pounds per tonne.
Minimum Fluctuation: 0.25 = 6.25 pounds.
Contract Months: Daily between spot and next three
months.

First Notice Day: **
Last Trading Day: **
Settlement: Cash and physical.
Trading Hours: 12:05 to 12:10 and 12:40 to 12:45.
15:20 to 15:25 and 16:00 to 16:05.

Volume—1986:	310,758 contracts.
Volume—1987:	291,680 contracts.

NICKEL

Unit:	6 metric tonnes.
Quotation:	Pounds per tonne.
Minimum Fluctuation:	One contract pound = 6 Pounds.
Contract Months:	Daily between spot and next three months.
First Notice Day:	**
Last Trading Day:	**
Settlement:	Cash and physical.
Trading Hours:	12:15 to 12:20 and 13:00 to 13:05. 15:45 to 15:50 and 16:25 to 16:30.
Volume—1986:	**
Volume—1987:	163,239 contracts.

SILVER (10,000 OUNCES)

Unit:	10,000 troy ounces.
Quotation:	US cents per ounce.
Minimum Fluctuation:	0.1 = $10.00.
Contract Months:	Daily between spot and next three months.
First Notice Day:	**
Last Trading Day:	**
Settlement:	Cash and physical.
Trading Hours:	11:45 to 11:50 and 13:05 to 13:10. 15:50 to 15:55 and 16:30 to 16:35.
Volume—1986:	**
Volume—1987:	7,694 contracts.

SILVER (2,000 TROY OUNCES)

Unit:	2,000 troy ounces.
Quotation:	US cents per ounce.
Minimum Fluctuation:	0.1 = $2.00.
Contract Months:	Daily between spot and next three months.
First Notice Day:	**
Last Trading Day:	**
Settlement:	Cash and physical.
Trading Hours:	11:45 to 11:50 and 13:05 to 13:10. 15:50 to 15:55 and 16:30 to 16:35.
Volume—1986:	**
Volume—1987:	27 contracts.

ZINC (HIGH-GRADE)

Unit:	25 metric tonnes.

Quotation:	Pounds per tonne.
Minimum Fluctuation:	0.25 = 6.25 pounds.
Contract Months:	Daily between spot and next three months.
First Notice Day:	**
Last Trading Day:	**
Settlement:	Cash and physical.
Trading Hours:	12:10 to 12:15 and 12:45 to 12:50.
	15:25 to 15:30 and 16:05 to 16:10.
Volume—1986:	**
Volume—1987:	238,910 contracts.

OPTIONS

GROUP: METALS

ALUMINUM (HIGH GRADE)

Unit:	One LME 25 metric tonnes aluminum futures contract.
Quotation:	US$ or Pounds per tonne—not all months.
Strike Price:	25 BP/US $25 per tonne intervals.
Contract Months:	January and every second month thereafter.
Last Trading Day:	First Wednesday of contract month.
Expiration:	**
Exercise:	**
Type:	**
Settlement:	**
Trading Hours:	** All day.
Volume—1986:	**
Volume—1987:	105 contracts.

ALUMINUM (PRIMARY)

Unit:	One LME 25 metric tonne aluminum futures contract.
Quotation:	US$ or Pounds per tonne—not all months.
Strike Price:	$25 or 25 Pounds per tonne intervals.
Contract Months:	January and every second month thereafter.
Last Trading Day:	First Wednesday of contract month.
Expiration:	**
Exercise:	**
Type:	**
Settlement:	**

Trading Hours:	** All day.
Volume—1986:	**
Volume—1987:	43,986 contracts.

COPPER (GRADE A)

Unit:	One LME 25 metric tonne copper futures contract.
Quotation:	Pounds per tonne.
Minimum Fluctuation:	0.50 Pounds per tonne.
Strike Price:	25 BP/US $25 per tonne intervals.
Contract Months:	January and every second month thereafter.
Last Trading Day:	First Wednesday of contract month.
Expiration:	**
Exercise:	**
Type:	**
Settlement:	**
Trading Hours:	** All day.
Volume—1986:	**
Volume—1987:	50,831 contracts.

LEAD

Unit:	One LME 25 metric tonne lead futures contract.
Quotation:	Pounds per tonne.
Minimum Fluctuation:	0.25 Pounds per tonne.
Strike Price:	20 BP/US $20 per tonne intervals.
Contract Months:	February and every second month thereafter.
Last Trading Day:	First Wednesday of contract month.
Expiration:	**
Trading Hours:	** All day.
Volume—1986:	**
Volume—1987:	244 contracts.

NICKEL

Unit:	One LME six metric tonne nickel futures contract.
Quotation:	Pounds per tonne.
Minimum Fluctuation:	One Pound per tonne.
Strike Price:	50 BP/US $50 per tonne intervals.
Contract Months:	February and every second month thereafter.
Last Trading Day:	First Wednesday of contract month.
Expiration:	**
Exercise:	**
Type:	**

Settlement:	**
Trading Hours:	** All day.
Volume—1986:	**
Volume—1987:	457 contracts.

ZINC (HIGH-GRADE)

Unit:	One LME 25 metric tonne zinc futures contract.
Quotation:	Pound per tonne.
Minimum Fluctuation:	0.25 Pound per tonne.
Strike Price:	20 BP/US $20 per tonne intervals.
Contract Months:	February and every second month.
Last Trading Day:	First Wednesday of contract month.
Expiration:	**
Exercise:	**
Type:	**
Settlement:	**
Trading Hours:	** All day.
Volume—1986:	**
Volume—1987:	1,035 contracts.

COUNTRY: HONG KONG *1987 Volume 4,535,239 contracts.*

HONG KONG FUTURES EXCHANGE

Established:	1976
System:	Open Outcry
Relationships:	None

FUTURES

GROUP: AGRICULTURE

SOYBEANS

Unit:	30,000 kilograms (500 bags of 60 kilograms) unselected China yellow soybeans.
Quotation:	Hong Kong dollars and cents.
Minimum Fluctuation:	20 Hong Kong cents per bag.
Contract Months:	Each consecutive month for up to six months.
First Notice Day:	**
Last Trading Day:	Fifteenth day of contract month at second session.
Settlement:	Physical.

Trading Hours: 9:00 to 10:50 and 12:50 to 14:50.
Volume—1986: 330,524 contracts.
Volume—1987: 635,975 contracts.

SUGAR

Unit: 50 long tons (112,000 pounds) raw sugar.

Quotation: US cents and hundredths cent per pound.

Minimum Fluctuation: One one-hundredth (1/100) cent, 1/100 = $11.20.

Contract Months: January, March, May, July, September, October.

First Notice Day: **

Last Trading Day: Business day preceding first day of contract month.

Settlement: Physical.
Trading Hours: 10:30 to 12:00 and 14:25 to 16:00.
Volume—1986: 273,800 contracts.
Volume—1987: 282,237 contracts.

GROUP: METALS

GOLD (100 OUNCES)

Unit: 100 troy ounces.
Quotation: US dollars and cents per troy ounce.
Minimum Fluctuation: $.10 = $10.00.
Contract Months: Even months, spot months plus two following months.

First Notice Day: **

Last Trading Day: Last business day of contract month at morning session.

Settlement: Physical.
Trading Hours: 9:00 to 12:00 and 14:00 to 17:30.
Volume—1986: 6,366 contracts.
Volume—1987: 5,698 contracts.

GROUP: INDEX

HANG SENG INDEX

Unit: 50 Hong Kong dollars times index.
Quotation: Points of index.
Minimum Fluctuation: One index point.
Contract Months: Three even months.
First Notice Day: **

Last Trading Day: Second business day of trading month.

Settlement:	Cash on business day following last trading day.
Trading Hours:	10:00 to 12:30 and 14:30 to 15:30.
Volume—1986:	825,279 contracts.
Volume—1987:	3,611,329 contracts.

COUNTRY: JAPAN 1987 Volume 34,717,190 contracts.

OSAKA SECURITIES EXCHANGE

Established:	1987—Futures
System:	Open Outcry
Relationships:	None

FUTURES

GROUP: INDEX

NIKKEI STOCK AVERAGE

Unit:	1,000 times Nikkei Stock Average
Quotation:	Yen per average.
Minimum Fluctuation:	10 yen per average.
Contract Months:	March, June, September, December.
First Notice Day:	na
Last Trading Day:	Third Day preceding settlement day, unless holiday then next day.
Settlement:	Cash on tenth day of contract month, unless holiday, then next day.
Trading Hours:	9:00 to 11:15 and 13:00 to 19:15.
Volume—1986:	nt
Volume—1987:	nt

OSAKA STOCK FUTURES 50

Unit:	Index of 50 exchange-listed stocks.
Quotation:	Average of per share price of 50 stocks.
Minimum Fluctuation:	10 sen or 1/10 yen.
Contract Months:	March, June, September, December.
First Notice Day:	**
Last Trading Day:	Sixth business day preceding delivery day of each contract month.
Delivery Day:	Fifteenth day of contract month.
Settlement:	Physical.
Trading Hours:	9:00 to 11:00 and 13:00 to 15:00

Volume—1986:   nt
Volume—1987:   200,480 contracts.

TOKYO COMMODITY EXCHANGE

Established: 1984
System: Call Session
Relationships: None

FUTURES

GROUP: METALS

GOLD

Unit: One kilogram gold bar.
Quotation: Japanese yen per gram.
Minimum Fluctuation: One yen per gram.
Contract Months: Odd-numbered month following a
                               current even-numbered month and
                               every even-numbered month
                               within one year after transaction
                               date in odd-numbered current
                               month.
First Notice Day: **
Last Trading Day: Third business day preceding delivery
                               day.
Delivery Day: End of contract month.
Settlement: Physical.
Trading Hours: Morning session calls:
                               09:10, 10:30 and 11:30.
                               Afternoon session calls:
                               13:10, 14:30 and 15:45.
Volume—1986:   1,030,438 units.
Volume—1987:   2,158,745 units.

PLATINUM

Unit: 500 grams platinum.
Quotation: Japanese yen per gram.
Minimum Fluctuation: One yen per gram.
Contract Months: Odd-numbered month following a
                               current even-numbered month and
                               every even-numbered month
                               within one year after transaction
                               date in odd-numbered current
                               month.

First Notice Day: **
Last Trading Day: Third business day preceding delivery day.

Delivery Day: End of contract month.
Settlement: Physical.
Trading Hours: After morning and afternoon silver session calls.

Volume—1986:   **
Volume—1987:   2,866,244 units.

SILVER
Unit: 30 kilograms silver.
Quotation: Japanese yen per gram.
Minimum Fluctuation: 10 sen or 0.1 yen per 10 gram.
Contract Months: Odd-numbered month following a current even-numbered month and every even-numbered month within one year after transaction date in odd-numbered current month.

First Notice Day: **
Last Trading Day: Third business day preceding delivery day.

Delivery Day: End of contract month.
Settlement: Physical.
Trading Hours: After morning and afternoon gold session calls.

Volume—1986:   **
Volume—1987:   1,471,815 units.

GROUP: SOFTS

RUBBER
Unit: 5,000 kilograms RSS No. 3 rubber.
Quotation: Japanese yen per kilogram.
Minimum Fluctuation: 10 sen or 0.1 yen per one kilogram.
Contract Months: Monthly within four months after current month and every even-numbered month within four months thereafter.

First Notice Day: **
Last Trading Day: Fifth business day preceding delivery day.

Delivery Day: End of contract month.
Settlement: Physical.

Trading Hours:

Morning session calls:
09:45 and 10:45.
Afternoon session calls:
13:45, 14:45 and 15:30.

Volume—1986: **
Volume—1987: **

COTTON YARN

Unit:

4,000 pounds 40-count single gray
weaving Z-twist Murufuji brand.

Quotation: Japanese yen per pound.
Minimum Fluctuation: 10 sen or 0.1 yen per one pound.
Contract Months: Monthly for six months.
First Notice Day: **
Last Trading Day:

Fourth business day preceding
delivery day.

Delivery Day: End of contract month.
Settlement: Physical.
Trading Hours:

Morning session calls:
08:50 and 10:00.
Afternoon session calls:
13:50 and 15:10.

Volume—1986: **
Volume—1987: **

WOOLEN YARN

Unit:

500 kilogram 48-count double worsted
weaving Z twist AG brand.

Quotation: Japanese yen per gram.
Minimum Fluctuation: One yen per one gram.
Contract Months: Monthly for six months.
First Notice Day: **
Last Trading Day:

Fourth business day preceding
delivery day.

Settlement: Physical.
Trading Hours: After morning and afternoon cotton
yarn session calls.

Volume—1986: **
Volume—1987: **

TOKYO GRAIN EXCHANGE

Established: **
System: Call Session
Relationships: None

FUTURES

GROUP: AGRICULTURE

AMERICAN SOYBEANS

Unit:	15 tons yellow IOM US soybeans.
Quotation:	Japanese yen per kilogram.
Minimum Fluctuation:	10 yen per 60 kilogram.
Contract Months:	Even-numbered months.
First Notice Day:	**
Last Trading Day:	Two days preceding last business day of contract month at third morning session.
Settlement:	Physical.
Trading Hours:	10:00 to 11:00 and 13:00 to 14:00.
Volume—1986:	2,997,827 contracts.
Volume—1987:	2,088,820 contracts.

CHINESE SOYBEANS

Unit:	250 bags yellow Chinese soybeans (People's Republic of China).
Quotation:	Japanese yen per kilogram bag.
Minimum Fluctuation:	10 yen per 60 kilogram bag.
Contract Months:	Six months.
First Notice Day:	**
Last Trading Day:	**
Settlement:	Physical.
Trading Hours:	10:00 to 11:00 and 13:00 to 14:00.
Volume—1986:	177,218 contracts.
Volume—1987:	13,212 contracts.

JAPANESE SOYBEANS

Unit:	40 bags No. 2 Hokkaido-produced small soybeans.
Quotation:	Japanese yen per kilogram bag.
Minimum Fluctuation:	10 yen per 60 kilogram bag.
Contract Months:	Three months.
First Notice Day:	**
Last Trading Day:	**
Settlement:	Physical.
Trading Hours:	15:00.
Volume—1986:	**
Volume—1987:	**

RED BEANS

Unit:	80 bags No. 2 Hokkaido-produced white beans.

Quotation:	Japanese yen per kilogram bag.
Minimum Fluctuation:	10 yen per 30 kilogram bag.
Contract Months:	Six months.
First Notice Day:	**
Last Trading Day:	**
Settlement:	Physical.
Trading Hours:	09:00 to 11:00 and 13:00 to 15:00.
Volume—1986:	2,045,635 contracts.
Volume—1987:	3,098,437 contracts.

WHITE BEANS

Unit:	40 bags No. 2 Hokkaido-produced white beans.
Quotation:	Japanese yen per kilogram bag.
Minimum Fluctuation:	10 yen per kilogram bag.
Contract Months:	Six months.
First Notice Day:	**
Last Trading Day:	**
Settlement:	Physical.
Trading Hours:	15:00.
Volume—1986:	**
Volume—1987:	**

POTATO STARCH

Unit:	100 bags No. 1 Hokkaido-produced refined powder potato starch.
Quotation:	Japanese yen per kilogram bag.
Minimum Fluctuation:	1 yen per 25 kilogram bag.
Contract Months:	Three months.
First Notice Day:	**
Last Trading Day:	**
Settlement:	Physical delivery.
Trading Hours:	15:00.
Volume—1986:	**
Volume—1987:	**

TOKYO STOCK EXCHANGE

Established:	1985
System:	Electronic
Relationships:	None (See CBT)

FUTURES

GROUP: INTEREST RATES

JAPANESE 10-YEAR GOVERNMENT BOND

Unit:	10-year Japanese yen bond.
Quotation:	**
Minimum Fluctuation:	0.01 yen per 100 yen.
Contract Months:	March, June, September, December.
First Notice Day:	**
Last Trading Day:	Ninth business day prior to delivery date.
Settlement:	Offsetting or physical.
Trading Hours:	9:00 to 11:00 and 13:00 to 15:00.
Volume—1986:	9,395,829 contracts.
Volume—1987:	18,284,198 contracts.

JAPANESE 20-YEAR GOVERNMENT BOND

Unit:	20-year Japanese yen bond.
Quotation:	**
Minimum Fluctuation:	0.01 yen per 100 yen.
Contract Months:	March, June, September, December.
First Notice Day:	**
Last Trading Day:	Ninth business day prior to delivery date.
Settlement:	Offsetting or physical.
Trading Hours:	9:00 to 11:15 and 13:00 to 15:00.
Volume—1986:	nt
Volume—1987:	nt

GROUP: INDEX

TOKYO STOCK PRICE INDEX (TOPIX)

Unit:	Tokyo Stock Price Index
Quotation:	Index Points.
Minimum Fluctuation:	1 TOPIX point.
Contract Months:	March, June, September, December.
First Notice Day:	na
Last Trading Day:	Third business day prior to each delivery date.
Settlement:	Offsetting or cash.
Trading Hours:	9:00 to 11:15 and 13:00 to 15:15.
Volume—1986:	na
Volume—1987:	na

TOKYO SUGAR EXCHANGE

FUTURES

GROUP: SOFTS

RAW SUGAR

Unit:	10 metric tonnes raw sugar.
Quotation:	**
Minimum Fluctuation:	**
Contract Months:	Odd numbered month for 20 months.
First Notice Day:	**
Last Trading Day:	**
Settlement:	Physical.
Trading Hours:	First session: 09:30.
	Second session: 10:30.
	Third session: 13:30.
	Fourth session: 14:30.
Volume—1986:	**
Volume—1987:	**

REFINED WHITE SOFT SUGAR

Unit:	9 metric tonnes refined white sugar.
Quotation:	**
Minimum Fluctuation:	**
Contract Months:	All months for six months.
First Notice Day:	**
Last Trading Day:	**
Settlement:	Physical.
Trading Hours:	First session: 09:30.
	Second session: 10:30.
	Third session: 13:30.
	Fourth session: 14:30.
Volume—1986:	**
Volume—1987:	**

COUNTRY: MALAYSIA   *1987 Volume 107,597 contracts.*

KUALA LUMPUR COMMODITY EXCHANGE

Established:	1980
System:	Open Outcry
Relationships:	None

FUTURES

GROUP: AGRICULTURE

COCOA

Unit:	10 metric tonnes.
Quotation:	US dollars per tonne.
Minimum Fluctuation:	One dollar per tonne.
Contract Months:	January, March, May, July, September, November and December.
First Notice Day:	**
Last Trading Day:	Twentieth of month or preceding business day.
Settlement:	Physical.
Trading Hours:	11:15 to 12:00 and 16:00 to 19:00.
Volume—1986:	nt
Volume—1987:	nt

CRUDE PALM OIL

Unit:	25 metric tonnes.
Quotation:	Malaysian dollar per tonne.
Minimum Fluctuation:	One dollar per tonne.
Contract Months:	Current month, next five months, plus alternate months up to one year.
First Notice Day:	**
Last Trading Day:	Fifteenth of month of preceding day.
Settlement:	Physical.
Trading Hours:	11:00 to 12:30 and 15:30 to 18:00.
Volume—1986:	41,303 contracts.
Volume—1987:	131,451 contracts.

RUBBER (SMR 20)

Unit:	20 metric tonnes for contract months. 60 metric tonnes for distant deliveries.
Quotation:	Next nine months.
Minimum Fluctuation:	Malaysian cents per kilogram.
Contract Months:	25 Malaysian cents per kilogram.
First Notice Day:	**
Last Trading Day:	**
Settlement:	Physical.
Trading Hours:	10:00 to 13:00 and 16:00 to 18:00.
Volume—1986:	1,020 contracts.
Volume—1987:	42 contracts.

RUBBER (SMR 20)

Unit:	10-tonne for single contract month. 30-tonne for delivery quarter.

Quotation:	Malaysian cents per kilogramme.
Minimum Fluctuation:	One-quarter (¼) cents per kilogramme.
Contract Month:	Current month, next three to five months and two distant quarters, plus alternate months up to one year.
First Notice Day:	**
Last Trading Day:	Last business day of month preceding contract month.
Settlement:	Physical.
Trading Hours:	10:00 to 13:00 and 16:00 to 18:00.
Volume—1986:	1,202 contracts (20 tonne)
Volume—1987:	79 contracts (20 tonne)

TIN

Unit:	Five tonnes.
Quotation:	US dollars per tonne.
Minimum Fluctuation:	Five dollars per tonne.
Contract Months:	Current month, next three months, plus alternate months up to one year.
First Notice Day:	**
Last Trading Day:	Third to last business day of month.
Settlement:	Physical.
Trading Hours:	12:15 to 13:00 and 16:00 to 18:00.
Volume—1986:	nt
Volume—1987:	6,441 tonnes (began 27 Oct 1987).

COUNTRY: THE NETHERLANDS   *1987 Volume 2,160,988 contracts.*

EUROPEAN OPTIONS EXCHANGE (EOE)

Established:	1978
System:	Open Outcry
Relationship:	Mutual Offset with American Stock Exchange, Montreal Exchange, Vancouver Stock Exchange, and Sydney Stock Exchange.

OPTIONS

GROUP: CURRENCIES

BRITISH POUND

Unit:	10,000 Pounds
Quotation:	DFL per 100 Pounds.
Minimum Fluctuation:	0.05 DFL.
Strike Price:	5 DFL intervals.
Contract Months:	March, June, September, December.
Last Trading Day:	Third Friday of contract month at 14:00.
Expiration:	Saturday following third Friday of LTD.
Exercise:	**
Type:	American.
Settlement:	**
Trading Hours:	10:00 to 16:30.
Volume—1986:	46,935 contracts.
Volume—1987:	44,176 contracts.

US DOLLAR

Unit:	$10,000.
Quotation:	DFL per $100.
Minimum Fluctuation:	0.05 DFL.
Strike Price:	5 DFL intervals.
Contract Months:	March, June, September, December.
Last Trading Day:	Third Friday of contract month at 14:00.
Expiration:	Saturday following third Friday of LTD.
Exercise:	**
Type:	American.
Settlement:	**
Trading Hours:	10:00 to 16:30.
Volume—1986:	484,696 contracts.
Volume—1987:	647,251 contracts.

GROUP: METALS

GOLD (10 OUNCES)—IOCC

Unit:	10 troy ounces for London delivery.
Quotation:	US dollars and cents per ounce.
Minimum Fluctuation:	$.10 = $1.00.
Strike Price:	$10 intervals.
Contract Months:	Next three months on February, May, August, November cycle.

Last Trading Day:	Third Friday in contract month at 14:00.
Expiration:	Saturday following third Friday of LTD.
Exercise:	**
Type:	American.
Settlement:	**
Trading Hours:	IOCC schedule: EOE: 10:00 to 16:30. VSE: 11:30 to 16:00. ME: 9:00 to 14:30. ASE: 11:00 to 13:00 (Summer). 10:30 to 12:30 (Winter).
Volume—1986:	233,601 contracts.
Volume—1987:	374,112 contracts.

SILVER (250 OUNCES)—IOCC

Unit:	250 troy ounces.
Quotation:	US dollars and cents per ounce.
Minimum Fluctuation:	$.01 = $2.50.
Strike Price:	$0.25 less than $5.00. $0.50 $5.00 to $15.00. $1.00 greater than $15.
Contract Months:	March, June, September, December.
Last Trading Day:	Third Friday in contract month at 14:00.
Expiration:	Saturday following third Friday of LTD.
Exercise:	**
Type:	American.
Settlement:	**
Trading Hours:	IOCC schedule: EOE: 10:00 to 16:30. VSE: 07:30 to 16:00. ASE: 11:00 to 13:00 (Summer). 10:30 to 12:30 (Winter).
Volume—1986:	9,522 contracts.
Volume—1987:	32,416 contracts.

GROUP: INTEREST RATES
DUTCH GOVERNMENT BONDS

Unit:	10,000 DFL principal.
Quotation:	Per 100 units.
Minimum Fluctuation:	0.10 DFL.
Strike Price:	2.50 pct of principal.

Contract Months:	February, May, August, November.
Last Trading Day:	Third Friday of contract month at 14:00.
Expiration:	Saturday following third Friday of LTD.
Exercise:	**
Type:	American.
Settlement:	**
Trading Hours:	11:30 to 16:30.
Volume—1986:	866,765 contracts.
Volume—1987:	634,928 contracts.

GROUP: INDEX

BOND INDEX

Unit:	100 DFL times OBL Bond-Index.
Quotation:	Index points.
Minimum Fluctuation:	0.05 DFL.
Strike Price:	2.50 DFL intervals.
Contract Months:	February, May, August, November. Options with a maturity of more than 9 months expire in November.
Last Trading Day:	Third Friday of contract month at 16:30.
Expiration:	Saturday following third Friday of LTD.
Exercise:	**
Type:	European.
Settlement:	**
Trading Hours:	10:30 to 16:30.
Volume—1986:	nt
Volume—1987:	nt

Note: Contract began trading in August 1988.

EOE STOCK INDEX

Unit:	100 DFL times EOE Dutch Stock Index.
Quotation:	Index points.
Minimum Fluctuation:	0.10 DFL.
Strike Price:	5.00 DFL intervals.
Contract Months:	January, April, July, October.
Last Trading Day:	Third Friday of contract month at 14:00.
Expiration:	Saturday following third Friday of LTD.

Exercise:	**
Type:	European.
Settlement:	**
Trading Hours:	10:30 to 16:30.
Volume—1986:	nt
Volume—1987:	388,576 contracts (began May).

MAJOR MARKET INDEX

Unit:	$100 times index.
Quotation:	Index points.
Minimum Fluctuation:	⅛ point above $3.
	¹⁄₁₆ point up to $3.
Strike Price:	Five point intervals.
Contract Months:	Three consecutive near-term expiration months.
Last Trading Day:	Third Friday of contract month at 14:00.
Expiration:	Saturday following third Friday of LTD.
Exercise:	**
Type:	European.
Settlement:	**
Trading Hours:	EOE: 12:00 to 16:30.
	AMEX: 10:00 to 16:10.
Volume—1986:	nt
Volume—1987:	39,529 contracts (began August).

FINANCIELE TERMIJNMARKT AMSTERDAM N.V. (FTA)

Established:	1987
System:	Open Outcry
Relationships:	None

FUTURES

GROUP: INTEREST RATES

GUILDER BOND FUTURE

Unit:	1000 Dutch fl times EOE-FTA Bond Index.
Quotation:	Points per index.
Minimum Fluctuation:	One one-hundredth of one point, .01 = 10 Dutch DFL.
Contract Months:	February, May, August, November.
First Notice Day:	na
Last Trading Day:	Last business day of contract month.
Settlement:	Cash.

Trading Hours:	10:45 to 16:30.
Volume—1986:	nt
Volume—1987:	**

COUNTRY: NEW ZEALAND   *1987 Volume 357,174 contracts.*

NEW ZEALAND FUTURES EXCHANGE

Established:	1985
System:	Electronic
Relationships:	None

FUTURES

GROUP: CURRENCIES

NEW ZEALAND DOLLAR

Unit:	$NZ100,000.
Quotation:	$NZ/$US
Minimum Fluctuation:	$0.00001
Contract Months:	Spot month plus the next two consecutive months then the financial quarters to one year.
Last Trading Day:	Two business days before the first Wednesday of the cash settlement month at 2:30 pm.
Settlement:	One business day prior to last trading day in contract month.
Trading Hours:	8:05 to 16:55.
Volume—1986:	nt
Volume—1987:	nt

US DOLLAR

Unit:	50,000 US dollars.
Quotation:	US$/NZ$
Minimum Fluctuation:	$0.00001.
Contract Months:	Spot month plus next three months plus March, June, September, December.
First Notice Day:	na
Last Trading Day:	First Wednesday after ninth day of cash settlement month.
Settlement:	Cash in New Zealand dollars two business days following last trading day.

Trading Hours: 8:15 to 16:45.
Volume—1986:   12,938 contracts.
Volume—1987:   16,191 contracts.

GROUP: INTEREST RATES

FIVE YEAR GOVERNMENT STOCK NO. 2

Unit: $100,000 face value New Zealand Government Stock, coupon rate of 10% per annum.

Minimum Fluctuation: 0.01 pct.

Contract Months: March, June, September, December.

First Notice Day: na

Last Trading Day: First Wednesday after ninth day of the settlement month.

Settlement: Cash on second business day after last trading day.

Trading Hours: 8:00 to 17:00.

Volume—1986:   nt

Volume—1987:   nt

90-DAY BANK ACCEPTED BILLS

Unit: $500,000 New Zealand principal.

Quotation: 100 minus price.

Minimum Fluctuation: 0.01 pct.

Contract Months: Spot plus next two months plus March, June, September, December.

First Notice Day: na

Last Trading Day: First Wednesday after ninth day of contract month at 12:30.

Settlement: First business day following last trading day.

Trading Hours: 08:10 to 16:50.

Volume—1986:   2,793 contracts.

Volume—1987:   37,774 contracts.

GROUP: INDEX

BARCLAYS SHARE PRICE INDEX

Unit: $20 New Zealand times index.

Quotation: In index points.

Minimum Fluctuation: **

Contract Months: Spot month plus next two months plus March, June, September, December.

First Notice Day: na

Last Trading Day:	Second to last business day of contract month.
Settlement:	Cash on business day following last trading day.
Trading Hours:	09:15 to 15:45.
Volume—1986:	nt
Volume—1987:	119,038 contracts.

COUNTRY: SINGAPORE   *1987 Volume 2,115,773 contracts.*

SINGAPORE INTERNATIONAL MONETARY EXCHANGE (SIMEX)

Established:	1983
System:	Open Outcry
Relationships:	Chicago Mercantile Exchange

FUTURES

GROUP: CURRENCIES

BRITISH POUND (CME LINK)

Unit:	62,500 BP.
Quotation:	US$/BP.
Minimum Fluctuation:	$0.0002 = $12.50.
Contract Months:	Spot, March, June, September, December.
First Notice Day:	Last trading day.
Last Trading Day:	Second business day preceding third Wednesday of contract month.
Settlement:	Physical.
Trading Hours:	8:25 to 17:15.
Volume—1986:	17,978 contracts.
Volume—1987:	8,324 contracts.

DEUTSCHE MARK (CME LINK)

Unit:	125,000 Deutsche mark.
Quotation:	US$/DM.
Minimum Fluctuation:	$0.0001 = $12.50.
Contract Months:	Spot, March, June, September, December.
First Notice Day:	Last trading day.
Last Trading Day:	Second business day preceding third Wednesday of contract month.

Settlement:	Physical.
Trading Hours:	8:20 to 17:10.
Volume—1986:	213,762 contracts.
Volume—1987:	130,802 contracts.

JAPANESE YEN (CME LINK)

Unit:	12,500,000 Japanese yen.
Quotation:	US$/JY.
Minimum Fluctuation:	$0.000001 = $12.50.
Contract Months:	Spot, March, June, September, December.
First Notice Day:	Last trading day.
Last Trading Day:	Second business day preceding third Wednesday of contract month.
Settlement:	Physical.
Trading Hours:	8:15 to 17:05.
Volume—1986:	111,339 contracts.
Volume—1987:	93,573 contracts.

GROUP: INTEREST RATES

EURODOLLAR 90-DAY TIME DEPOSIT (CME LINK)

Unit:	US $1,000,000 principal.
Quotation:	Percent of par in basis points.
Minimum Fluctuation:	0.01 = $25.00.
Contract Months:	Spot, March, June, September, December.
First Notice Day:	na
Last Trading Day:	Second London business day preceding third Wednesday of contract month.
Settlement:	Cash.
Trading Hours:	8:30 to 17:20.
Volume—1986:	459,847 contracts.
Volume—1987:	1,519,630 contracts.

GROUP: INDEX

NIKKEI STOCK AVERAGE

Unit:	500 Japanese yen times Nikkei stock average futures price.
Quotation:	Points per index.
Minimum Fluctuation:	0.05 = 2,500 yen.
Contract Months:	Spot, March, June, September, December.
First Notice Day:	na
Last Trading Day:	Third Wednesday of contract month.
Settlement:	Cash.

Trading Hours:	8:00 to 14:15.
	8:00 to 10:15. Saturday
	(when TSE is open; not on SIMEX
	holidays.)
Volume—1986:	33,593 contracts.
Volume—1987:	363,439 contracts.

OPTIONS

GROUP: INTEREST RATES

EURODOLLAR 90-DAY TIME DEPOSIT

Unit:	One SIMEX $1,000,000 Eurodollar futures contract.
Quotation:	Points of 100 percent.
Minimum Fluctuation:	One one-hundredth (.01) of one point.
Point Value:	$25.00.
Strike Price:	.50 intervals under 88.00.
	.25 intervals above 88.00.
Contract Months:	March, June, September, December.
Last Trading Day:	Second London business day before third Wednesday of contract month.
Expiration:	Last trading day at 19:30.
Settlement:	Cash.
Exercise:	Automatic.
Type:	American.
Trading Hours:	8:30 to 17:20.
Volume—1986:	nt
Volume—1987:	Legan late 1987.

JAPANESE YEN

Unit:	One SIMEX JY12,500,000 Japanese yen futures.
Quotation:	Points of 1000 percent.
Minimum Fluctuation:	0.001 ($0.000001) = US$12.50.
Strike Price:	0.01 intervals.
Contract Months:	March, June, September, December, and Serial Months.
Last Trading Day:	Two Fridays before third Wednesday of contract month.
Expiration:	Last trading day at 19:30.
Settlement:	Cash.
Exercise:	Automatic.
Type:	American.

Trading Hours:	8:15 to 17:05.
Volume—1986:	nt
Volume—1987:	Began trading late 1987.

DEUTSCHE MARK

Unit:	One SIMEX DM125,000 Deutsche mark futures.
Quotation:	Point of 100 percent.
Minimum Fluctuation:	0.01 ($0.0001) = US$12.50.
Strike Price:	Intervals of one cent.
Contract Months:	March, June, September, December, and Serial Months.
Last Trading Day:	Two Fridays before third Wednesday of contract month.
Expiration:	Last trading day at 19:30.
Settlement:	Cash.
Exercise:	Automatic.
Type:	American.
Trading Hours:	8:20 to 17:10.
Volume—1986:	nt
Volume—1987:	Began trading late 1987.

COUNTRY: SWEDEN   1987 Volume 376,771 contracts.

STOCKHOLM OPTIONS MARKET (SOM)

Established:	1985
System:	Electronic
Relationships:	None

FORWARDS

GROUP: INDEX

OMX INDEX

Unit:	OMX Index on 30 stocks traded most heavily on Stockholm Stock Exchange. About SEK 60,000.
Quotation:	Index points.
Minimum Fluctuation:	**
Contract Months:	January, March, May, July, September, November.
First Notice Day:	One day preceding expiration date.
Last Trading Day:	Fourth Friday in expiration month.
Settlement:	Cash or physical.
Trading Hours:	10:00 to 16:00.

Volume—1986:	nt
Volume—1987:	159,447 (began 3 April 1987).

OPTIONS

GROUP: INTEREST RATES

FIVE-YEAR SWEDISH TREASURY NOTE

Unit:	1,000,000 SEK principal.
Quotation:	Percentage of option.
Minimum Fluctuation:	One hundredth of an option.
Strike Price:	20 basis point intervals.
Contract Months:	March, June, September, December.
Last Trading Day:	**
Expiration:	LTD at 12:00 noon.
Exercise:	By instruction.
Type:	European.
Settlement:	Cash or physical.
Trading Hours:	9:30 to 15:00.
Volume—1986:	376,771 contracts.
Volume—1987:	763,164 contracts.

Note: Not available for international trading.

GROUP: INDEX

OMX STOCK INDEX

Unit:	OMX Index, on 30 stocks traded most heavily on the Stockholm Stock Exchange. About SEK 60,000.
Quotation:	Percentage of option.
Minimum Fluctuation:	Hundredth of an option.
Strike Price:	20 index points intervals.
Contract Months:	January, March, May, July, September, November.
Last Trading Day:	Fourth Friday in contract month.
Expiration:	Close of business, LTD.
Exercise:	By instruction.
Type:	European.
Settlement:	Cash or physical.
Trading Hours:	10:00 to 16:00.
Volume—1986:	nt
Volume—1987:	6,738,654 contracts.

SWEDISH OPTIONS AND FUTURES EXCHANGE (SOFE)

Established:	1987
System:	Open Outcry and Electronic Trading
Relationships:	None

231

FORWARDS

GROUP: INDEX

SX 16 STOCK INDEX

Unit:	100 times SX 16 index of the Stockholm Stock Exchange.
Quotation:	Index points, 0.01 Multiples.
Minimum Fluctuation:	0.05 SEK.
Contract Months:	Monthly.
First Notice Day:	na
Last Trading Day:	Last trading day before expiration.
Settlement:	Cash on fourth Friday of contract month.
Trading Hours:	9:45 to 16:00 floor trading. 9:45 to 22:00 electronic trading.
Volume—1986:	nt
Volume—1987:	9,274 contracts.

OPTIONS

GROUP: INDEX

SX 16 STOCK INDEX

Unit:	100 times index.
Quotation:	Index points, 0.01 Multiples.
Minimum Fluctuation:	0.05 SEK.
Strike Price:	10 SEK intervals.
Contract Months:	Monthly.
Last Trading Day:	Last trading day before expiration.
Expiration:	Fourth Friday of contract month.
Exercise:	By instruction.
Type:	European.
Settlement:	Cash.
Trading Hours:	9:45 to 16:00 floor trading. 9:45 to 22:00 electronic trading.
Volume—1986:	nt
Volume—1987:	1,843,272 contracts.

COUNTRY: UNITED STATES   *1987 United States Volume 407,155,166 contracts.*

AMERICAN STOCK EXCHANGE (AMEX)

Established:	1791 (as the Curbstone Brokers)
System:	Open Outcry & Electronic

Relationships: The AMEX MMI stock index contract is also listed at the European Options Exchange in Amsterdam.

OPTIONS

GROUP: INDEX

COMPUTER TECHNOLOGY INDEX

Unit	$100 times index.
Quotation:	Index points.
Minimum Fluctuation:	⅛ point above $3.
	¹⁄₁₆ point up to $3.
	0.01 = $1.00.
Strike Price:	Five-point intervals.
Contract Months:	Three consecutive near-term months, plus March, June, September, December.
Last Trading Day:	Third Friday of contract month.
Expiration:	Last trading day at 16:10.
Exercise:	Automatic if in the money by 1/4.
Type:	American.
Settlement:	Cash.
Trading Hours:	9:30 to 16:10.
Volume—1986:	22,907 contracts.
Volume—1987:	23,558 contracts.

INSTITUTIONAL INDEX

Unit:	$100 times index.
Quotation:	Index points.
Minimum Fluctuation:	⅛ point above $3.
	¹⁄₁₆ point up to $3.
	0.01 = $1.00.
Strike Price:	0.05 intervals.
Contract Months:	Three consecutive near-term months, plus March, June, September, December.
Last Trading Day:	Third Friday of contract month.
Expiration:	Last trading day at 16:15.
Exercise:	Automatic if in the money by 1/4.
Type:	European.
Settlement:	Cash.
Trading Hours:	9:30 to 16:15.
Volume—1986:	502,864 contracts.
Volume—1987:	1,780,468 contracts.

MAJOR MARKET INDEX

Unit:	$100 times index.

Quotation:	Index points.
Minimum Fluctuation:	⅛ point above $3.
	¹⁄₁₆ point up to $3.
	0.01 = $1.00.
Strike Price:	0.05 intervals.
Contract Months:	Three consecutive near-term months, plus March, June, September, December.
Last Trading Day:	Third Friday of contract month.
Expiration:	Last trading day by 16:15.
Exercise:	Automatic if in the money by 3/4.
Type:	American.
Settlement:	Cash.
Trading Hours:	AMEX: 9:30 to 16:15.
	EOE: 12:00 to 16:30.
Volume—1986:	15,643,399 contracts.
Volume—1987:	14,545,669 contracts.

OIL INDEX

Unit:	$100 times index.
Quotation:	Index points.
Minimum Fluctuation:	⅛ point above $3.
	¹⁄₁₆ point up to $3.
	0.01 = $1.00.
Strike Price:	0.05 intervals.
Contract Months:	Three consecutive near-term months, plus January, April, July, October.
Last Trading Day:	Third Friday of contract month.
Expiration:	Last trading day by 16:00.
Exercise:	Automatic if in the money by 3/4.
Type:	American.
Settlement:	Cash.
Trading Hours:	9:30 to 16:10.
Volume—1986:	116,672 contracts.
Volume—1987:	91,160 contracts.

GROUP: INTEREST RATES

UNITED STATES TREASURY BILLS

Unit:	$1,000,000 principal.
Quotation:	Percent of par in basis points.
Minimum Fluctuation:	0.01 = $25.00.
Strike Price:	⅕ of one point or 0.2 pct intervals.
Contract Months:	March, June, September, December.
Last Trading Day:	Of expiration month on which a one-year T Bill has 13 weeks remaining to maturity.

Expiration:	Tuesday at 15:00.
Exercise:	Automatic.
Type:	American.
Settlement:	Physical.
Trading Hours:	9:30 to 15:00.
Volume—1986:	502 contracts.
Volume—1987:	0

UNITED STATES TREASURY NOTES

Unit:	$100,000 principal.
Quotation:	Percent of par in basis points. 32 basis points equals one note point.
Minimum Fluctuation:	$\frac{1}{32} = \$31.25.$
Strike Price:	0.02 intervals.
Contract Months:	February, May, August, November.
Last Trading Day:	The eighth last business day of contract month.
Expiration:	Friday by 15:00.
Exercise:	Automatic if in the money.
Type:	American.
Settlement:	Physical.
Trading Hours:	9:30 to 15:00.
Volume—1986:	23,472 contracts.
Volume—1987:	24,662 contracts.

CHICAGO BOARD OF TRADE (CBOT)

Established:	1848
System:	Open Outcry
Relationships:	Chicago Board Options Exchange

FUTURES

GROUP: AGRICULTURE

CORN

Unit:	5,000 bushels.
Quotation:	US cents and quarter cents per bushel.
Minimum Fluctuation:	$.025 = $12.50.
Contract Months:	March, May, July, September, December. Year runs December to September.
First Notice Day:	The last business day of the month preceding the contract month.
Last Trading Day:	The eighth last business day of contract month at 12-noon.
Settlement:	Physical.

Hours:	9:30 to 13:15.
Volume—1986:	6,160,298 contracts.
Volume—1987:	7,253,212 contracts.

OATS

Unit:	5,000 bushels.
Quotation:	US cents and quarter cents per bushel.
Minimum Fluctuation:	$.025 = $12.50.
Contract Months:	March, May, July, September, December.
First Notice Day:	The last business day of the month preceding the contract month.
Last Trading Day:	The eighth last business day of contract month.
Settlement:	Physical.
Hours:	9:30 to 13:15.
Volume—1986:	140,952 contracts.
Volume—1987:	291,108 contracts.

SOYBEANS

Unit:	5,000 bushels.
Quotation:	US cents and quarter cents per bushel.
Minimum Fluctuation:	$.025 = $12.50.
Contract Months:	January, March, May, July, August, September, November.
First Notice Day:	The last business day of the month preceding the contract month.
Last Trading Day:	The eighth to last business day of contract month.
Settlement:	Physical.
Hours:	9:30 to 13:15.
Volume—1986:	6,133,668 contracts.
Volume—1987:	7,378,760 contracts.

SOYBEAN MEAL

Unit:	100 tons.
Quotation:	US dollars and cents per ton.
Minimum Fluctuation:	$.10 = $10.00.
Contract Months:	January, March, May, July, August, September, October, December. Year runs September to August.
First Notice Day:	The last business day of the month preceding the contract month.
Last Trading Day:	The eighth to last business day of contract month.
Settlement:	Physical.
Hours:	9:30 to 13:15.

Volume—1986:	3,049,005 contracts.
Volume—1987:	3,797,970 contracts.

SOYBEAN OIL

Unit:	60,000 pounds.
Quotation:	Dollars and cents per hundredweight.
Minimum Fluctuation:	$.01 = $6.00.
Contract Months:	January, March, May, July, August, September, October, December.
First Notice Day:	The last business day of the month preceding the contract month.
Last Trading Day:	The eighth to last business day of contract month.
Settlement:	Physical.
Hours:	9:30 to 13:15.
Volume—1986:	3,182,963 contracts.
Volume—1987:	3,912,417 contracts.

WHEAT (SOFT WINTER)

Unit:	5,000 bushels.
Quotation:	US cents and quarter cents per bushel.
Minimum Fluctuation:	$.025 = $12.50.
Contract Months:	July, September, December, March, May.
First Notice Day:	The last business day of the month preceding the contract month.
Last Trading Day:	The eighth to last business day of contract month.
Settlement:	Physical.
Hours:	9:30 to 13:15.
Volume—1986:	2,090,316 contracts.
Volume—1987:	1,929,306 contracts.

GROUP: METALS

GOLD

Unit:	100 troy ounces.
Quotation:	US dollars and cents per troy ounce.
Minimum Fluctuation:	$.10 = $10.00.
Contract Months:	Current month, next two calendar months and any February, April, June, August, October, December.
First Notice Day:	The last business day of the month preceding the contract month.
Last Trading Day:	Fifth to last business day of delivery month.
Settlement:	Refined gold.

Trading Hours:	7:20 to 13:40 CST Monday to Thursday.
	17:00 to 20:00 CDT Sunday to Thursday.
	18:00 to 21:00 CST Sunday to Thursday.
Volume—1986:	nt
Volume—1987:	24,893 contracts.

GOLD

Unit:	One kilogram or 32.5 troy ounces gold.
Quotation:	US dollars and cents per troy ounce.
Minimum Fluctuation:	$.10 = $32.15.
Contract Months:	Current month, next two calendar months and any February, April, June, August, October, December.
First Notice Day:	The last business day of the month preceding the contract month.
Last Trading Day:	Fourth to last business day preceding contract month.
Settlement:	Refined gold.
Trading Hours:	7:20 to 13:40.
Volume—1986:	124,546 contracts.
Volume—1987:	159,627 contracts.

SILVER

Unit:	1000 troy ounces of silver.
Quotation:	US dollars and cents per troy ounce.
Minimum Fluctuation:	$.001 = $1.00.
Contract Months:	Current calendar month and two following months and any February, April, June, August, October, December within 17-month period beginning with current month.
First Notice Day:	The last business day of the month preceding the contract month.
Last Trading Day:	Fifth to last business day of contract month.
Settlement:	Refined silver.
Trading Hours:	7:25 to 13:25.
Volume—1986:	511,239 contracts.
Volume—1987:	509,965 contracts.

SILVER

Unit:	5000 troy ounces.

Quotation:	US dollars and cents per troy ounce.
Minimum Fluctuation:	$.001 = $5.00.
Contract Months:	Current calendar month, two following months and any February, April, June, August, October, December.
First Notice Day:	Business day preceding contract month.
Last Trading Day:	Fifth to last business day of contract month.
Settlement:	Refined silver.
Trading Hours:	7:25 to 13:25, Monday to Friday. CDT 18:00 to 21:30, Sunday to Thursday. CST 17:00 to 20:30, Sunday to Thursday.
Volume—1986:	nt
Volume—1987:	12,092 contracts.

GROUP: INTEREST RATES

30-DAY FIXED-RATE

Unit:	$5,000,000 principal.
Quotation:	100.00 minus Federal funds rate.
Minimum Fluctuation:	.001 = $41.67.
Contract Months:	First four calendar months, plus March, June, September, December.
First Notice Day:	na
Last Trading Day:	Last business day of contract month.
Settlement:	Cash settled against average daily Federal funds rate for contract month.
Trading Hours:	7:20 to 14:00.
Volume—1986:	nt
Volume—1987:	nt

Note: Contract to begin trading 3 October 1988.

UNITED STATES FIVE-YEAR TREASURY NOTE

Unit:	$100,000 principal.
Quotation:	Percent of par in basis points. 32 basis points equals 1 bond point.
Minimum Fluctuation:	$\frac{1}{32}$ = $31.25.
Contract Months:	March, June, September, December.
First Notice Day:	The last business day of the month preceding the contract month.

Last Trading Day: The eighth last business day of contract month.

Settlement: Physical.

Trading Hours: 8:00 to 14:00

Volume—1986:   nt

Volume—1987:   nt

UNITED STATES 10-YEAR TREASURY NOTE

Unit: $100,000 principal.

Quotation: Percent of par in basis points. 32 basis points equals 1 bond point.

Minimum Fluctuation: $\frac{1}{32}$ = $31.25.

Contract Months: March, June, September, December.

First Notice Day: The last business day of the month preceding the contract month.

Last Trading Day: The eighth last business day of contract month.

Settlement: Physical.

Trading Hours: 7:20 to 14:00. Monday to Friday. CDT 17:00 to 20:30, Sunday to Thursday. CST 18:00 to 21:30, Sunday to Thursday.

Volume—1986:   4,426,476 contracts.

Volume—1987:   5,253,791 contracts.

UNITED STATES TREASURY BONDS

Unit: $100,000 principal.

Quotation: Percent of par in basis points.

Minimum Fluctuation: $\frac{1}{32}$ = $31.25.

Contract Months: March, June, September, December.

First Notice Day: The last business day of the month preceding the contract month.

Last Trading Day: Last business day of contract month.

Settlement: Physical.

Trading Hours: 7:20 to 14:00. Monday to Friday. CDT 17:00 to 20:30, Sunday to Thursday. CST 18:00 to 21:30, Sunday to Thursday.

Volume—1986:   52,598,811 contracts.

Volume—1987:   66,841,474 contracts.

GROUP: INDEX

MAJOR MARKET INDEX—MAXI

Unit: $250 times index.

Quotation:	Points of index.
Minimum Fluctuation:	0.05 = $12.50.
Contract Months:	Monthly.
First Notice Day:	na
Last Trading Day:	Third Friday of contract month.
Settlement:	Cash.
Trading Hours:	8:15 to 15:15.
Volume—1986.	1,738,916 contracts.
Volume—1987:	2,630,887 contracts.

CBOE 250 STOCK INDEX

Unit:	$500 times CBOE 250 stock index.
Quotation:	Index points.
Minimum Fluctuation:	0.05 = $25.00.
Contract Months:	January, February, March, June, September, December.
First Notice Day:	na
Last Trading Day:	First business day preceding first Saturday following third Friday of contract month.
Settlement:	Cash.
Trading Hours:	8:30 to 15:15.
Volume—1986:	nt
Volume—1987:	nt

Note: Trading to begin 3 November 1988.

MUNICIPAL BOND INDEX

Unit:	$1000 times index.
Quotation:	Percent of par in basis points. 32 basis points equals 1 bond point.
Minimum Fluctuation:	$\frac{1}{32}$ = $31.25.
Contract Months:	March, June, September, December.
First Notice Day:	na
Last Trading Day:	The eighth last business day of contract month.
Settlement:	Cash on last trading day based on Bond Buyer Muncipal Bond Index.
Trading Hours:	7:20 to 14:00.
Volume—1986:	906,980 contracts.
Volume—1987:	1,613,107 contracts.

OPTIONS

GROUP: AGRICULTURE

CORN

Unit:	One CBT 5,000 bushel corn futures contract.

Quotation:	US cents per bushel.
Minimum Fluctuation:	$.0012 = $6.25.
Strike Price:	$.10 intervals.
Contract Months:	Same as CBT corn futures: March, May, July, September and December.
Last Trading Day:	Last Friday at least 5 business days preceding first notice day of underlying futures at 12 noon.
Expiration:	Saturday at 10:00.
Exercise:	Automatic if in the money by 0.10.
Type:	American
Settlement:	Futures.
Trading Hours:	9:30 to 13:15.
Volume—1986:	575,634 contracts.
Volume—1987:	661,519 contracts.

SOYBEANS

Unit:	One CBT 5,000 bushel soybean futures contract.
Quotation:	US dollar and cents per bushel.
Minimum Fluctuation:	$.0012 = $6.25.
Strike Price:	25 cent per bushel intervals.
Contract Months:	January, March, May, July, August, September and November.
Last Trading Day:	Last Friday at least 5 business days preceding first notice day in underlying soybean futures contract.
Expiration:	Saturday at 10:00.
Exercise:	Automatic if in the money by 0.30.
Type:	American
Settlement:	Futures.
Trading Hours:	9:30 to 13:15.
Volume—1986:	775,139 contracts.
Volume—1987:	1,242,072 contracts.

SOYBEAN MEAL

Unit:	One CBT 100 tons soybean meal futures contract.
Quotation:	US cents per ton.
Minimum Fluctuation:	$.05 = $5.00.
Strike Price:	$5 per ton intervals for prices less than $200.
	$10 per ton intervals for prices greater than or equal to $200.

Contract Months: Same as CBT Soybeans Meal Futures: January, March, May, July, August, September, October and December.

Last Trading Day: Friday at least five business days preceding first notice day in underlying soybean meal futures contract at 12-noon.

Expiration: Saturday at 10:00.
Exercise: Automatic if in the money by $10.00.
Type: American.
Settlement: Futures.
Trading Hours: 9:30 to 13:15.
Volume—1986: nt
Volume—1987: 81,213 contracts.

SOYBEAN OIL

Unit: One CBT 60,000 pounds soybean oil futures contract.

Quotation: US cents per pound.
Minimum Fluctation: $.005 = $3.00.
Strike Price: $.01 intervals.
Contract Months: Same as CBT Soybean Oil futures: January, March, May, July, August, September, October and December.

Last Trading Day: Last Friday at least five business days preceding first notice day in underlying soybean oil futures contract at 12-noon.

Expiration: Saturday at 10:00.
Exercise: Automatic if in the money by 0.01.
Type: American.
Settlement: Futures.
Trading Hours: 9:30 to 13:15.
Volume—1986: nt
Volume—1987: 85,735 contracts.

WHEAT (SOFT WINTER)

Unit: One CBT 5,000 bushel wheat futures contract.

Quotation: US cents per bushel.
Minimum Fluctuation: $.0012 = $6.25.
Strike Price: $.10 intervals.
Contract Months: March, May, July, September, December

Last Trading Day: Last Friday preceding first notice day of underlying wheat futures contract by at least five business days at 12-noon.

Expiration: Saturday at 10:00.

Exercise: Automatic if in the money by 0.20.

Type: American.

Settlement: Futures.

Trading Hours: 09:30 to 15:15.

Volume—1986: 9,314 contracts.

Volume—1987: 124,598 contracts.

GROUP: METALS

SILVER

Unit: One CBT 1000 troy ounce silver futures contract.

Quotation: Cents per troy ounce.

Minimum Fluctuation: $.01 = $1.00.

Strike Price: $.25 intervals for prices below $8.00.
$.50 intervals for prices from $8.00 to $20.00.
$1.00 intervals for prices above $20.00.

Contract months: February, April, June, August, October and December.

Last Trading Day: Last Friday at least five business days prior to first notice day in underlying silver futures contract at 13:25.

Expiration: Saturday at 10:00.

Exercise: Automatic if in the money by 0.50.

Type: American.

Settlement: Futures.

Trading Hours: 8:05 to 13:25.

Volume—1986: 3,081 contracts.

Volume—1987: 10,009 contracts.

GROUP: INTEREST RATES

UNITED STATES 10-YEAR TREASURY NOTE

Unit: One CBT $100,000 long-term United States Treasury note futures contract.

Quotation: $1/64$ of one percent.
64 basis points equal one bond point.

Minimum Fluctuation: $1/64 = 15.625.

Strike Price: One bond point.

Contract Months:	Same as CBT US T-notes future contract: March, June, September and December.
Last Trading Day:	Last Friday at least five business days prior to first notice day of underlying CBT US T-Note futures contract at 12-noon.
Expiration:	Saturday at 10:00.
Exercise:	Automatic if in the money by 2 bond pts.
Type:	American.
Settlement:	Futures.
Trading Hours:	7:20 to 14:00. CDT 18:00 to 21:30, Sunday to Thursday. CST 17:00 to 20:30, Sunday to Thursday.
Volume—1986:	1,000,682 contracts.
Volume—1987:	1,421,852 contracts.

UNITED STATES TREASURY BOND

Unit:	One CBT $100,000 US Treasury bond futures contract.
Quotation:	¹⁄₆₄ of one percent. 64 basis points equal one bond point.
Minimum Fluctuation:	¹⁄₆₄ = $15.625.
Strike Price:	Two bond points (200 basis points).
Contract Months:	March, June, September, December.
Last Trading Day:	Last Friday at least five business days preceding first notice day of underlying futures contract at 12-noon.
Expiration:	Saturday at 10:00.
Exercise:	Automatic if in the money by 2 bond pts.
Type:	American.
Settlement:	Futures.
Trading Hours:	7:20 to 14:00. CDT 18:00 to 21:30, Sunday to Thursday. CST 17:00 to 20:30, Sunday to Thursday.
Volume—1986:	17,314,349 contracts.
Volume—1987:	21,720,402 contracts.

GROUP: INDEX

MUNICIPAL BOND INDEX

Unit:	One CBT Municipal Bond Index futures contract.
Quotation:	Points of index.
	64 points = 1 index point.
Minimum Fluctuation:	$\frac{1}{64}$ = $15.625.
Strike Price:	Two index points.
Contract Months:	March, June, September and December.
Last Trading Day:	Last trading day in underlying Municipal Bond Index futures contract at 14:00.
Expiration:	Last trading day at 20:00.
Exercise:	Automatic.
Type:	American.
Settlement:	Futures.
Trading Hours:	7:20 to 14:00.
Volume—1986:	nt
Volume—1987:	118,632 contracts.

CHICAGO BOARD OPTIONS EXCHANGE (CBOE)

Established:	1973
System:	Electronic & Open Outcry
Relationships:	Chicago Board of Trade

OPTIONS

GROUP: INTEREST RATES

UNITED STATES FIVE-YEAR TREASURY NOTE

Unit:	$100,000, 5-year US Treasury Note.
Quotation:	32 basis points equals one bond point.
Minimum Fluctuation:	$\frac{1}{32}$ = $31.25.
Contract Months:	March, June, September, December.
Last Trading Day:	Third Friday of contract month.
Expiration:	Saturday at 16:00.
Exercise:	By instruction.
Type:	American.
Settlement:	Physical.
Trading Hours:	8:00 to 14:00.
Volume—1986:	49,528 contracts.
Volume—1987:	33,011 contracts.

UNITED STATES TREASURY BOND

Unit:	$100,000 principal.

Quotation:	32 basis points equals one bond point.
Minimum Fluctuation:	$\frac{1}{32} = \$31.25$.
Strike Price:	One-point intervals.
Contract Months:	March, June, September, December.
Last Trading Day:	Third Friday of contract month.
Expiration:	Saturday at 16:00.
Exercise:	By instruction.
Type:	American.
Settlement:	Physical.
Trading Hours:	8:00 to 14:00.
Volume—1986:	271,493 contracts.
Volume—1987:	174,465 contracts.

GROUP: INDEX

STANDARD & POOR'S 100 STOCK INDEX

Unit:	100 times index.
Quotation:	Index points.
Minimum Fluctuation:	$\frac{1}{8}$ point premium above $3.
	$\frac{1}{16}$ up to $3.
	0.01 = $1.00.
Strike Price:	0.05 intervals.
Contract Months:	Four sequential months.
Last Trading Day:	Third Friday of contract month.
Expiration:	Last Trading Day at 15:00.
Exercise:	Automatic if in the money $\frac{1}{4}$ point.
Type:	American.
Settlement:	Cash.
Trading Hours:	8:30 to 15:15.
Volume—1986:	113,151,085 contracts.
Volume—1987:	101,827,077 contracts.

STANDARD & POOR'S 500 STOCK INDEX

Unit:	100 times index.
Quotation:	Index points.
Minimum Fluctuation:	$\frac{1}{8}$ point premium above $3.
	$\frac{1}{16}$ up to $3.
	0.01 = $1.00.
Strike Price:	0.05 intervals.
Contract Months:	March, June, September, October, December.
Last Trading Day:	Third Thursday of contract month, NSX.
	Third Friday of contract month, SPX.
Expiration:	Last trading day at 15:00.
Exercise:	Automatic if in the money $\frac{1}{4}$ point.

Type: European.
Settlement: Cash.
Trading Hours: 8:30 to 14:00.
Volume—1986:   1,682,808 contracts.
Volume—1987:   620,793 contracts.

CHICAGO MERCANTILE EXCHANGE (CME)

Established: 1919
System: Open Outcry
Relationships: Mutual Offset System with Singapore International Monetary Exchange in Singapore.

FUTURES

GROUP: AGRICULTURE

FEEDER CATTLE

Unit: 44,000 pounds.
Quotation: US cents per pound.
Minimum Fluctuation: .025 = $11.00.
Contract Months: January, March, April, May, August, September, October, November.
First Notice Day: na
Last Trading Day: Last Thursday of contract month.
Settlement: Cash.
Trading Hours: 9:05 to 13:00.
Volume—1986:   411,441 contracts.
Volume—1987:   645,877 contracts.

LIVE CATTLE

Unit: 40,000 pounds.
Quotation: US cents per pound.
Minimum Fluctuation: $.025 = $10.00.
Contract Months: February and alternate months.
First Notice Day: Third business day preceding contract day.
Last Trading Day: Twentieth calendar day of contract month.
Settlement: Physical.
Trading Hours: 9:05 to 13:00.
Volume—1986:   4,690,538 contracts.
Volume—1987:   5,229,294 contracts.

LIVE HOGS

Unit: 30,000 pounds.
Quotation: US cents per pound.
Minimum Fluctuation: $.025 = $7.50.

Contract Months:	February, April, June, July, August, October, December.
First Notice Day:	First day preceding contract day.
Last Trading Day:	Twentieth calendar day of contract month.
Settlement:	Physical.
Trading Hours:	9:10 to 13:00.
Volume—1986:	1,936,864 contracts.
Volume—1987:	2,040,478 contracts.

PORK BELLIES (FROZEN)

Unit:	40,000 pounds.
Quotation:	US cents per pound.
Minimum Fluctuation:	$.025 = $10.00.
First Notice Day:	First business day preceding contract day.
Last Trading Day:	Business day preceding last five business days of contract month.
Settlement:	Physical.
Trading Hours:	9:10 to 13:00.
Volume—1986:	1,100,339 contracts.
Volume—1987:	1,097,010 contracts.

LUMBER (RANDOM LENGTH)

Unit:	150,000 board feet.
Quotation:	US cents per board foot.
Minimum Fluctuation:	$.10 = $15.00.
Contract Months:	January and alternate months.
First Notice Day:	Any business day following last trading day.
Last Trading Day:	Business day preceding sixteenth calendar day of contract month.
Settlement:	Physical.
Trading Hours:	9:00 to 13:05.
Volume—1986:	502,530 contracts.
Volume—1987:	437,089 contracts.

GROUP: CURRENCIES

AUSTRALIAN DOLLAR

Unit:	100,000 Australian dollars.
Quotation:	US$/A$.
Minimum Fluctuation:	$0.0001 = $10.00.
Contract Months:	March, June, September, December.
First Notice Day:	Last trading day.
Last Trading Day:	Second business day preceding third Wednesday of contract month.

Settlement: Physical.
Delivery Day: Third Wednesday of contract month.
Trading Hours: 7:20 to 14:00.
Volume—1986:   nt
Volume—1987:   53,335 contracts.

BRITISH POUND

Unit: 62,500 British pounds.
Quotation: US$/BP.
Minimum Fluctuation: $0.0002 = $12.50.
Contract Months: March, June, September, December.
First Notice Day: Last trading day.
Last Trading Day: Second business day preceding third
                           Wednesday of contract month.

Settlement: Physical.
Delivery Day: Third Wednesday of contract month.
Trading Hours: 7:20 to 14:00.
Volume—1986:   2,701,330 contracts.
Volume—1987:   2,592,177 contracts.

Note: The size of this contract was changed from $25,000 in 1988.

CANADIAN DOLLAR

Unit: 100,000 Canadian dollars.
Quotation: US$/CD.
Minimum Fluctuation: $0.0001 = $10.00.
Contract Months: March, June, September, December.
First Notice Day: Last trading day.
Last Trading Day: Second business day preceding third
                           Wednesday of contract month.

Settlement: Physical.
Delivery Day: Third Wednesday of contract month.
Trading Hours: 7:20 to 14:00.
Volume—1986:   734,071 contracts.
Volume—1987:   914,563 contracts.

DEUTSCHE MARK

Unit: 125,000 Deutsche marks.
Quotation: US$/JY.
Minimum Fluctuation: $0.0001 = $12.50.
Contract Months: March, June, September, December.
First Notice Day: Last trading day.
Last Trading Day: Second business day preceding third
                           Wednesday of contract month.

Settlement: Physical.
Delivery Day: Third Wednesday of contract month.
Trading Hours: 7:20 to 14:00.

Volume—1986:	6,582,145 contracts.
Volume—1987:	6,037,048 contracts.

FRENCH FRANC

Unit:	250,000 French francs.
Quotation:	US$/FF.
Minimum Fluctuation:	$0.00005 = $12.50.
Contract Months:	March, June, September, December.
First Notice Day:	Last trading day.
Last Trading Day:	Second business day preceding third Wednesday of contract month.
Settlement:	Physical.
Delivery Day:	Third Wednesday of contract month.
Trading Hours:	7:20 to 14:00.
Volume—1986:	2,685 contracts.
Volume—1987:	10,437 contracts.

JAPANESE YEN

Unit:	12,500,000 Japanese yen.
Quotation:	US$/JY.
Minimum Fluctuation:	$0.000001 = $12.50.
Contract Months:	March, June, September, December.
First Notice Day:	Last trading day.
Last Trading Day:	Second business day preceding third Wednesday of contract month.
Settlement:	Physical.
Delivery Day:	Third Wednesday of contract month.
Trading Hours:	7:20 to 14:00.
Volume—1986:	3,969,777 contracts.
Volume—1987:	5,358,556 contracts.

SWISS FRANC

Unit:	125,000 Swiss francs.
Quotation:	US$/SF.
Minimum Fluctuation:	$0.0001 = $12.50.
Contract Months:	March, June, September, December.
First Notice Day:	Last trading day.
Last Trading Day:	Second business day preceding third Wednesday of contract month.
Settlement:	Physical.
Delivery Day:	Third Wednesday of contract month.
Trading Hours:	7:20 to 14:00.
Volume—1986:	4,998,430 contracts.
Volume—1987:	5,268,276 contracts.

EUROPEAN CURRENCY UNIT

Unit:	125,000 European currency units.

Quotation:	US$/ECU.
Minimum Fluctuation:	$0.0001 = $12.50.
Contract Months:	March, June, September, December.
First Notice Day:	Last trading day.
Last Trading Day:	Second business day preceding third Wednesday of contract month.
Settlement:	Physical.
Delivery Day:	Third Wednesday of contract month.
Trading Hours:	7:10 to 14:00.
Volume—1986:	43,826 contracts.
Volume—1987:	300 contracts.

GROUP: INTEREST RATES

EURODOLLAR 90-DAY TIME DEPOSIT

Unit:	$1,000,000 principal.
Quotation:	Percent of par in basis points. 100 basis points equals one Euro point.
Minimum Fluctuation:	0.01 = $25.00.
Contract Months:	March, June, September, December.
First Notice Day:	na
Last Trading Day:	Second London business day preceding third Wednesday of contract month.
Settlement:	Cash.
Trading Hours:	7:20 to 14:00.
Volume—1986:	10,824,914 contracts.
Volume—1987:	20,416,216 contracts.

UNITED STATES 90-DAY TREASURY BILLS

Unit:	$1,000,000 principal.
Quotation:	Percent of par in basis points. 100 basis points equals one bill point.
Minimum Fluctuation:	0.01 = $25.00.
Contract Months:	March, June, September, December.
First Notice Day:	Last trading day.
Last Trading Day:	Business day preceding issue date of contract month.
Settlement:	Physical.
Trading Hours:	7:20 to 14:00.
Volume—1986:	1,815,162 contracts.
Volume—1987:	1,927,006 contracts.

GROUP: INDEX

STANDARD & POOR'S 500 STOCK INDEX

Unit:	$500 times index.

Quotation:	Points of index.
Minimum Fluctuation:	.05 = $25.00.
Contract Months:	March, June, September, December.
First Notice Day:	na
Last Trading Day:	Third Thursday of contract month.
Settlement:	Cash.
Trading Hours:	8:30 to 15:15.
Volume—1986:	19,505,273 contracts.
Volume—1987:	19,044,673 contracts.

OPTIONS

GROUP: AGRICULTURE

FEEDER CATTLE

Unit:	One CME 44,000-pound feeder cattle futures contract.
Quotation:	US cents per pound.
Minimum Fluctuation:	$.025 = $11.00.
Strike Price:	$.02 intervals.
Contract Months:	January, March, April, May, August, September, October, November.
Last Trading Day:	Last Thursday of contract month.
Expiration:	Business day following LTD at 19:00.
Exercise:	Automatic.
Type:	American.
Settlement:	Cash.
Hours:	9:05 to 13:00.
Volume—1986:	nt
Volume—1987:	134,830 contracts.

LIVE CATTLE

Unit:	One CME 40,000-pound live cattle futures contract.
Quotation:	US cents per pound.
Minimum Fluctuation:	$.025 = $10.00.
Strike Price:	$.02 intervals.
Contract Months:	February and alternate months.
Last Trading Day:	Friday at least three business days preceding first business day of contract month.
Expiration:	Last trading day at 19:00.
Exercise:	Automatic.
Type:	American.
Settlement:	Futures.
Trading Hours:	9:05 to 13:00.

Volume—1986:	718,099 contracts.
Volume—1987:	1,222,397 contracts.

LIVE HOGS

Unit:	One CME 30,000-pound live hog futures contract.
Quotation:	US cents per pound.
Minimum Fluctuation:	$.025 = $7.50.
Strike Price:	$.02 intervals.
Contract Months:	February, April, June, July, August, October, December.
Last Trading Day:	Friday at least three business days preceding first business day of contract month.
Expiration:	Last trading day at 19:00.
Exercise:	Automatic by instruction.
Type:	American.
Settlement:	Futures.
Trading Hours:	9:10 to 13:00.
Volume—1986:	105,516 contracts.
Volume—1987:	147,859 contracts.

FROZEN PORK BELLIES

Unit:	One CME 40,000-pound frozen pork belly futures contract.
Quotation:	US cents per pound.
Minimum Fluctuation:	$.025 = $10.00.
Strike Price:	Two cent intervals.
Contract Months:	February, March, May, July, August.
Last Trading Day:	Friday three business days preceding first business day of contract month.
Expiration:	Last trading day at 19:00.
Exercise:	Automatic by instruction.
Type:	American.
Settlement:	Futures.
Trading Hours:	9:10 to 13:00.
Volume—1986:	1,981 contracts.
Volume—1987:	15,112 contracts.

LUMBER (RANDOM LENGTH)

Unit:	One IOM 150,000 board feet lumber futures contract.
Quotation:	US cents per board feet.
Minimum Fluctuation:	$.10 = $15.00.
Strike Price:	$5 intervals.

Contract Months:	January, March, May, July, September, November.
Last Trading Day:	Last Friday preceding contract month.
Expiration:	Last trading day at 19:00.
Exercise:	Automatic by instruction.
Type:	American.
Settlement:	Futures.
Trading Hours:	9:00 to 13:05.
Volume—1986:	nt
Volume—1987:	6,483 contracts.

GROUP: CURRENCIES

AUSTRALIAN DOLLAR

Unit:	100,000 Australian dollars.
Quotation:	US$/A$.
Minimum Fluctuation:	$.0001 = $10.00.
Strike Price:	$.01 intervals.
Contract Months:	All calendar months.
Last Trading Day:	Two Fridays preceding third Wednesday of contract month.
Expiration:	Last trading day at 19:00.
Exercise:	Automatic by instruction.
Type:	American.
Settlement:	Futures.
Trading Hours:	7:20 to 14:00.
Volume—1986:	nt
Volume—1987:	nt

BRITISH POUND

Unit:	One IMM 62,500 British pound futures contract.
Quotation:	US$/BP.
Minimum Fluctuation:	$.02 = $12.50.
Strike Price:	$.025 intervals.
Contract Months:	All calendar months.
Last Trading Day:	Two Fridays preceding third Wednesday of contrct month.
Expiration:	Last trading day at 19:00.
Exercise:	Automatic by instruction.
Type:	American.
Settlement:	Futures.
Trading Hours:	7:20 to 14:00.
Volume—1986:	496,591 contracts.
Volume—1987:	569,062 contracts.

CANADIAN DOLLAR

Unit:	One IMM 100,000 Canadian dollar futures contract.
Quotation:	US$/CD$.
Minimum Fluctuation:	$.001 = $10.
Strike Price:	$.005 intervals.
Contract Months:	All calendar months.
Last Trading Day:	Two Fridays preceding third Wednesday of contract month.
Expiration:	Last trading day at 19:00.
Exercise:	Automatic by instruction.
Type:	American.
Settlement:	Futures.
Trading Hours:	7:20 to 14:00.
Volume—1986:	26,465 contracts.
Volume—1987:	48,690 contracts.

DEUTSCHE MARK

Unit:	One IMM 125,000 Deutsche mark futures contract.
Quotation:	US$/DM.
Minimum Fluctuation:	$.01 = $12.50.
Strike Price:	$.01 intervals.
Contract Months:	All calendar months.
Last Trading Day:	Two Fridays preceding third Wednesday of contract month.
Expiration:	Last trading day at 19:00.
Exercise:	Automatic by instruction.
Type:	American.
Settlement:	Futures.
Trading Hours:	7:20 to 14:00.
Volume—1986:	2,205,579 contracts.
Volume—1987:	3,125,687 contracts.

JAPANESE YEN

Unit:	One IMM 12,500,000 Japanese yen futures contract.
Quotation:	US$/JY.
Minimum Fluctuation:	$.00001 = $12.50.
Strike Price:	$.00001 intervals.
Contract Months:	All calendar months.
Last Trading Day:	Two Fridays preceding third Wednesday of contract month.
Expiration:	Last trading day at 19:00.
Exercise:	Automatic by instruction.
Type:	American.

Settlement:	Futures.
Trading Hours:	7:20 to 14:00.
Volume—1986:	864,586 contracts.
Volume—1987:	2,250,813 contracts.

SWISS FRANC

Unit:	One IMM 125,000 Swiss franc contract.
Quotation:	US$/SF.
Minimum Fluctuation:	$.01 = $12.50.
Strike Price:	$.01 intervals.
Contract Months:	All calendar months.
Last Trading Day:	Two Fridays preceding third Wednesday of contract month.
Expiration:	Last trading day at 19:00.
Exercise:	Automatic by instruction.
Type:	American.
Settlement:	Futures.
Trading Hours:	7:20 to 14:00.
Volume—1986:	817,897 contracts.
Volume—1987:	1,053,323 contracts.

GROUP: INTEREST RATES

EURODOLLAR 90-DAY TIME DEPOSIT

Unit:	One IMM $1,000,000 Eurodollar futures contract.
Quotation:	Points of 100 percent.
Minimum Fluctuation:	$.01 = $25.00.
Strike Price:	50 cent intervals for strikes under 88.00.
	25 cent intervals for strikes above 88.00.
Contract Months:	March, June, September, December.
Last Trading Day:	Second London business day preceding third Wednesday of contract month.
Expiration:	Last trading day at 19:00.
Exercise:	Automatic by instruction.
Type:	American.
Settlement:	Cash.
Trading Hours:	7:20 to 14:00.
Volume—1986:	1,757,426 contracts.
Volume—1987:	2,569,957 contracts.

UNITED STATES 90-DAY TREASURY BILLS

Unit:	One IMM $1,000,000 90-day US Treasury bill futures contract.

Quotation:	Points of 100 percent.
Minimum Fluctuation:	$.01 = $25.00.
Strike Price:	50 cent intervals for strikes above 91.00.
	25 cent intervals for strikes below 91.00.
Contract Months:	March, June, September, December.
Last Trading Day:	Friday at least six business days preceding first business day of contract month.
Expiration:	Last trading day at 19:00.
Exercise:	Automatic by instruction.
Type:	American.
Settlement:	Futures.
Trading Hours:	7:20 to 14:00.
Volume—1986:	63,768 contracts.
Volume—1987:	11,634 contracts.

GROUP: INDEX

STANDARD & POOR'S 500 STOCK INDEX

Unit:	One IOM S&P 500 futures contract.
Quotation:	Points of index.
Minimum Fluctuation:	$.05 = $25.00.
Strike Price:	0.05 intervals.
Contract Months:	All calendar months.
Last Trading Day:	Third Thursday of contract month for March, June, September, December (quarterly).
	Third Friday of contract month for non-quarterly months.
Expiration:	Third Friday at 19:00 for quarterly months.
	Third Saturday at noon for non-quarterly months.
Exercise:	Automatic for quarterly months.
	Automatic by instruction for non-quarterly months.
Type:	American.
Settlement:	Cash for quarterly months.
	Futures for non-quarterly months.
Trading Hours:	8:30 to 15:15.
Volume—1986:	1,886,445 contracts.
Volume—1987:	1,877,295 contracts.

COFFEE, SUGAR AND COCOA EXCHANGE (CSCE)

Established: 1888
System: Open Outcry
Relationships: None

FUTURES

GROUP: SOFTS

COCOA

Unit:	Ten metric tons or 22,046 pounds.
Quotation:	US dollars per metric ton.
Minimum Fluctuation:	$1.00 = $10.00.
Contract Months:	March, May, July, September, December.
First Notice Day:	Ten business days before the 1st business day of the contract month.
Last Trading Day:	Eleven business days prior to the last business day of the contract month.
Settlement:	Physical.
Trading Hours:	9:30 to 14:15.
Volume—1986:	777,765 contracts.
Volume—1987:	895,465 contracts.

COFFEE "C"

Unit:	37,500 pounds.
Quotation:	US cents per pound.
Minimum Fluctuation:	$.01 = $3.75.
Contract Months:	March, May, July, September, December.
First Notice Day:	Seven business days before the 1st business day of the contract month.
Last Trading Day:	Eight business days prior to the last business day of the contract month.
Settlement:	Physical.
Trading Hours:	9:45 to 14:28, 14:30 closing call.
Volume—1986:	1,073,142 contracts.
Volume—1987:	964,586 contracts.

SUGAR NO. 11 (WORLD)

Unit:	50 long tons or 112,000 pounds.
Quotation:	US cents per pound.
Minimum Fluctuation:	$.01 = $11.20.
Contract Months:	January, March, May, July, September, October.

First Notice Day:	First business day after last trading day.
Last Trading Day:	Last business day of month preceding contract month.
Settlement:	Physical.
Trading Hours:	10:00 to 13:43, 13:45 closing call.
Volume—1986:	3,583,814 contracts.
Volume—1987:	3,853,499 contracts.

SUGAR NO. 14 (DOMESTIC)

Unit:	50 long tons (112,000 pounds).
Quotation:	US cents per pound.
Minimum Fluctuation:	$.01 = $11.20.
Contract Months:	January, March, May, July, September, November.
First Notice Day:	First business day after last trading day.
Last Trading Day:	Eighth calendar day of month preceding contract month.
Settlement:	Physical.
Trading Hours:	10:00 to 13:43, 13:45 closing call.
Volume—1986:	72,526 contracts.
Volume—1987:	69,928 contracts.

WORLD WHITE SUGAR

Unit:	50 metric tons.
Quotation:	US cents per ton.
Minimum Fluctuation:	$.20 = $10.00.
Contract Months:	January, March, May, July, October, traded in 18-month cycle.
First Notice Day:	First business day after last trading day.
Last Trading Day:	Fifteenth of month preceding contract month.
Settlement:	Physical.
Trading Hours:	9:45 to 13:43, 13:45 closing call.
Volume—1986:	nt
Volume—1987:	903 contracts.

GROUP: INDEX

CPI-W (Consumer Price Index for Urban Wage Earners & Clerical Workers) Base year of 1967 equals 100.

Unit:	$1000 times index.
Quotation:	Points of index.
Minimum Fluctuation:	0.01 = $10.00.

Contract Months: January, April, July, October, extending 12 months from current trading date. Contract months of January and July listed for period beyond 12 months but less than 36 months from current trading date.

First Notice Day: na

Last Trading Day: Market close on second exchange business day.

Settlement: Cash on value of CPI-W released that contract month.

Trading Hours: 9:30 to 14:30.

Volume—1986:   8,776 contracts.

Volume—1987:   2 contracts.

OPTIONS

GROUP: SOFTS

COCOA

Unit: One CSCE 10-metric-tons cocoa futures contract.

Quotation: US dollars per metric ton.

Minimum Fluctuation: $1.00 = $10.00.

Strike Price: $100 intervals for strikes below $3,600.
$200 intervals for strikes above $3,600.

Contract Months: March, May, July, September, December.

Last Trading Day: First Friday of month preceding contract month of underlying futures contract.

Expiration: Last trading day at 21:00.

Exercise: Automatic if in the money 200 basis pts.

Type: American.

Settlement: Futures.

Trading Hours: 9:30 to 15:00.

Volume—1986:   999 contracts.

Volume—1987:   13,910 contracts.

COFFEE "C"

Unit: One CSCE 37,500-pound coffee "C" futures contract.

Quotation: US cents per pound.

Minimum Fluctuation: $.01 = $3.75.
Strike Price: $.05 intervals less than 200 cents.
                         $.10 cent intervals greater than 200 cents.
Contract Months: March, May, July, September, December.
Last Trading Day: First Friday of month preceding contract month of underlying futures contract.
Expiration: Last trading day at 21:00.
Exercise: Automatic if in the money 200 basis pts.
Type: American.
Settlement: Futures.
Trading Hours: 9:45 to 14:43, 14:45 closing call.
Volume—1986:   5,319 contracts.
Volume—1987:   25,639 contracts.

SUGAR NO. 11 (WORLD)

Unit: One CSCE 50-long-tons sugar No. 11 futures contract.
Quotation: US cents per pound.
Minimum Fluctuation: $.01 = $11.20.
Strike Price: Varies.
Contract Months: January, March, May, July, September, October.
Last Trading Day: Second Friday of month before underlying futures contract expires.
Expiration: Last day of trading at 21:00.
Exercise: Automatic if in the money 200 basis pts.
Type: American.
Settlement: Futures.
Trading Hours: 9:30 to 14:30.
Volume—1986:   254,491 contracts.
Volume—1987:   432,927 contracts.

COMMODITY EXCHANGE INCORPORATED (COMEX)

Established: 1933
System: Open Outcry
Relationships: Gold is also traded on the Sydney Futures Exchange.

FUTURES

GROUP: METALS

ALUMINUM

Unit:	40,000 pounds.
Quotation:	US cents per pound.
Minimum Fluctuation:	$.0005 = $20.00.
Contract Months:	Current calendar month, next two calendar months and any February, April, June, August, October, December within 23-month period from current month.
First Notice Day:	Business day preceding contract month.
Last Trading Day:	Third to last business day on contract month.
Settlement:	Physical.
Trading Hours:	9:30 to 14:10.
Volume—1986:	52,627 contracts.
Volume—1987:	8,500 contracts.

Note: Contract size and delivery specifications will change in May 1989.

COPPER

Unit:	25,000 pounds copper.
Quotation:	US cents per pound.
Minimum Fluctuation:	$.05 = $12.50.
Contract Months:	Current calendar month, next two calendar months and any January, March, May, July, September, December within 23-month period beginning with current month.
First Notice Day:	Business day preceding contract month.
Last Trading Day:	Fourth to last business day of maturing contract month.
Settlement:	Copper.
Trading Hours:	9:25 to 14:00.
Volume—1986:	1,872,209 contracts.
Volume—1987:	2,569,178 contracts.

Note: Delivery specification changed on July 29, 1988.

GOLD

Unit:	100 troy ounces.
Quotation:	US cents per troy ounce.
Minimum Fluctuation:	$.10 = $10.00.

263

Contract Months:	Current calendar month, next two calendar months and any February, April, June, August, October, December within 23-month period from current month.
First Notice Day:	Business day preceding contract month.
Last Trading Day:	Third to last business day of contract month.
Settlement:	Gold.
Trading Hours:	9:00 to 14:30.
Volume—1986:	8,400,175 contracts.
Volume—1987:	10,239,805 contracts.

SILVER

Unit:	5000 troy ounces.
Quotation:	US cents per troy ounce.
Minimum Fluctuation:	$.001 = $5.00.
Contract Months:	Current calendar month, next two calendar months and any January, March, May, July, September, December within 23-month period from current month.
First Notice Day:	Business day preceding contract month.
Last Trading Day:	Third business day of contract month.
Settlement:	Refined silver. See COMEX regulations.
Trading Hours:	9:05 to 14:25.
Volume—1986:	3,849,687 contracts.
Volume—1987:	5,055,652 contracts.

GROUP: INDEX

MOODY'S CORPORATE BOND INDEX

Unit:	$500 times index.
Quotation:	Points of index.
Minimum Fluctuation:	0.05 = $25.00.
Contract Months:	March, June, September, December in 23-month period from current calendar month.
First Notice Day:	na
Last Trading Day:	First day of contract month on which exchange and NYSE are open for trading.
Settlement:	Cash. Index value at close.

Trading Hours:	8:20 to 15:00.
Volume—1986:	nt
Volume—1987:	11,482 contracts.

OPTIONS

GROUP: METALS

COPPER

Unit:	One COMEX 25,000-pound copper futures contract.
Quotation:	US cents per pound.
Minimum Fluctuation:	$.0005 = $12.50.
Strike Price:	$.01 intervals for strikes less than or equal to 40 cents.
	$.02 intervals for strikes 40 to 80 cents.
	$.05 intervals for strikes above 80 cents.
Contract Months:	March, May, July, September, December.
Last Trading Day:	Second Friday of month preceding contract month of underlying futures contract.
Expiration:	Last trading day at 16:00.
Exercise:	Automatic if in the money by $300.
Type:	American.
Settlement:	Futures.
Trading Hours:	9:50 to 14:00.
Volume—1986:	127,501 contracts.
Volume—1987:	612,850 contracts.

GOLD

Unit:	One COMEX 100 troy ounce gold futures contract.
Quotation:	US cents per troy ounce.
Minimum Fluctuation:	$.10 = $10.00.
Strike Price:	$10 intervals for strikes below $400.
	$20 intervals for strikes $400 to $600.
	$30 intervals for strikes $600 to $900.
	$40 intervals for strikes above $900.
Contract Months:	February, April, June, August, October, December.
Last Trading Day:	Second Friday of month preceding contract month of underlying futures contract.

Expiration:	Last trading day at 16:00.
Exercise:	Automatic if in the money by $300.
Type:	American.
Settlement:	Futures.
Trading Hours:	9:00 to 14:30.
Volume—1986:	1,646,791 contracts.
Volume—1987:	2,080,067 contracts.

SILVER

Unit:	One COMEX 5,000 troy ounce silver futures contract.
Quotation:	US cents per troy ounce.
Minimum Fluctuation:	$.001 = $5.00.
Strike Price:	$.25 intervals for strikes below $5.
	$.50 intervals for strikes $5 to $15.
	$1.00 intervals for strikes above $15.
Contract Months:	March, May, July, September, December.
Last Trading Day:	Second Friday of month preceding contract month of underlying futures contract.
Expiration:	Last trading day at 16:00.
Exercise:	Automatic if in the money by $300.
Type:	American.
Settlement:	Futures.
Trading Hours:	9:05 to 14:25.
Volume—1986:	579,425 contracts.
Volume—1987:	918,064 contracts.

KANSAS CITY BOARD OF TRADE (KCBT)

Established:	1856 (Futures 1876)
System:	Open Outcry
Relationships:	None

FUTURES

GROUP: AGRICULTURE

WHEAT (HARD RED WINTER)

Unit:	5,000 bushels.
Quotation:	US cents per bushel.
Minimum Fluctuation:	$.012 = $12.50.
Contract Months:	March, May, June, September, December.

First Notice Day:	Business day preceding contract month.
Last Trading Day:	The eighth business day preceding end of contract month.
Settlement:	Physical.
Trading Hours:	9:30 to 13:15.
Volume—1986:	744,023 contracts.
Volume—1987:	971,095 contracts.

GROUP: INDEX

VALUE LINE STOCK INDEX

Unit:	$500 times futures price.
Quotation:	Points of index.
Minimum Fluctuation:	0.05 = $25.00.
Contract Months:	March, June, September, December.
First Notice Day:	na
Last Trading Day:	Third Friday of contract month.
Settlement:	Cash.
Trading Hours:	9:00 to 15:15.
Volume—1986:	953,985 contracts.
Volume—1987:	505,551 contracts.

MINI VALUE LINE STOCK INDEX

Unit:	$100 times futures price.
Quotation:	Points of index.
Minimum Fluctuation:	0.05 = $5.00.
Contract Months:	March, June, September, December.
First Notice Day:	na
Last Trading Day:	Third Friday of contract month.
Settlement:	Cash.
Trading Hours:	9:00 to 15:15.
Volume—1986:	18,678 contracts.
Volume—1987:	28,457 contracts.

OPTIONS

GROUP: AGRICULTURE

WHEAT (HARD RED WINTER)

Unit:	One KBOT 5,000-bushel hard red winter wheat futures contract.
Quotation:	US cents per bushel.
Minimum Fluctuation:	$.012 = $6.25.
Strike Price:	$.10 intervals.
Trading Months:	March, May, July, September, December.

Last Trading Day: Friday at least 10 business days
                                  preceding first notice day of
                                  underlying futures contract at
                                  13:00.
Expiration: Saturday at 10:00.
Exercise: By instruction.
Type: American.
Settlement: Futures.
Trading Hours: 9:30 to 13:20.
Volume—1986:   18,302 contracts.
Volume—1987:   33,228 contracts.

MIDAMERICA COMMODITY EXCHANGE (MIDAM)

Established: **
System: Open Outcry
Relationships: Merged with the Chicago Board of Trade in 1987.

FUTURES

GROUP: AGRICULTURE

LIVE CATTLE

Unit: 22,000 pounds.
Quotation: US cents per pound.
Minimum Fluctuation: $0.025 = $5.00.
Contract Months: February, April, June, August, October,
                                 December.
First Notice Day: Third business day preceding first
                                 delivery day.
Last Trading Day: Twentieth calendar day of contract
                                 month.
Settlement: Physical.
Trading Hours: 9:05 to 13:15.
Volume—1986:   58,752 contracts.
Volume—1987:   44,112 contracts.

LIVE HOGS

Unit: 15,000 pounds.
Quotation: US cents per pound.
Minimum Fluctuation: $0.025 = $3.75.
Contract Months: February, April, June, July, August,
                                 September, October, December.
First Notice Day: Business day preceding 1st delivery
                                 day.
Last Trading Day: Twentieth calendar day of contract
                                 month.

268

Settlement:	Physical.
Trading Hours:	9:10 to 13:15.
Volume—1986:	80,818 contracts.
Volume—1987:	44,364 contracts.

CORN

Unit:	1,000 bushels.
Quotation:	US cents per bushel.
Minimum Fluctuation:	$.0125 = $6.25.
Contract Months:	March, May, July, September, December.
First Notice Day:	Last business day of previous month.
Last Trading Day:	The eighth last business day of contract month.
Settlement:	Physical.
Trading Hours:	9:30 to 13:30.
Volume—1986:	406,694 contracts.
Volume—1987:	311,722 contracts.

OATS

Unit:	1,000 bushels.
Quotation:	US cents per bushel.
Minimum Fluctuation:	$.0125 = $6.25.
Contract Months:	March, May, July, September, December.
First Notice Day:	Last business day of previous month.
Last Trading Day:	The eighth last business day of contract month.
Settlement:	Physical.
Trading Hours:	9:30 to 13:30.
Volume—1986:	2,169 contracts.
Volume—1987:	6,958 contracts.

SOYBEANS

Unit:	1,000 bushels.
Quotation:	US cents per bushel.
Minimum Fluctuation:	$.0125 = $6.25.
Contract Months:	January, March, May, July, August, September, November.
First Notice Day:	Last business day of previous month.
Last Trading Day:	The eighth last business day of contract month.
Settlement:	Physical.
Hours:	9:30 to 13:30.
Volume—1986:	680,156 contracts.
Volume—1987:	417,620 contracts.

SOYBEAN MEAL

Unit:	20 tons.
Quotation:	US cents per ton.
Minimum Fluctuation:	$.10 = $2.00.
Contract Months:	January, March, May, July, August, September, October, December.
First Notice Day:	na
Last Trading Day:	Eighth to last business day of contract month.
Settlement:	Cash.
Trading Hours:	9:30 to 13:30.
Volume—1986:	2,256 contracts.
Volume—1987:	3,191 contracts.

WHEAT (SOFT WINTER)

Unit:	1,000 bushels.
Quotation:	US cents per bushel.
Minimum Fluctuation:	$.0125 = $6.50.
Contract Months:	March, May, July, September, December.
First Notice Day:	Last business day of previous month.
Last Trading Day:	Eighth to last business day of contract month.
Settlement:	Physical.
Trading Hours:	9:30 to 13:30.
Volume—1986:	344,749 contracts.
Volume—1987:	189,610 contracts.

ROUGH RICE—CRCE

Unit:	2,000 cwt. U.S. No. 2 Long Grain Rough Rice.
Quotation:	US cents per cwt.
Minimum Fluctuation:	$0.0005 = $10.00.
Contract Months:	January, March, May, September, November.
First Notice Day:	Last business day of previous month.
Last Trading Day:	Eighth to last business day of contract month.
Settlement:	Physical.
Trading Hours:	9:15 to 13:30.
Volume—1986:	3,095 contracts.
Volume—1987:	31,114 contracts.

GROUP: METALS

NEW YORK GOLD

Unit:	33.2 troy ounces.
Quotation:	US cents per troy ounce.
Minimum Fluctuation:	$.10 = $3.32.
Contract Months:	Monthly.
First Notice Day:	Last business day of previous month.
Last Trading Day:	Third to last business day of contract month.
Settlement:	Physical.
Trading Hours:	8:00 to 13:40.
Volume—1986:	21,111 contracts.
Volume—1987:	17,957 contracts.

NEW YORK SILVER

Unit:	1,000 troy ounces.
Quotation:	US cents per troy ounce.
Minimum Fluctuation:	$.001 = $1.00.
Contract Months:	Monthly.
First Notice Day:	Last business day of previous month.
Last Trading Day:	Third to last business day of contract month.
Settlement:	Physical.
Trading Hours:	8:05 to 13:40.
Volume—1986:	9,342 contracts.
Volume—1987:	9,578 contracts.

PLATINUM

Unit:	25 troy ounces.
Quotation:	US cents per troy ounce.
Minimum Fluctuation:	$.10 = $2.50.
Contract Months:	Current month and January, April, July, October.
First Notice Day:	First business day of contract month.
Last Trading Day:	Fourth to last business day of contract month.
Settlement:	Physical.
Trading Hours:	8:00 to 13:40.
Volume—1986:	5,944 contracts.
Volume—1987:	4,342 contracts.

GROUP: CURRENCIES

BRITISH POUND

Unit:	12,500 pounds.
Quotation:	US$/BP.

Minimum Fluctuation:	$0.0005 = $6.25.
Contract Months:	March, June, September, December.
First Notice Day:	Two business days preceding third Wednesday of contract month.
Last Trading Day:	Same as First Notice Day.
Settlement:	Physical.
Trading Hours:	7:20 to 13:34.
Volume—1986:	17,270 contracts.
Volume—1987:	10,979 contracts.

CANADIAN DOLLAR

Unit:	50,000 Canadian dollars.
Quotation:	US$/CD.
Minimum Fluctuation:	$0.0001 = $6.25.
Contract Months:	March, June, September, December.
First Notice Day:	Two business days preceding third Wednesday of contract month.
Last Trading Day:	Same as First Notice Day.
Settlement:	Physical.
Trading Hours:	7:20 to 13:36.
Volume—1986:	6,150 contracts.
Volume—1987:	7,749 contracts.

DEUTSCHE MARK

Unit:	62,500 Deutsche marks.
Quotation:	US$/DM.
Minimum Fluctuation:	$0.0001 = $6.25.
Contract Months:	March, June, September, December.
First Notice Day:	Two business days preceding third Wednesday of contract month.
Last Trading Day:	Same as First Notice Day.
Settlement:	Physical.
Trading Hours:	7:20 to 13:30.
Volume—1986:	74,662 contracts.
Volume—1987:	85,009 contracts.

JAPANESE YEN

Unit:	6,250,000 yen.
Quotation:	US$/JY.
Minimum Fluctuation:	$0.000001 = $6.25.
Contract Months:	March, June, September, December.
First Notice Day:	Two business days preceding third Wednesday of contract month.
Last Trading Day:	Same as First Notice Day.
Settlement:	Physical.

Trading Hours:	7:20 to 13:32.
Volume—1986:	47,601 contracts.
Volume—1987:	58,836 contracts.

SWISS FRANC

Unit:	62,500 francs.
Quotation:	US$/SF.
Minimum Fluctuation:	$0.0001 = $6.25.
Contract Months:	March, June, September, December.
First Notice Day:	Two business days preceding third Wednesday of contract month.
Last Trading Day:	Same as First Notice Day.
Settlement:	Physical.
Trading Hours:	7:20 to 13:36.
Volume—1986:	102,019 contracts.
Volume—1987:	97,571 contracts.

GROUP: INTEREST RATES

UNITED STATES 90-DAY TREASURY BILLS

Unit:	$500,000 principal.
Quotation:	Percent of par in basis points.
Minimum Fluctuation:	0.01 = $12.50.
Contract Months:	March, June, September, December.
First Notice Day:	na
Last Trading Day:	Business day preceding issue date of contract month.
Settlement:	Cash.
Trading Hours:	7:20 to 14:15.
Volume—1986:	34,690 contracts.
Volume—1987:	25,592 contracts.

UNITED STATES TREASURY BONDS

Unit:	$50,000 principal.
Quotation:	Percent of par in basis points.
Minimum Fluctuation:	$\frac{1}{32}$ = $15.625.
Contract Months:	February, March, May, June, August, September, November, December.
First Notice Day:	Last business day of previous month.
Last Trading Day:	Eighth to last business day of contract month.
Settlement:	Physical.
Trading Hours:	8:00 to 14:15.
Volume—1986:	467,639 contracts.
Volume—1987:	1,015,454 contracts.

OPTIONS

GROUP: AGRICULTURE

SOYBEANS

Unit:	One MidAm 1,000-bushel soybean futures contract.
Quotation:	US cents per bushel.
Minimum Fluctuation:	$.0125 = $1.00.
Strike Price:	$.25 intervals.
Contract Months:	January, March, May, July, August, September, November.
Last Trading Day:	Last Friday at least 10 business days before first notice day of underlying soybean futures contract.
Expiration:	Saturday at 10:00.
Exercise:	Automatic if in the money by 0.30.
Type:	American.
Settlement:	Future.
Trading Hours:	9:30 to 13:30.
Volume—1986:	6,635 contracts.
Volume—1987:	12,317 contracts.

WHEAT (SOFT WINTER)

Unit:	One MidAm 1,000-bushel wheat futures contract.
Quotation:	US cents per bushel.
Minimum Fluctuation:	$.0125 = $1.00.
Strike Price:	$.10 intervals.
Contract Months:	March, May, July, September, December.
Last Trading Day:	Last Friday at least 10 business days preceding first notice day of underlying futures contract.
Expiration:	Saturday at 10:00.
Exercise:	Automatic if in the money by 0.20.
Type:	American.
Settlement:	Future.
Trading Hours:	9:30 to 13:30.
Volume—1986:	7,492 contracts.
Volume—1987:	530 contracts.

GROUP: METALS

GOLD

Unit:	One MidAm 33.2-ounce gold futures contract.
Quotation:	US cents per troy ounce.
Minimum Fluctuation:	$0.025 = $2.50.
Strike Price:	$10 intervals for strikes under $300.
	$20 intervals for strikes $300 to $500.
	$30 intervals for strikes $500 to $800.
	$40 intervals for strikes above $800.
Contract Months:	February, April, June, August, October, December.
Last Trading Day:	Friday, five business days preceding first notice day for underlying futures contract.
Expiration:	Saturday at 10:00.
Exercise:	Automatic if in the money by $25.00.
Type:	American.
Settlement:	Future.
Trading Hours:	8:00 to 13:40.
Volume—1986:	91 contracts.
Volume—1987:	74 contracts.

MINNEAPOLIS GRAIN EXCHANGE (MGE)

Established:	1881
System:	Open Outcry
Relationships:	None

FUTURES

GROUP: AGRICULTURE

WHEAT (HARD RED SPRING)

Unit:	5,000 bushels hard red spring wheat.
Quotation:	Cents and quarter-cents per bushel.
Minimum Fluctuation:	$.012 = $6.25.
Contract Months:	September, December, March, May, July.
First Notice Day:	Last business day of month preceding contract month.
Last Trading Day:	Eighth to last business day of contract month.
Settlement:	Physical.
Trading Hours:	9:30 to 13:15.

Volume—1986:	283,900 contracts.
Volume—1987:	310,599 contracts.

HIGH FRUCTOSE CORN SYRUP

Unit:	48,000 pounds high fructose corn syrup.
Quotation:	Cents per cwt.
Minimum Fluctuation:	$.01 = $4.80.
Contract Months:	March, May, July, September, December.
First Notice Day:	Last business day of month preceding contract month.
Last Trading Day:	Eighth to last business day of contract month at noon.
Settlement:	Physical.
Trading Hours:	9:00 to 13:25.
Volume—1986:	nt
Volume—1987:	5,963 contracts.

WHITE WHEAT

Unit:	5,000 bushels.
Quotation:	Cents and quarter cents per bushel.
Minimum Fluctuation:	$.25 = $12.50.
Contract Months:	September, December, March, May, July.
First Notice Day:	Last business day of month preceding contract month.
Last Trading Day:	Eighth to last business day of contract month.
Settlement:	Physical.
Trading Hours:	9:30 to 13:15.
Volume—1986:	686 contracts.
Volume—1987:	1,415 contracts.

OPTIONS

GROUP: AGRICULTURE

WHEAT (HARD RED SPRING)

Unit:	One MGE 5,000-bushel futures contract.
Quotation:	Cents and eighth cents per bushel.
Minimum Fluctuation:	$.012 = $6.25.
Strike Price:	$.10 intervals.
Contract Months:	September, December, March, May, July.

Last Trading Day:	First Friday at least 10 business days preceding first notice day of underlying futures contract at 13:00.
Expiration:	Saturday at 10:00.
Exercise:	By Instruction.
Type:	American.
Settlement:	Future.
Trading Hours:	9:30 to 13:15.
Volume—1986:	3,259 contracts.
Volume—1987:	1,229 contracts.

NEW YORK COTTON EXCHANGE (NYCE)

Established:	1870
System:	Open Outcry
Relationships:	Affiliate, The New York Futures Exchange
	The Citrus Associates

FUTURES

GROUP: SOFTS

FROZEN CONCENTRATE ORANGE JUICE (FCOJ)

Unit:	15,000 pounds orange solids.
Quotation:	Cents and hundredths of cent per pound.
Minimum Fluctuation:	$.05 = $7.50.
Contract Months:	January, March, May, July, September, November.
First Notice Day:	First business day of contract month.
Last Trading Day:	Ninth business day preceding last delivery day.
Settlement:	Physical.
Trading Hours:	10:15 to 14:45.
Volume—1986:	211,543 contracts.
Volume—1987:	266,641 contracts.

COTTON NO. 2

Unit:	50,000 pounds net weight (approximately 100 bales).
Quotation:	Cents and hundredths of cent.
Minimum Fluctuation:	$.01 = $5.00.
Contract Months:	Current month and 17 succeeding months. Active: March, May, July, October, December.

First Notice Day: Five business days from end of contract month to preceding spot month.

Last Trading Day: 17 business days from end of spot month.

Settlement: Physical.

Trading Hours: 10:30 to 15:00.

Volume—1986: 1,015,392 contracts.

Volume—1987: 1,395,980 contracts.

GROUP: CURRENCIES

EUROPEAN CURRENCY UNIT (ECU)

Size: 100,000 European currency units.

Quotation: US$/ECU.

Minimum Fluctuation: 0.01 = $10.00.

Contract Months: March, June, September, December.

First Notice Day: na

Last Trading Day: Three business days preceding third Thursday of contract month.

Settlement: Physical.

Trading Hours: 8:20 to 14:40.

Volume—1986: 72,195 contracts.

Volume—1987: 42,198 contracts.

GROUP: INTEREST RATES

UNITED STATES FIVE-YEAR TREASURY NOTE (FYTR™)

Unit: $100,000 principal.

Quotation: One sixty-fourth of a point.
64 basis points equals one note point.

Minimum Fluctuation: $\frac{1}{64}$ = $15.625.

Contract Months: March, June, September, December.

First Notice Day: First business day preceding first delivery day.

Last Trading Day: Seven business days preceding last business day of expiring month at 13:00.

Settlement: Physical.

Trading Hours: 9:00 to 15:00.

Volume—1986: nt

Volume—1987: 383,613 contracts (began 6 May 1987).

GROUP: INDEX

UNITED STATES DOLLAR INDEX

Unit: $500 times US dollar index.

Quotation: Percentage of value as of March, 1973
                             to two decimal points.
Minimum Fluctuation: 0.01 = $5.00.
Contract Months: March, June, September, December.
First Notice Day: na
Last Trading Day: Third Wednesday of expiring contract
                             month.
Settlement: Cash.
Trading Hours: 8:20 to 14:40.
Volume—1986:   166,494 contracts.
Volume—1987:   403,783 contracts.

OPTIONS

GROUP: SOFTS

FROZEN CONCENTRATE ORANGE JUICE (FCOJ)
Unit: One 15,000-pounds FCOJ futures
                             contract.
Quotation: Cents and hundredth-cents.
Minimum Fluctuation: $.005 = $7.50.
Strike Price: $2.50 intervals.
Contract Months: January, March, May, July, September,
                             November.
Last Trading Day: First Friday of month preceding
                             futures contract month.
Expiration: Saturday at 12:00.
Exercise: By Instruction.
Type: American.
Settlement: Future.
Trading Hours: 10:15 to 14:45.
Volume—1986:   3,354 contracts.
Volume—1987:   685 contracts.

COTTON NO. 2
Unit: One NYCE 50,000-pounds cotton
                             futures contract.
Quotation: Cents and hundredths of a cent.
Minimum Fluctuation: $.01 = $5.00.
Strike Price: $.01 intervals for strikes below 0.74.
                             $.02 intervals for strikes above 0.75.
Contract Months: March, May, July, October, December.
Last Trading Day: First Friday of month preceding
                             contract month.
Expiration: Saturday at 12:00.

Exercise:	By instruction.
Type:	American.
Settlement:	Future.
Trading Hours:	10:30 to 15:00.
Volume—1986:	60,507 contracts.
Volume—1987:	73,480 contracts.

GROUP: INDEX

UNITED STATES DOLLAR INDEX

Unit:	One NYCE US dollar index futures contract.
Quotation:	Points and hundredths of a point.
Minimum Fluctuation:	$.01 = $5.00.
Strike Price:	0.02 intervals.
Contract Months:	March, June, September, December.
Last Trading Day:	Two Fridays preceding third Wednesday of expiring contract month.
Expiration:	Saturday after last trading day at noon.
Exercise:	Last trading day at 17:00.
Type:	American.
Settlement:	Future.
Trading Hours:	8:20 to 14:40.
Volume—1986:	198 contracts (began 3 September 1986).
Volume—1987:	14,538 contracts.

FIVE YEAR US TREASURY NOTE (FYTR®)

Unit:	$100,000 principal.
Quotation:	$\frac{1}{64}$ of a note point. 64 basis points equals one note point.
Minimum Fluctuation:	$\frac{1}{64}$ = $15.625.
Strike Price:	Intervals of $\frac{1}{2}$ of one futures point.
Contract Months:	March, June, September, December.
Last Trading Day:	Friday, at least 5 business days prior to the first business day of the expiring month.
Expiration:	Last trading day at 17:00.
Exercise:	By instruction.
Type:	American.
Settlement:	Future.
Trading Hours:	8:20 to 15:00.
Volume:	nt
Volume:	nt

NEW YORK FUTURES EXCHANGE (NYFE)

Established: 1980
System: Open Outcry
Relationships: None

FUTURES

GROUP: INDEX

COMMODITY RESEARCH BUREAU'S (CRB) FUTURES PRICE INDEX

Unit:	$500 times index.
Quotation:	Percentage of points per index.
Minimum Fluctuation:	0.05 = $25.00.
Contract Months:	March, May, July, September, December. Four months listed at all times.
First Notice Day:	na
Last Trading Day:	Third Friday of contract month at 15:30.
Settlement:	Cash.
Trading Hours:	9:00 to 15:30.
Volume—1986:	59,324 contracts.
Volume—1987:	136,832 contracts.

NEW YORK STOCK EXCHANGE COMPOSITE STOCK INDEX

Unit:	$500 times NYSE Stock Index futures.
Quotation:	Index points.
Minimum Fluctuation:	0.05 = $25.00.
Contract Months:	March, June, September, December.
First Notice Day:	na
Last Trading Day:	Third Friday of contract month or preceding, if not a business day.
Settlement:	Cash.
Trading Hours:	9:30 to 16:15.
Volume—1986:	3,123,668 contracts.
Volume—1987:	2,915,915 contracts.

RUSSELL 2000 INDEX

Unit:	$500 times Russell Stock Index.
Quotation:	Index points.
Minimum Fluctuation:	0.05 = $25.00.
Contract Months:	March, June, September, December. Four months traded at all times.
First Notice Day:	na
Last Trading Day:	Third Friday of contract month or preceding, if not a business day.

Settlement:	Cash.
Trading Hours:	9:15 to 16:10.
Volume—1986:	nt
Volume—1987:	5,644 contracts.

RUSSELL 3000 INDEX

Unit:	$500 times Russell Stock Index.
Quotation:	Index points.
Minimum Fluctuation:	0.05 of a point.
Contract Months:	March, June, September, December.
First Notice Day:	na
Last Trading Day:	Third Friday of contract month or preceding, if not a business day.
Settlement:	Cash.
Trading Hours:	9:15 to 16:10.
Volume—1986:	nt
Volume—1987:	10,734 contracts.

OPTIONS

GROUP: INDEX

NYSE COMPOSITE STOCK INDEX

Unit:	One NYSE composite index futures contract.
Quotation:	Points and one one-hundredths of a point.
Minimum Fluctuation:	0.05 = $.25.
Strike Price:	Two hundred point (2.00) intervals.
Contract Months:	March, June, September, December.
Last Trading Day:	Last trading day of underlying futures contract.
Expiration:	Last trading day at 18:00.
Exercise:	Automatic.
Type:	American.
Settlement:	Future.
Trading Hours:	9:30 to 16:15.
Volume—1986:	296,303 contracts.
Volume—1987:	206,631 contracts.

NEW YORK MERCANTILE EXCHANGE (NYME)

Established:	1884
System:	Open Outcry
Relationships:	None

FUTURES

GROUP: METALS

PALLADIUM

Unit:	100 troy ounces.
Quotation:	U.S. dollars and cents per troy ounce.
Minimum Fluctuation:	$.05 = $5.00.
Contract Months:	March, June, September, December. Trading conducted over 15 months commencing with current month and next two consecutive months before moving into quarterly cycle.
First Notice Day:	Last business day prior contract month.
Last Trading Day:	Four business days prior end of contract month.
Settlement:	Physical.
Trading Hours:	8:50 to 14:20.
Volume—1986:	145,562 contracts.
Volume—1987:	160,284 contracts.

PLATINUM

Unit:	50 troy ounces.
Quotation:	U.S. dollars and cents per troy ounce.
Minimum Fluctuation:	$.10 = $5.00.
Contract Months:	January, April, July, October. Trading conducted over 15 months commencing with current month and next two consecutive months before moving into quarterly cycle.
First Notice Day:	Last business day prior contract month.
Last Trading Day:	Four business days prior end of contract month.
Settlement:	Physical.
Trading Hours:	9:00 to 14:30.
Volume—1986:	1,624,635 contracts.
Volume—1987:	1,361,546 contracts.

GROUP: ENERGY

CRUDE OIL

Unit:	1,000 U.S. barrels (42,000 gallons).
Quotation:	Dollars and cents per barrel.
Minimum Fluctuation:	$.01 = $10.00.

Contract Months:	18 consecutive months with current month.
First Notice Day:	First day after last trading day.
Last Trading Day:	Third business day prior to 25th calendar day.
Settlement:	Physical.
Trading Hours:	9:45 to 15:10.
Volume—1986:	8,313,529 contracts.
Volume—1987:	14,581,614 contracts.

NO. 2 HEATING OIL

Unit:	1,000 US barrels (42,000 gallons).
Quotation:	Dollars and cents per gallon.
Minimum Fluctuation:	$.01 = $4.20.
Contract Months:	18 consecutive months with current calendar month.
First Notice Day:	First day after last trading day.
Last Trading Day:	Last business day of month preceding contract month.
Settlement:	Physical.
Trading Hours:	9:50 to 15:05.
Volume—1986:	3,275,044 contracts.
Volume—1987:	4,293,395 contracts.

PROPANE

Unit:	42,000 U.S. gallons (1,000 barrels).
Quotation:	Dollars and cents per gallon.
Minimum Fluctuation:	$.01 = $4.20.
Contract Months:	18 consecutive months with current calendar month.
First Notice Day:	First day after last trading day.
Last Trading Day:	Last business day of month preceding contract month.
Settlement:	Physical.
Trading Hours:	9:40 to 15:05.
Volume—1986:	nt
Volume—1987:	15,312 contracts.

OPTIONS

GROUP: METALS

CRUDE OIL

Unit:	One NYMEX 1,000 US barrels crude oil futures contract.
Quotation:	Dollars and cents per barrel.
Minimum Fluctuation:	$.01 = $10.00.

Strike Price:	$1.00 intervals.
Contract Months:	Six consecutive months.
Last Trading Day:	Second Friday of month preceding contract month of underlying.
Expiration:	Last trading day at 16:30.
Exercise:	Automatic if in the money $300.
Type:	American.
Settlement:	Future.
Trading Hours:	9:45 to 15:10.
Volume—1986:	135,266 contracts.
Volume—1987:	3,117,037 contracts.

NO. 2 HEATING OIL

Unit:	One NYMEX 42,000 US gallons heating oil futures contract.
Quotation:	Dollars and cents per gallon.
Minimum Fluctuation:	$.01 = $4.20.
Strike Price:	$.02 intervals.
Contract Months:	Six consecutive months.
Last Trading Day:	Second Friday of month preceding contract month of underlying futures contract.
Expiration:	Last trading day at 16:30.
Exercise:	Automatic if in the money $300.
Type:	American.
Settlement:	Future.
Trading Hours:	9:50 to 15:05.
Volume—1986:	nt
Volume—1987:	143,605 contracts.

NEW YORK STOCK EXCHANGE (NYSE)

Established:	1983, Index option.
System:	Specialist
Relationships:	None

OPTIONS

GROUP: INDEX

NYSE COMPOSITE INDEX

Unit:	$100 times index.
Quotation:	Index points.
Minimum Fluctuation:	$\frac{1}{16}$ point = $6.25.
Strike Price:	Five point intervals.
Contract Months:	Next three months.

Last Trading Day:	Third Thursday.
Expiration:	Last trading day at 16:15.
Exercise:	Automatic if in the money ¼ pt.
Type:	American.
Settlement:	Cash.
Trading Hours:	9:30 to 16:15.
Volume—1986:	2,749,705 contracts.
Volume—1987:	2,047,075 contracts.

PACIFIC STOCK EXCHANGE (PSE)

Established:	1957
System:	Order Book Official/Market Maker
Relationships:	None

OPTIONS

GROUP: INDEX

FINANCIAL NEWS COMPOSITE INDEX (FNCI)

Unit:	$100 times index.
Quotation:	Index points.
Minimum Fluctuation:	—
Strike Price:	Five-point intervals.
Contract Months:	Four consecutive months.
Last Trading Day:	Third Friday of contract month.
Expiration:	Last trading day at 13:15.
Exercise:	Automatic if in the money by ¾ point.
Type:	European.
Settlement:	Cash.
Trading Hours:	6:30 to 13:15.
Volume—1986:	nt
Volume—1987:	(began November 1987)

PHILADELPHIA STOCK EXCHANGE (PHLX)

Established:	1790
System:	Open Outcry
Relationships:	None

OPTIONS

GROUP: CURRENCIES

AUSTRALIAN DOLLAR

Unit:	50,000 Australian dollars.
Quotation:	US$/AD.

Minimum Fluctuation:	.0001 = $5.00.
Strike Price:	One cent intervals.
Contract Months:	March, June, September, December, plus next two months.
Last Trading Day:	Friday preceding third Wednesday.
Expiration:	Last trading day.
Exercise:	By instruction preceding LTD.
Type:	American & European.
Settlement:	Physical.
Trading Hours:	8:00 to 14:30.
	19:00 to 23:00.
Volume—1986:	nt
Volume—1987:	268,345 contracts.

BRITISH POUND

Unit:	12,500 British pounds.
Quotation:	US$/BP.
Minimum Fluctuation:	.0005 = $6.25.
Strike Price:	Five cent intervals.
Contract Months:	March, June, September, December, plus next two months.
Last Trading Day:	Friday preceding third Wednesday.
Expiration:	Last trading day.
Exercise:	By instruction preceding LTD.
Type:	American & European.
Settlement:	Physical.
Trading Hours:	8:00 to 14:30.
Volume—1986:	967,505 contracts.
Volume—1987:	1,880,469 contracts.

CANADIAN DOLLAR

Unit:	50,000 Canadian dollars.
Quotation:	US$/CD.
Minimum Fluctuation:	.0001 = $5.00.
Strike Price:	One cent intervals.
Contract Months:	March, June, September, December, plus next two months.
Last Trading Day:	Friday preceding third Wednesday.
Expiration:	Last trading day.
Exercise:	By instruction preceding LTD.
Type:	American & European.
Settlement:	Physical.
Trading Hours:	8:00 to 14:30.
Volume—1986:	170,305 contracts.
Volume—1987:	208,151 contracts.

DEUTSCHE MARK

Unit:	62,500 Deutsche marks.
Quotation:	US$/DM.
Minimum Fluctuation:	.0001 = $6.25.
Strike Price:	One cent intervals.
Contract Months:	March, June, September, December, plus next two months.
Last Trading Day:	Friday preceding third Wednesday.
Expiration:	Last trading day.
Exercise:	By instruction preceding LTD.
Type:	American & European.
Settlement:	Physical.
Trading Hours:	8:00 to 14:30.
	19:00 to 23:00.
Volume—1986:	2,487,037 contracts.
Volume—1987:	4,263,942 contracts.

FRENCH FRANC

Unit:	125,000 French francs.
Quotation:	US$/FF.
Minimum Fluctuation:	.00005 = $6.25.
Strike Price:	One-half cent (.005) intervals.
Contract Months:	March, June, September, December, plus next two months.
Last Trading Day:	Friday preceding third Wednesday.
Expiration:	Last trading day.
Exercise:	By instruction preceding LTD.
Type:	American & European.
Settlement:	Physical.
Trading Hours:	8:00 to 14:30.
Volume—1986:	45,248 contracts.
Volume—1987:	81,305 contracts.

JAPANESE YEN

Unit:	6,250,000 Japanese yen.
Quotation:	US$/JY.
Minimum Fluctuation:	.000001 = $6.25.
Strike Price:	.01 cent intervals.
Contract Months:	March, June, September, December, plus next two months.
Last Trading Day:	Friday preceding third Wednesday.
Expiration:	Last trading day.
Exercise:	By instruction preceding LTD.
Type:	American & European.
Settlement:	Physical.

Trading Hours:	8:00 to 14:30.
	19:00 to 23:00.
Volume—1986:	1,885,026 contracts.
Volume—1987:	2,465,026 contracts.

SWISS FRANC

Unit:	62,500 Swiss francs.
Quotation:	US$/SF.
Minimum Fluctuation:	.0001 = $6.25.
Strike Price:	One-cent intervals.
Contract Months:	March, June, September, December, plus next two months.
Last Trading Day:	Friday preceding third Wednesday.
Expiration:	Last trading day.
Exercise:	By instruction preceding LTD.
Type:	American & European.
Settlement:	Physical.
Trading Hours:	8:00 to 14:30.
Volume—1986:	2,337,287 contracts.
Volume—1987:	1,316,500 contracts.

EUROPEAN CURRENCY UNIT (ECU)

Unit:	62,500 European currency units.
Quotation:	US$/ECU.
Minimum Fluctuation:	.0001 = $6.25.
Strike Price:	Two cent intervals.
Contract Months:	March, June, September, December, plus next two months.
Last Trading Day:	Friday preceding third Wednesday.
Expiration:	Last trading day.
Exercise:	By instruction preceding LTD.
Type:	American & European.
Settlement:	Physical.
Trading Hours:	8:00 to 14:30.
Volume—1986:	12,831 contracts.
Volume—1987:	1,892 contracts.

GROUP: INDEX

VALUE LINE INDEX

Unit:	$100 times index.
Quotation:	Index points.
Minimum Fluctuation:	$\frac{1}{16}$ = $6.25.
Strike Price:	Five-point intervals.
Contract Months:	March, June, September, December, plus next two months.

Last Trading Day:	Third Friday.
Expiration:	Last trading day.
Exercise:	By instruction.
Type:	European.
Settlement:	Cash.
Trading Hours:	9:30 to 16:15.
Volume—1986:	1,236,174 contracts.
Volume—1987:	84,427 contracts.

9

International Holidays

1989 HOLIDAYS

	AUS	CAN	FRA	GB	HK	JAP	NZ	USA	
JAN	2	2	2	2	2	2	2	2	NEW YEARS
						15			ADULTS DAY
								16	MLKING DAY
	26								AUSTRALIA DAY
FEB							6		WAITANGI DAY
					6				LUNAR NEW YEAR
						11			NATIONAL FD DAY
								20	PRESIDENTS DAY
MAR						20			EQUINOX
	24	24	24	24	24		24	24	GOOD FRIDAY
	27	27			27		27		EASTER MONDAY
APR	25						25		ANZAC DAY
MAY			1						MAY DAY
						5			CHILDREN'S DAY
		22							VICTORIA DAY
								29	MEMORIAL DAY

291

	AUS	CAN	FRA	GB	HK	JAP	NZ	USA	
JUN							5		QUEEN'S BIRTHDAY
	12								QUEEN'S BIRTHDAY
					19				QUEEN'S BIRTHDAY
JUL		1							CANADA DAY
								4	INDEPENDENCE DAY
AUG			15						ASSUMPTION DAY
					28				LIBERATION DAY
				31					SUMMER HOLIDAY
SEPT		4						4	LABOR DAY
						15			RESPECT THE AGED
					15				CHINESE MIDAUTUMN
						16			EQUINOX
OCT		9							THANKSGIVING DAY
								9	COLUMBUS DAY
					9				CHUNG YEUNG FESTIVAL
						10			PHYSICAL CULTURE
							23		LABOR DAY
NOV			1						ALL SAINTS DAY
								30	THANKSGIVING DAY
DEC	25	25	25	25	25		25	25	CHRISTMAS DAY
	26	26		26	26		26		BOXING DAY

Note: Religious Holidays, Bank Holidays, and major Conventions occur when Exchanges are open and may affect trading liquidity.

Bibliography

Aftalion, Florin and Poncet, Patrice. *Le MATIF (Le Marche a Terme D'Instruements Financiers)*, 2nd ed., Paris: Presses Universitaires de France, 1987.

Alchien, Armin S. and Demsetz, Harold. "The Property Rights Paradigm," *The Journal of Economic History* 33 (1) (March 1973): 24–27.

The Globalization of the International Financial Markets: Implications and Opportunities, Arthur Andersen, March, 1988.

Anderson, Ronald W., ed. *The Industrial Organization of Futures Markets.* Lexington, MA: Lexington Books. 1984.

Andreas, A.T. *History of Chicago*, 3 vols. (Chicago: A.T. Andreas Company, Publishers, 1885), 1:581.

Baer, G. and Saxon, O.G. *Commodity Exchanges and Futures Trading* (NY: 1949) 130–31.

Baer, Julius Bernard, 1881 – *Commodity Exchanges and Futures Trading; Principles & Operating Methods* (NY: Harper) 1949.

Bakken, Henry H. "Futures Trading—Origin, Development and Present Economic Status," in E.A. Gaumnitz, ed. *Futures Trading Seminar: A Commodity Marketing Forum for College Teachers of Economics*, vol. 3 (Madison, Wisconsin: 1966) 1–13.

Black, Deborah. *Success and Failure of Futures Contracts: Theory & Empirical Evidence.* NY: Saloman Brothers Center for Study of Financial Instruments. Graduate School of Business, New York University, 1986.

Brown, Brendan, and Geisst, Charles R. *Financial Futures Markets.* NY: St. Martin's Press, 1983.

SIMEX and the Globalization of Financial Futures, Times Books International (Kifford Press), pp. 50–59.

Clearing Directory and Handbook. Washington: FIA (Annual).

Colbert, Elias. *Chicago Historical and Statistical Sketch of the Garden City* (Chicago: P.T. Sherlock, 1868) pp. 47–52.

Customer Account Protection Study. National Futures Association, November 20, 1986.

"The Financial Safeguard System of the Chicago Mercantile Exchange," Chicago Mercantile Exchange, April 1988.

Demsetz, Harold. "The Cost of Transacting," *The Quarterly Journal of Economics*, 82 (1) (February 1960): 40–46.

Demsetz, Harold. "The Exchange and Enforcement of Property Rights," *The Journal of Law and Economics* 7 (October 1964): 16–19.

Dowling, S. W. *The Exchanges of London.* London: 1929.

Factors Relating to the Feasibility of a Singapore-Based Financial Futures Market, Continental Illinois National Bank of Chicago, prepared for the Chicago Mercantile Exchange, 1981.

Friedman, Milton. *The Need for Futures Markets in Currencies*, December 20, 1971. Prepared for the Chicago Mercantile Exchange.

Fulscher, Mitchell. *Seminar Presentation for the Chicago Mercantile Exchange*, June, 1988, Tokyo, Japan.

Futures Trading, Market Interrelationships & Industry Structure. Chicago: Program in Law & Economics, University of Chicago Law School, 1983. (ICU# 84-610-842)

Gale, Edwin O. *Reminiscences of Early Chicago and Vicinity* (Chicago: Fleming H. Revell, 1902), pp. 260–61.

Grabbe, Orlin, Jr. *International Financial Markets*, NY: Elsevier, 1986.

Gregory, Owen K. "The Early History of the Chicago Board of Trade: A Study of Institutional Development." *International Futures Trading Seminar Proceeding*, Vol. VI. Chicago: 1979, pp. 166–176.

ICCH Commodities and Financial Futures Yearbook. London: Landell Mills Commodities Studies, Ltd., 1984.

Irwin, Harold S. *Evolution of Futures Trading.* Madison, Wisconsin: 1954.

Kubarych, Roger M. *Foreign Exchange Markets in the United States*, Revised Edition. NY: Federal Reserve Bank of New York.

Leuthold, Junkus, Cordier. *The Theory and Practice of Futures Markets*, To be published by Lexington Books, Lexington, MA: 1988.

Lurie, Jonathan. *The CBOT 1859–1905, The Dynamics of Self-Regulation.* Urbana, IL: University of Illinois Press, 1979.

Markham, Jerry W. *The History of Commodity Futures Trading and Its Regulation.* NY: Praeger, 1987.

M.C. Brackenbury & Co., *Dealing on the London Metal Exchange and Commodity Markets.* NY: Nichols, 1976.

Mutual Offset System: Simex, Chicago Mercantile Exchange, 1984.

Nicholas, David. *Commodities Futures Trading: A Guide to Information Sources and Computerized Services.* London: Mansell, 1985.

Paul, Allen B. "Past and Future of the Commodities Exchanges," *Agricultural History*, pp. 287–305.

Pierce, Bessie Louise. *History of Chicago*, 3 vols. (NY: Alfred A. Knopf, 1937) 1:129–31.

Powers, Mark. *Computerized Trading—A Framework for Analysis*, Commodity Trading Futures Commission, 1977, pp. 7–11.

Rees, Graham L. *Britain's Commodity Markets.* London: Paul Elek, 1972.

Registration Guidelines: A Compliance Guide, National Futures Association, 1986.

Roberts, Gerald, ed. *Guide to World Commodity Markets.* NY: Nichols Publishing, 1985.

Rudolf Wolff Co. *Wolff's Guide to London Metal Exchange*, 2nd ed. London: Metal Bulletin Books, 1984.

Stein, Jerome L. *The Economics of Futures Markets.* Oxford and NY: B. Blackwell, 1987.

Streit, Manfred E., ed. *Futures Markets: Modelling, Managing and Monitoring Futures Trading.* Oxford: B. Blackwell, 1983. (Published in cooperation with European Institute)

Taylor, Charles H., ed. *History of the Board of Trade of City of Chicago* (3 vols.; Chicago, 1917).

Teweles, R., Harlow, C., and Stone, H. *The Commodity Futures Game: Who Wins? Who Loses? Why?* (McGraw-Hill), pp. 8–9.

Williams, Jeffrey Carr. *The Economic Function of Futures Markets.* Yale University Dissertation. University Microfilms International: 1981.

Williams, Jeffrey Carr. "The Origins of Futures Markets," *Agricultural History*, pp. 306–325.

Woy, James B. *Commodity Futures Trading, A Bibliographic Guide.* NY: Bowker, 1976.

Yeutter, Clayton. *History of Futures Markets.* CME.

Index

ADP Comtrend, 76–77
Advisor, defined, 39
Agriculture, Department of, 47
American, defined, 72
American *vs.* British terminology, 68
American Stock Exchange (AMEX), 18, 116
  contract specification at, 232–235
  volume of, 142
Amsterdam Pork and Potato Exchange (APPE) 114
Andersen (Arthur) and Company, 87, 93
Arb clerks, 31–32
Arbitragers, 30–31, 33
Asset for asset swaps, defined, 71
Asset for debt swaps, defined, 71
Associated member, defined, 39
Associated Person (AP), 39, 50
Association for Futures Investment (AFI), 137
Association Market (AM) membership, 12
Association of Futures Brokers and Dealers (AFBD), 137
Auditor, internal, 90
Australia:
  contract specification in, 164–169
  futures and options exchanges in, 105–106

Australian Financial Futures Market (AFFM), 57
Automated Trading System, 57

Bakken, Henry H., 6, 7
Baltic Futures Exchange (BFE), 57, 108–109
  contract specification at, 187–191
  volume of, 142
Baltic International Freight Futures Exchange Ltd., The (BIFFEX), 108
  contract specification at, 187
Banque Commerce Commercial, 57
Barclays Bank, 57
Bolsa Brasileira de Futuros (BBF, Brazilian Futures Exchange), 106
Bolsa de Mercadorias de São Paulo (BMSP, São Paulo Commodities Exchange), 106
Bolsa Mercantil and de Futuros (BMF), 15, 106
  contract specification at, 169–174
  volume of, 142
Bond contract, 12
Bourse de Commerce du Paris, 57
Bourse de Montreal, *see* Montreal Exchange
Brazil:
  contract specification in, 169–174
  futures and options exchanges in, 106

Brazilian Futures Exchange, *see* Bolsa
   Brasileira de Futuros
Bretton Woods agreement (1944),
   10–11
Bridge Data, 76
British *vs.* American terminology, 68
Broker(s):
   authorized, 89
   Floor, 33–40, 47
   Introducing (IB), 40, 47
"Bucket shop," 50

Canada:
   contract specification in, 174–183
   futures and options exchanges in, 106–
      107
Central Bank of France, 35
Chambre de Compensation des
   Instruments Financiers de Paris
   (CCIFP), 133
Chia, Robert K. G., *SIMEX and the
   Globalization of Financial Futures*
   (with D. Soh), 20
Chicago Board of Trade (CBOT), 9, 13, 42,
   43, 51, 56, 116–117
   Association Market (AM) membership of,
      12
   Clearing Corporation, 55, 133
   contacts listed on, 123–124
   contract specification at, 235–246
   development of, 21
   evening and early morning trading at,
      14, 22, 30, 96
   fiduciary responsibility at, 61
   floor personnel at, 36
   Ginnie Mae Government Mortgage
      contract of, 12
   history of, 8
   leadership at, 37
   margining system of, 60
   and options trading, 17–18
   price information at, 45
   and Tokyo Stock Exchange, 22–23
   United States Thirty-Year Treasury Bond
      contract of, 12, 15, 17
   volume of, 142
Chicago Board Options Exchange (CBOE),
   13, 17, 18, 22, 117
   contract specification at, 246–248
   volume of, 142
Chicago Butter and Egg Board, 9, 10. *See
   also* Chicago Mercantile Exchange
Chicago Mercantile Exchange (CME), 9, 10,
   13, 43, 56, 118

   and arbitragers, 30
   and birth of financial futures, 10, 11, 12
   Clearinghouse, 133
   contracts listed on, 124–125
   contract specification at, 248–258
   and electronic trading, 96, 98
   Eurodollar contracts of, 17, 21
   financial safeguard system of, 61–62
   floor personnel at, 36, 51
   GLOBEX of, 14, 77, 95–96, 98, 99
   International Monetary Market at, 12,
      15
   leadership at, 37
   London office of, 14
   margining system of, 59, 60, 61
   and mutual-offset system, 20, 35
   physical plant at, 44
   price information at, 45
   Reuters' joint venture with, 77, 95–96
   and Standard & Poor's 500 stock index,
      18
   telephone system at, 42
   volume of, 142
   and worldwide clearinghouse links, 55
Chicago Produce Exchange, 9–10
Chicago Rice and Cotton Exchange, 120
Chicago School of Finance, 68
China, futures exchanges in, 25
CHO-AI-MAI-A-KAI rules, 5, 6, 7
Citrus Associates of New York Cotton
   Exchange Inc., 120
Clearing firm, 53–55, 61, 62
   defined, 39
Clearinghouse, 53–55
   defined, 38
   directory, 133–136
   and electronic trading, 98
   and fiduciary responsibility, 61–62
   and ICCH, 56–58
   links, worldwide, 55–56
   and margining systems, 58–61
Coffee, Sugar & Cocoa Exchange (CSCE),
   18–19, 36, 56, 119
   Clearing Corporation, 134
   contracts listed on, 125
   contract specification at, 259–262
   volume of, 142
Commodity Clearing Corporation, 56, 134
Commodity Communications, 76
Commodity Exchange of New York
   (COMEX), 30, 38, 56, 62, 119
   Clearing Association Inc., 134
   contracts listed on, 126
   contract specification at, 262–266

and exchange links, 19, 21
volume of, 142
Commodity Futures Trading Commission
(CFTC), 18–19, 38, 49, 94, 137–138
formation of, 47
and Joint Audit Committee, 56
and margining systems, 58, 59
Commodity Pool Operator (CPO), 40, 47–49
Commodity Quotations, 76
Commodity Quote Graphics, 76
Commodity Research Bureau, 43
Commodity Trading Advisor (CTA), 40, 47
Communication, see Information
Communications, intermarket, 63–65
British vs. American terminology, 68
interest rate terminology, 69–71
language barriers between markets, 65–67
options terms, 72
Compagnie des Commissionaires Agrèes
(CCA, Paris Futures Exchange), 14–15, 108
contract specification at, 185–186
Computerized Trade Reconstruction (CTR), 49
Computers, 73, 93. See also Electronic trading
for communication of market data, 74–75
comparative charting capabilities of
software run on, 75–78
role of, in market decisions, 79–87
CompuTrac, 78, 79
Conduct, forms of, 3, 4
Continental Illinois National Bank, 21
Continuous clearing, 49–50
Contracts:
index, alphabetical, 153–161
volume listing of, 143–151
volume and value of, 16–17
Contract terms, defined, 3, 4
Control(s):
systems, management internal, 88–91
trading operation, 87–88
Counts of Champagne, 4
Currency swap, defined, 70
CXL, defined, 67

Debt swap, defined, 70–71
Delta, defined, 72
Dojima Rice Market, 5
Dojima Rice Trading Board, 5

Dow Jones Industrial Average, 32
Dow Jones News Service, 77
DRT, defined, 66
Dumb terminal, 74
Duration, defined, 70
Duties, segregation of, 89

Economic Index Market, 119
Electronic trading, 93
pathways to 24-hour, 94–99
European, defined, 72
European Options Exchange (EOE,
Europese Optiebeurs), 22, 114
contract specification at, 220–224
European Stock Options Clearing
Corporation (ESOCC), 134
Exchange links, introduction of, 19, 21–22

Federation of Commodity Associations, 138
Federation of Oils, Seeds and Fats
Association Ltd. (FOFSA International), 108
Feranti-Packard electronic price
information boards, 43–44
Fiamass, 76
Fiduciary responsibility, 61–62
Filled and not endorsed, defined, 67
Financial futures, birth of, 10–12
Financial Instrument Exchange (FINEX), 120
Financial safeguards, 61–62
Financiele Termijnmarkt Amsterdam NV
(FTA), 114
contract specification at, 224–225
First National Bank of Chicago, 11
Floor Broker, 47
defined, 39–40
FOK, defined, 66–67
Forward contracts, 4
FRA, defined, 70
France:
contract specification in, 183–186
futures and options exchanges in, 108
Fraud, 88, 91
Frazer, Jim, 76
Friedman, Milton, 10, 11
FRN, defined, 70
FSA, defined, 70
Fulscher, Mitchell, 87–88
Futures Commission Merchant (FCM), 47, 62
defined, 39
Futures Council, 35

Futures exchange:
vs. clearinghouse, 53
defined, 38
Futures Industry Association (FIA), 17, 49, 138

Gamma, defined, 72
Ginnie Mae Government Mortgage contract (GNMA-CDR), 12
GLOBEX, 14, 77, 95–96, 98–99
Gould, Lincoln, 19–20
Government Instrument Market, 12. *See also* Association Market (AM) membership
Grain trading, 8–9, 16, 50
Granger, W. C., 4
Great Britain:
contract specification in, 187–209
futures and options exchanges in, 108–110
Guilbert, François, 35–36

Hang Seng Index, 25, 35, 52
Harlow, C., 3
Hedging activity, recognition of, 90–91
Hokkaido Grain Exchange, 110
Holidays, international, 291–292
Hong Kong:
contract specification in, 209–211
futures and options exchange in, 120
Hong Kong Commodity Exchange, 25
Hong Kong Futures Exchange (HKFE), 25, 35, 52, 110
contracts listed on, 129–130
contract specification at, 209–211
and ICCH, 57
volume of, 142
Hong Kong Silver and Gold Society, 25
Hong Kong Stock Exchange (HKSE), 25, 95, 96

Illinois-Michigan Canal, 8
Implied volatility, defined, 72
Index and Options Market (IOM), 118
Individual market makers, 32–33, 40
Information:
effective and efficient use of, 41–42
options-related, 45–46
physical plant and order flow, 42–44
relay of price, 44–45
Insolvency, 61, 62
Inspection and grading, specific rules of, 3, 4
Institutional hedgers, 27–30
Institutional market makers, 31–32

Intelligent terminal, 74
Interest rate swaps, defined, 71
Interest rate terminology, 69–71
Internal audit, 90
International Commodities Clearing House, Ltd. (ICCH), 20, 21, 34, 39
continuous clearing at, 49
directory, 134–136
founding of, 56
margining system of, 59
role of, 56–58
International Federation of Stock Exchanges, 139
International Monetary Market (IMM), 11–12, 15, 118
International Options Clearing Corporation (IOCC), 136
International Petroleum Exchange of London Ltd. (IPE), 57, 109
contract specification at, 191–192
volume of, 142
International Stock Exchange (ISE), 109
contract specification at, 192–194
INTEX, 57, 77
Introducing Broker (IB), 47
defined, 40
Irwin, H. S., 9

Japan:
birth of futures contract in, 5–8
contract specification in, 211–218
futures and options exchanges in, 22–25, 110–113
Joint Audit Committee, 56

Kanmon Commodity Exchange (Kanmon Shohin Torihikijo), 110
Kansas City Board of Trade (KCBT), 56, 119
Clearing Corporation, 136
contract specification at, 266–268
volume of, 142
Knight Ridder, 76, 78
Kobe Grain Exchange (Kobe Kokumotsu Torihikijo), 111
Kobe Raw Silk Exchange (Kobe Kiito Torihikijo), 111
Kobe Rubber Exchange (Kobe Gomu Torihikijo), 111
Kuala Lumpur Commodity Exchange (KLCE), 114
contract specification at, 218–220
volume of, 142

Labys, C. W. J., 4

Language barriers between markets, 65–67,
97. *See also* Terminology
Leadership, 37–38
Lettre de faire, 4–5, 9
LIBOR (London Interbank offered rate), 69,
70
Lille Potato Futures Market (LPFM), 108
contract specification at, 183–184
volume of, 142
Limits, position, 88–89
Lloyds Bank, 57
Locals, 32–33
defined, 40
London Commodity Exchange, 20
London Futures and Options Exchange
(FOX), 57, 109
contract specification at, 194–197
volume of, 142
London Grain Futures Market (LGFM), 108
contract specification at, 187–189
London International Financial Futures
Exchange, The (LIFFE), 4, 12, 22, 43,
109
continuous clearing at, 49–50
contracts listed on, 127–128
contract specification at, 197–204
and exchange links, 19, 21
financial futures traded at, 15
and ICCH, 57
institutional interest at, 35
margining system of, 60
price information at, 45
volume of, 142
London Meat Futures Exchange (LMFE),
108
contract specification at, 189
London Metal Exchange Ltd. (LME), 35, 110
contracts listed on, 128–129
contract specification at, 204–209
volume of, 142
London Potato Futures Association (LPFA),
108
contract specification at, 189–190
London Produce Clearing House for Sugar
and Coffee, 56. *See also* International
Commodities Clearing House, Ltd.
London Stock Exchange (LSE), 96, 110
London Traded Options Market, *see* Traded
Options Market
London Wool Terminal Market Association,
19
Lynch, Phil, 63

Maebashi Dried Cocoon Exchange, 111

Major Market Index, 22
Malaysia:
contract specification in, 218–220
futures and options exchange in, 114
Management:
internal control systems, 88–91
reporting system, 90–91
Manila International Futures Exchange
(MIFE), 115
Manual, procedures, 88
Marché à Terme des Instruments
Financiers (MATIF), 12, 14–15, 34, 108
continuous clearing at, 50
contracts listed on, 129
contract specification at, 184–185
establishment of, 35
and ICCH, 58
institutional interest at, 35
and local membership, 35–36
regulation of, 51
volume of, 142
Margining systems, 58–61
Market, defined, 66
Market data, communication of, 74–75
Market decisions, role of computers in, 79–
87
Market makers:
individual, 32–33, 40
institutional, 31–32
Market participants, 38–40
around the world, 34–37
Marketplace, designation of location of, 3–
4
Markets, language barriers between, 65–67
Maturity transformation, 69
Melamed, Leo. 10, 11, 95, 96
Member, defined, 40
MidAmerica Commodity Exchange
(MIDAM), 120
contract specification at, 268–275
volume of, 142
Midland Bank, 57
Midwest Stock Exchange (MSE), 13
Ministry for International Trade and
Industry (MITI, Japan), 24
Ministry of Finance (MOF, Japan), 15, 22,
23
Ministry of Fisheries and Forestries (MFF,
Japan), 24
Minneapolis Grain Exchange (MGE), 56,
120
Clearinghouse, 136
contract specification at, 275–277
volume of, 142

Mismatches, *see* Out-trades
MOC, defined, 66
Money manager, defined, 40
Montreal Exchange, The (ME, Bourse de
    Montreal), 106–107
    contract specification at, 174–177
    volume of, 142
Multitasking, 75
Mutual-offset trading system, 8, 35
    introduction of, 19, 20–21

Nagoya Grain and Sugar Exchange (Nagoya
    Kokumotsu Sato Torihikijo), 111
Nagoya Textile Exchange (Nagoya Seni
    Torihikijo), 111
National Association of Securities Dealers
    (NASD), 139
National Futures Association (NFA), 39, 40,
    49, 51, 139
    and fiduciary responsibility, 61, 62
    functions of, 47
    on order entry and checking
        terminology, 66
National Westminster Bank, 57
Netherlands:
    contract specification in, 220–225
    futures and options exchanges in, 114
New York Cotton Exchange (NYCE), 120
    contracts listed on, 126–127
    contract specification at, 277–280
    volume of, 142
New York Futures Exchange (NYFE), 56,
    120
    contract specification at, 281–282
    volume of, 142
New York Mercantile Exchange (NYMEX),
    36, 38, 56, 120–121
    Clearinghouse, 136
    continuous clearing at, 50
    contracts listed on, 127
    contract specification at, 282–285
    margining system of, 59
    volume of, 142
New York Stock Exchange (NYSE), 18, 23,
    30, 32
    contract specification at, 285–286
    volume of, 142
New Zealand:
    contract specification in, 225–227
    futures and options exchange in, 115
New Zealand Futures Exchange (NZFE), 19,
    57, 115
    contracts listed on, 130
    contract specification at, 225–227

NIF, defined, 70
Nikkei Stock Average Index, 21, 24
Not filled, defined, 67
Not held, defined, 66

OCO, defined, 67
Opening-only, defined, 66
Options Clearing Corporation, 136
Options-related information, 45–46
Options terms, 72
Options trading, 17–19
Order entry and checking terminology, 66–
    67
Order flow, physical plant and, 42–44
Osaka Grain Exchange (Osaka Kokumotsu
    Torihikijo), 112
Osaka Securities Exchange (OSE), 24, 112
    contract specification at, 211–212
    volume of, 142
Osaka Stock Futures 50 (OSF50), 24
Osaka Sugar Exchange (Osaka Sato
    Torihikijo), 112
Osaka Textile Exchange, 112
Out-trades, 6, 50

Pacific Rim markets, 19–25
Pacific Stock Exchange (PSE), 18
    contract specification at, 286
Parallel loans, defined, 71
Paris Futures Exchange, *see* Compagnie des
    Commissionaires Agrèes
Paris Sugar Exchange, 4
Partial fill, defined, 67
"Passing the book," 63
Pech, Bernard, 58
Philadelphia Board of Trade (PBOT), 121
Philadelphia Stock Exchange (PHLX). 14,
    18, 110–111
    contract specification at, 286–290
    volume of, 142
Philippines, futures and options exchange
    in, 115
Physical plant and order flow, 42–44
Position limits, 88–89
Powers, Mark, 94–95
Price information, relay of, 44–45
Price limit, defined, 66
Price MIT, defined, 66
Procedures manual, 88
Put option, 18

Quotron, 76

Regulation, 47–49

current status of futures, 49–50
  of exchanges outside U.S., 51–52
Reuters, 76, 77, 78
  and GLOBEX, 14, 77, 95
  joint venture of, with CME, 77, 95
Rice trading, 5–7, 16
Royal Bank of Scotland, 57
Royal Exchange, 4, 8

Saitori companies, 23
São Paulo Commodities Exchange, *see*
  Bolsa de Mercadorias de São Paulo
Securities and Exchange Commission
  (SEC). 18, 56, 58, 139
Securities and Investments Board (SIB),
  139
Securities Dealers Association of Japan
  (Nihon Shokengyo Kyokai), 139
Shearson Lehman Hutton, 63
Singapore:
  contract specification in, 227–230
  futures and options exchange in, 115
Singapore International Monetary Exchange
  Ltd., The (SIMEX), 22, 24, 96, 115
  contracts listed on, 130–131
  contract specification at, 227–230
  mutual-offset system between CME and,
    20, 21, 35
  volume of, 142
Soh, Doreen, *SIMEX and the Globalization
  of Financial Futures* (with R. K. G.
  Chia), 20
Soya Bean Meal Futures Association Ltd.
  (SOMFA), 108
  contract specification at, 191
Spreaders, 33
Standard & Poor's:
  100 stock index, 18
  500 stock index, 18, 30, 33
Standard Chartered Bank, 57
Stockholm Options Market (SOM), 115
  contract specification at, 230–231
  volume of, 142
Stock market crash (October 1987), 32, 53–
  54, 55
Stone, H., 3
Strips, defined, 70
Sweden:
  contract specification in, 230–232
  futures and options exchanges in, 115–
  116
Sweden Options and Futures Exchange
  (SOFE), 115–116
  contract specification at, 231–232

Swiss Commodities, Futures and Options
  Association (SCFOA), 140
Swiss Options and Financial Futures
  Exchange (SOFFEX), 116
Switzerland, futures and options exchange
  in, 116
Sydney Futures Exchange, Ltd. (SFE), 12,
  105–106
  continuous clearing at, 50
  contracts listed on, 131
  contract specification at, 164–169
  evening sessions at, 14
  and exchange links, 19, 21
  growth of, 15
  and ICCH, 57
  multilevel memberships of, 34
  90-Day Bank Acceptance Rate at, 69
  volume of, 142
Sydnay Stock Exchange Ltd. (SSE), 105

Task Management, 43
Taylor, Barry, 50
Taylor, Charles, 8
Telerate, 57, 76, 77–78
Terminology:
  British *vs.* American, 68
  interest rate, 69–71
  options, 72
  order entry and checking, 66–67
Teweles, R., 3
Theta, defined, 72
Time contract, 9
"To arrive" contracts, 9
Tokyo Commodity Exchange (TCE, Tokyo
  Kogyohin Torihikijo), 24, 112
  contract specification at, 212–214
  volume of, 142
Tokyo Grain Exchange, The (TGE), 24, 113
  contract specification at, 214–216
  volume of, 142
Tokyo Stock Exchange (TSE), 12, 22, 34,
  113
  computerization of, 96
  contract specification at, 216–217
  regulation of, 51
  and Tokyo Stock Price Index (TOPIX),
  23–24
  volume of, 142
  yen bond contract of, 15–16, 23–24
Tokyo Stock Price Index (TOPIX),
  23–24
Tokyo Sugar Exchange (TSUE, Tokyo Sato
  Torihikijo), 113
  contract specification at, 218

Toronto Futures Exchange (TFE), 107
    contract specification at, 177–178
    volume of, 142
Toronto Stock Exchange (TSEX), 107
    contract specification at, 178–179
    volume of, 142
Toyohashi Cocoon Exchange, 113
Traded Options Market (TOM), 113
    contract specification at, 192–194
Traders, 32–33
    authorized, 88
Trade tables, 45–46
Trans-Canada Options Corporation, 136
Trustee Savings Bank, 57

United Dominion Trust, 57
United States:
    contract specification in, 232–290
    early futures trading in, 8–10
    futures and options exchanges in, 116–121
United States Banker's Acceptance Rate, 69
United States Thirty-Year Treasury Bond
    contract, 12, 15, 17
United States Treasury bills, 28, 31
United States Treasury bonds, 30, 31, 77

Value, defined, 72
Vancouver Stock Exchange (VSE), 107
    contract specification at, 179–181
    volume of, 142
Vega, defined, 72
Verification, 90
Volume:
    distribution by country and exchange,
        141–142
    listing of contracts, 143–151
    and value of contracts, 16–17
Volume Investors, 62

Wilmouth, Robert, 17, 51
Windstrup, Glen, 43
Winnipeg Commodity Exchange (WCE),
    107
    contract specification at, 181–183
    volume of, 142
Wool trading, 19–20
Working, defined, 67
World Trade Center, 36

Yokahama Raw Silk Exchange, 113